DESCENDING STORIES

SHOWA
GENROKU
RAKUGO
SHINJU

Haruko Kumota

THE STORY SO FAR

YOTARO'S ODYSSEY

Yotaro falls in love with Yakumo Yurakutei's *rakugo* when he hears it in prison. Once free, he becomes Yakumo's apprentice and is soon made a *zenza.* As his appreciation for *rakugo* grows, the incredible *rakugo* of the late Sukeroku takes hold of him and he commits an unthinkable faux pas at a solo recital by his teacher. Facing expulsion, Yotaro begs forgiveness. Yakumo relents, but extracts three promises from his student. Then he begins to tell the tale of his own promise with Sukeroku...

YAKUMO AND SUKEROKU

Yakumo Yurakutei VII takes two apprentices on the same day: Kikuhiko and Hatsutaro. Promoted to *shin'uchi* together, the two are soon popular *rakugo* artists, with Hatsutaro adopting the name "Sukeroku," and Kikuhiko finding his own style at last.

But Sukeroku argues with his shisho and is expelled from the lineage. Wounded, he disappears with Miyokichi, Kikuhiko's former lover. Not long after, Yakumo makes a deathbed confession to Kikuhiko of his secret connection to the Sukeroku name. Bereaved and alone, Kikuhiko goes in search of Sukeroku at a hot springs town in the countryside, in order to make him inherit the Yakumo name. Sukeroku has abandoned *rakugo*, but, at Kikuhiko's insistence, the two Yurakutei disciples put on a successful joint show.

CAST OF CHARACTERS

Yakumo and Sukeroku

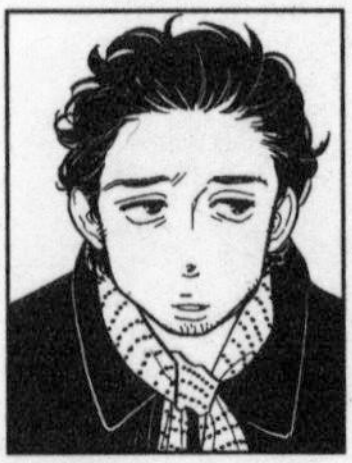

Sukeroku
Apprentice of Yakumo VII, making him a brother apprentice to Kikuhiko, until his expulsion.

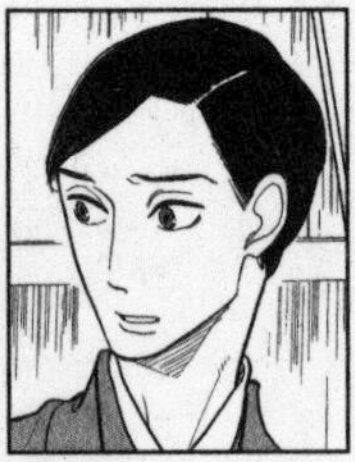

Kikuhiko
Yakumo Yurakutei VIII as a young *zenza*. The same age as Sukeroku.

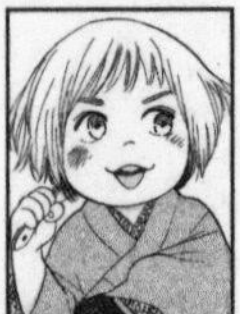

Konatsu
Konatsu in her youth. Daughter of Sukeroku and Miyokichi.

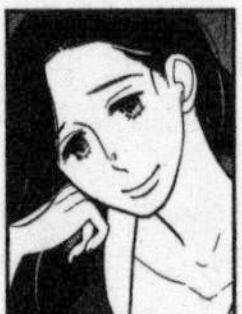

Miyokichi (Yurie)
Konatsu's mother. Dies falling from a window with Sukeroku.

Yotaro's Odyssey

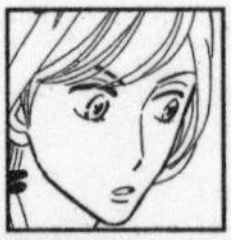

Konatsu
Sukeroku's only daughter, taken in by Yakumo.

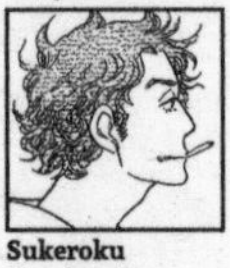

Sukeroku Yurakutei
Legendary *rakugo* artist hailed as a genius before his untimely death.

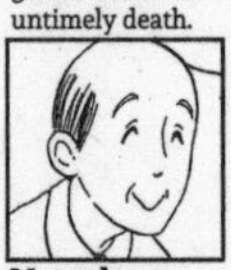

Matsuda-san
Faithful servant and driver of Yakumo VIII, and Yakumo VII before him.

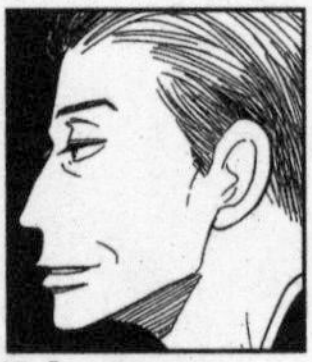

Yakumo Yurakutei VIII
Renowned as the Showa period's last great master of *rakugo.*

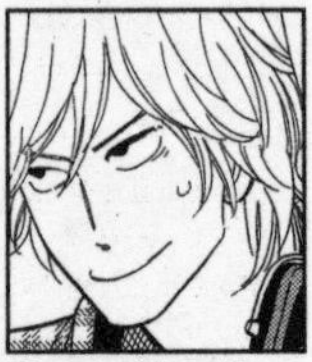

Yotaro (Kyoji)
Reformed street tough who became Yakumo's apprentice.

That night, however, Miyokichi reappears, hinting at a joint suicide with Kikuhiko. Driven by a hunch, Sukeroku bursts in to stop them, and the scene ends in tragedy as he and Miyokichi fall to their deaths together. Taking in their child Konatsu in memory of the two, Kikuhiko inherits the Yakumo name himself, in order to put an end to the story...

SUKEROKU AGAIN

Taking the promises he made to Yakumo to heart, Yotaro diligently polishes his craft. With the *rakugo* world fading and only one *yose* left in Tokyo, he is finally promoted to *shin'uchi*—adopting the name "Sukeroku III." Meanwhile, Konatsu reveals that she is pregnant. Yotaro marries her, becoming father to her child.

Seeing his apprentice struggle to find his own *rakugo*, Yakumo sets him a challenge: to perform the story "*Inokori*" at their father-and-son recital. But, on the day of the recital, Yakumo barely finishes his first story before collapsing on the stage. As his shisho is rushed to hospital, Yotaro remains to perform a stunning "*Inokori.*"

One week later, Yakumo comes to. But his future remains uncertain...

Cast of Characters

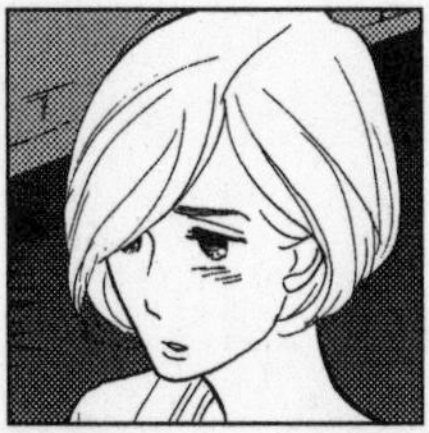

Konatsu
Only daughter of the late Sukeroku II, taken in by Yakumo. Had a child without revealing the father. Now married to Yotaro.

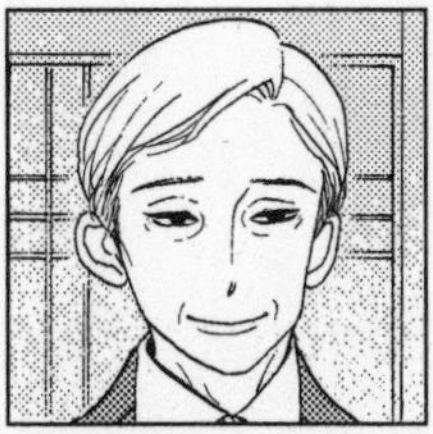

Yakumo Yurakutei VIII
Now the most powerful figure in the world of *rakugo* and president of the *Rakugo* Association. Accepted no apprentices except Yotaro, leaving nobody to inherit the Yakumo name.

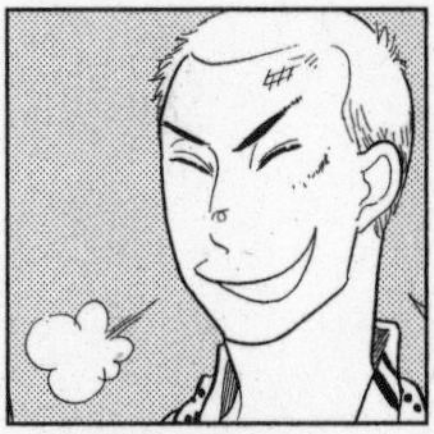

Sukeroku Yurakutei III (a.k.a. Yotaro)
Promoted to *shin'uchi*, Yotaro inherits the Sukeroku name and marries Konatsu to form a family. Loves *rakugo* with all his heart.

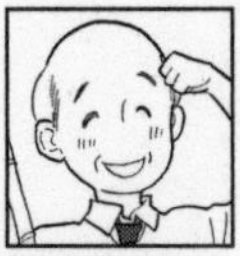

Matsuda-san
Faithful servant and driver of Yakumo VIII. Part of the Yurakutei family in all but name.

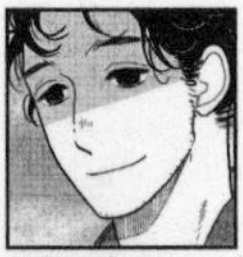

Sukeroku Yurakutei II
Konatsu's deceased father, whose *rakugo* remains legendary.

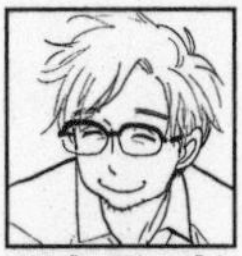

Eisuke Higuchi
A.k.a. "Sensei." Popular writer and fan of Yotaro.

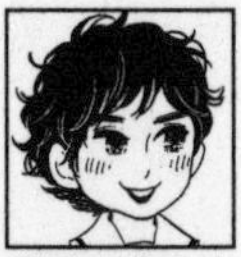

Shinnosuke
Yotaro and Konatsu's son, whose real father remains a secret.

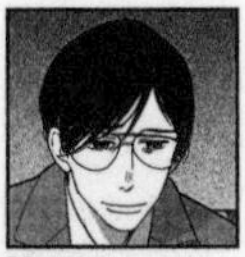

Mangetsu
Former *rakugo* artist and devoted admirer of Yakumo. Made it big working in television.

DESCENDING STORIES

SHOWA
GENROKU
RAKUGO
SHINJU

Contents

Sukeroku Again

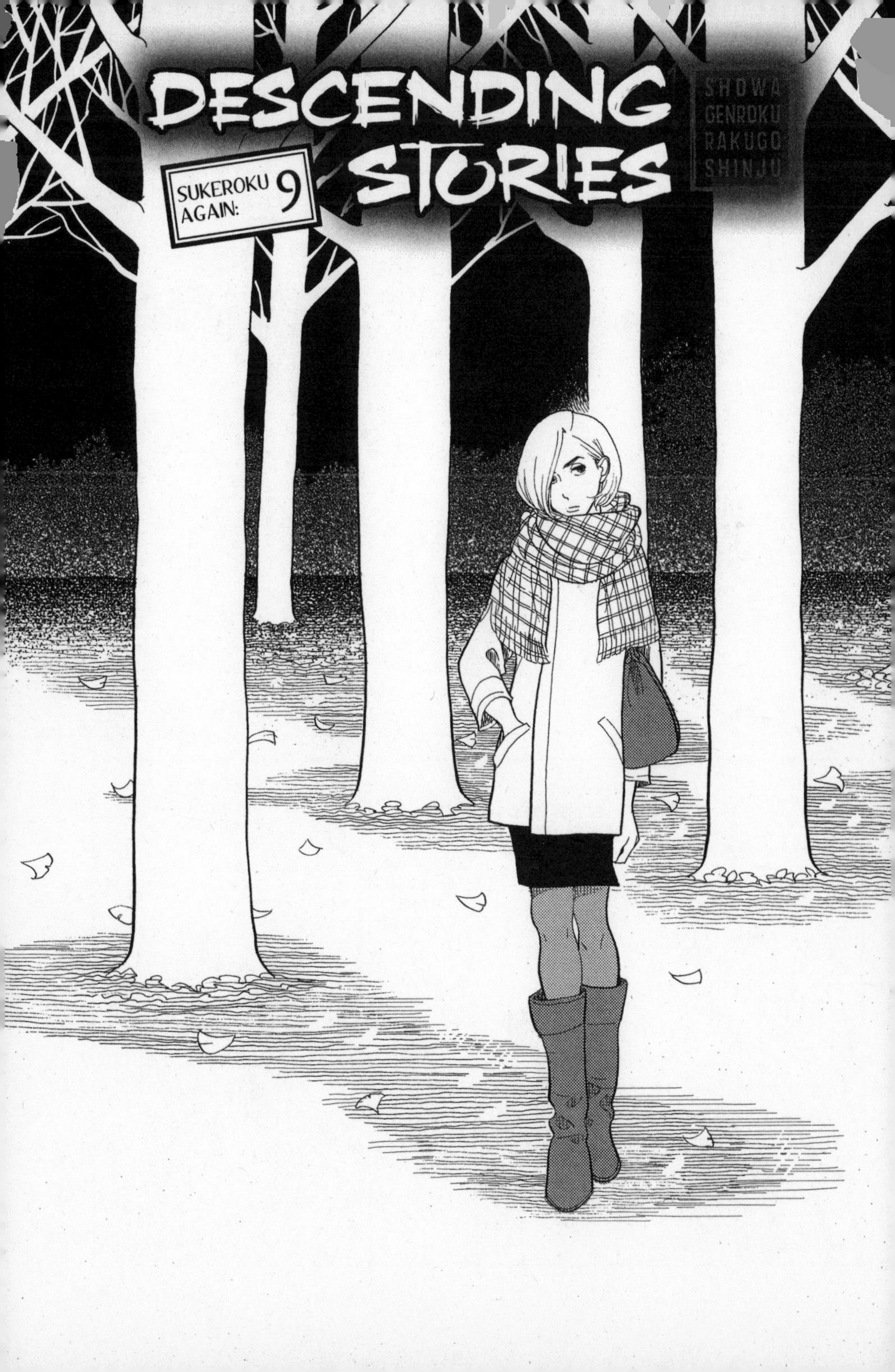
DESCENDING STORIES
SHOWA GENROKU RAKUGO SHINJU
SUKEROKU AGAIN: 9

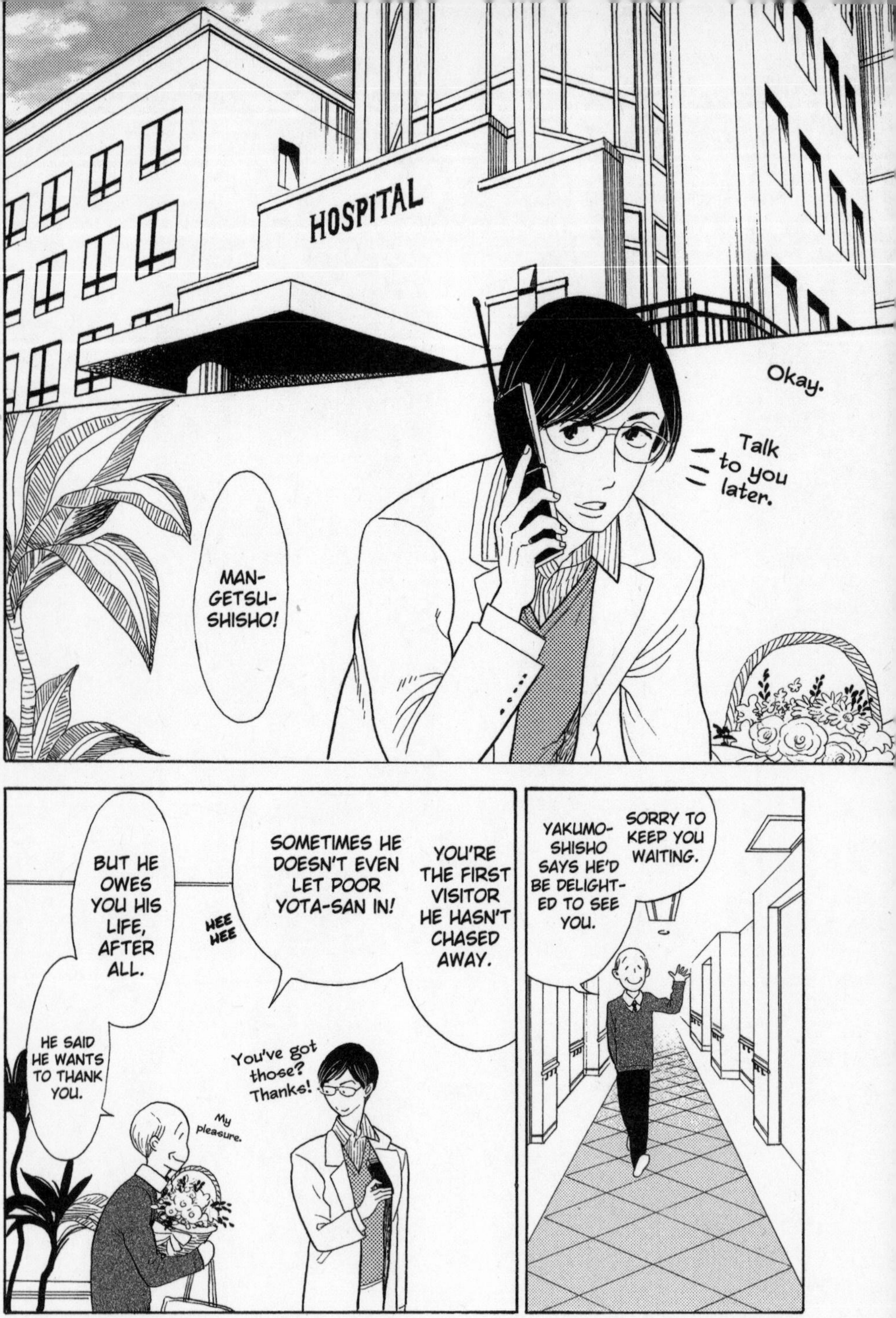

HOSPITAL
Okay.
Talk to you later.
MAN-GETSU-SHISHO!
SORRY TO KEEP YOU WAITING.
YAKUMO-SHISHO SAYS HE'D BE DELIGHT-ED TO SEE YOU.
YOU'RE THE FIRST VISITOR HE HASN'T CHASED AWAY.
SOMETIMES HE DOESN'T EVEN LET POOR YOTA-SAN IN!
HEE HEE
BUT HE OWES YOU HIS LIFE, AFTER ALL.
You've got those? Thanks!
My pleasure.
HE SAID HE WANTS TO THANK YOU.

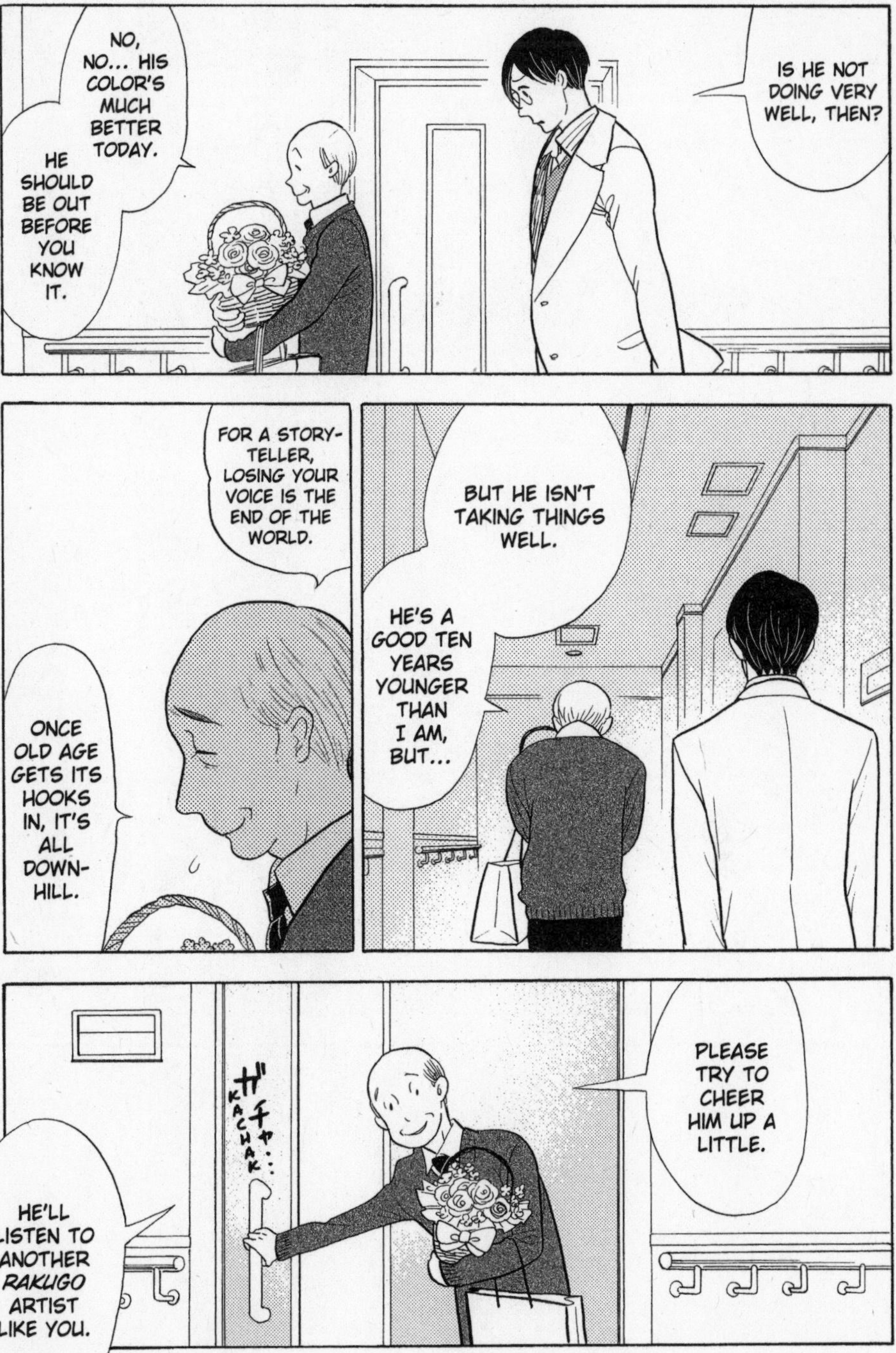
IS HE NOT DOING VERY WELL, THEN?
NO, NO... HIS COLOR'S MUCH BETTER TODAY.
HE SHOULD BE OUT BEFORE YOU KNOW IT.
BUT HE ISN'T TAKING THINGS WELL.
HE'S A GOOD TEN YEARS YOUNGER THAN I AM, BUT...
FOR A STORY-TELLER, LOSING YOUR VOICE IS THE END OF THE WORLD.
ONCE OLD AGE GETS ITS HOOKS IN, IT'S ALL DOWN-HILL.
PLEASE TRY TO CHEER HIM UP A LITTLE.
ガチャ…
KACHAK
HE'LL LISTEN TO ANOTHER *RAKUGO* ARTIST LIKE YOU.

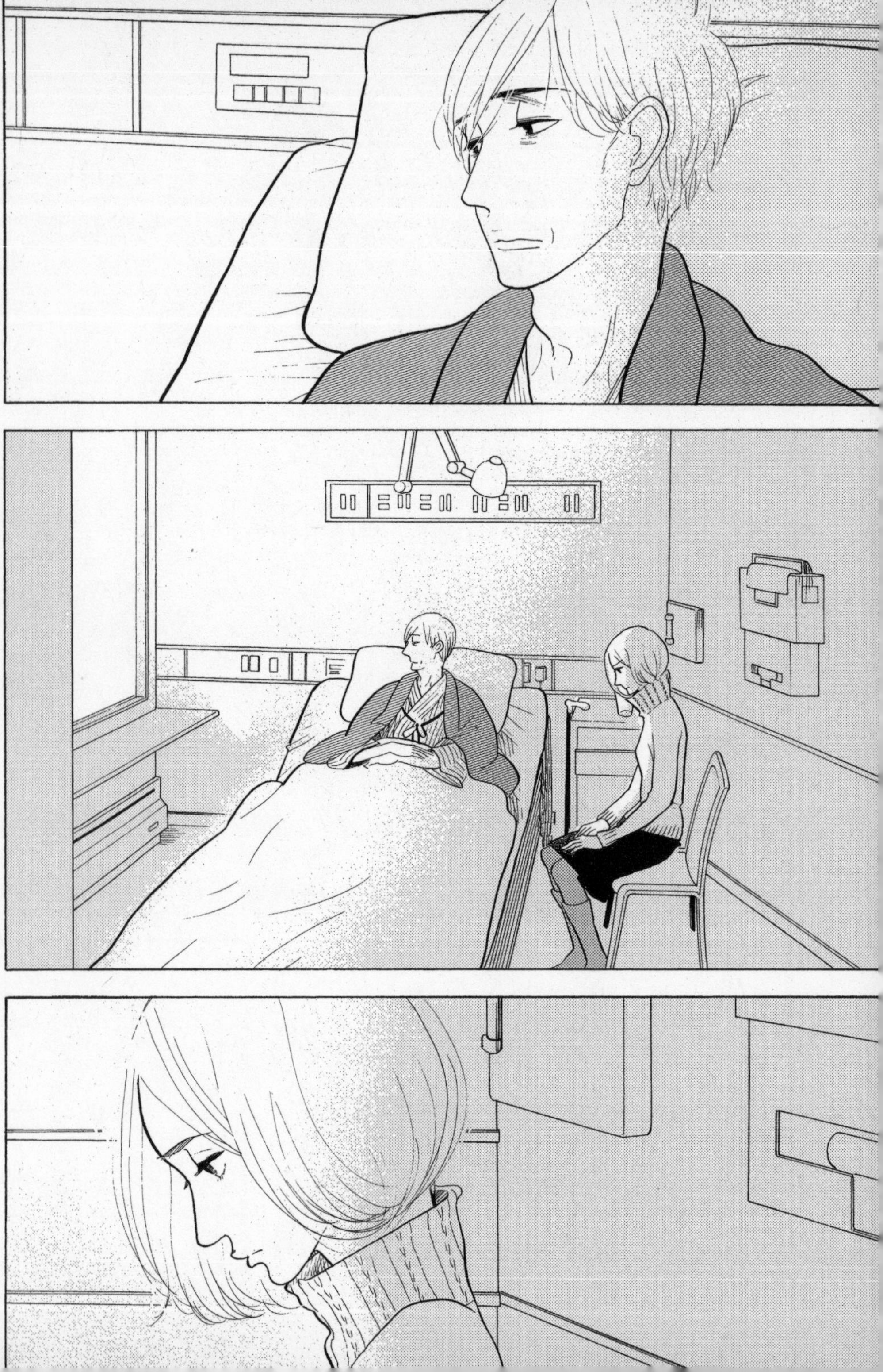

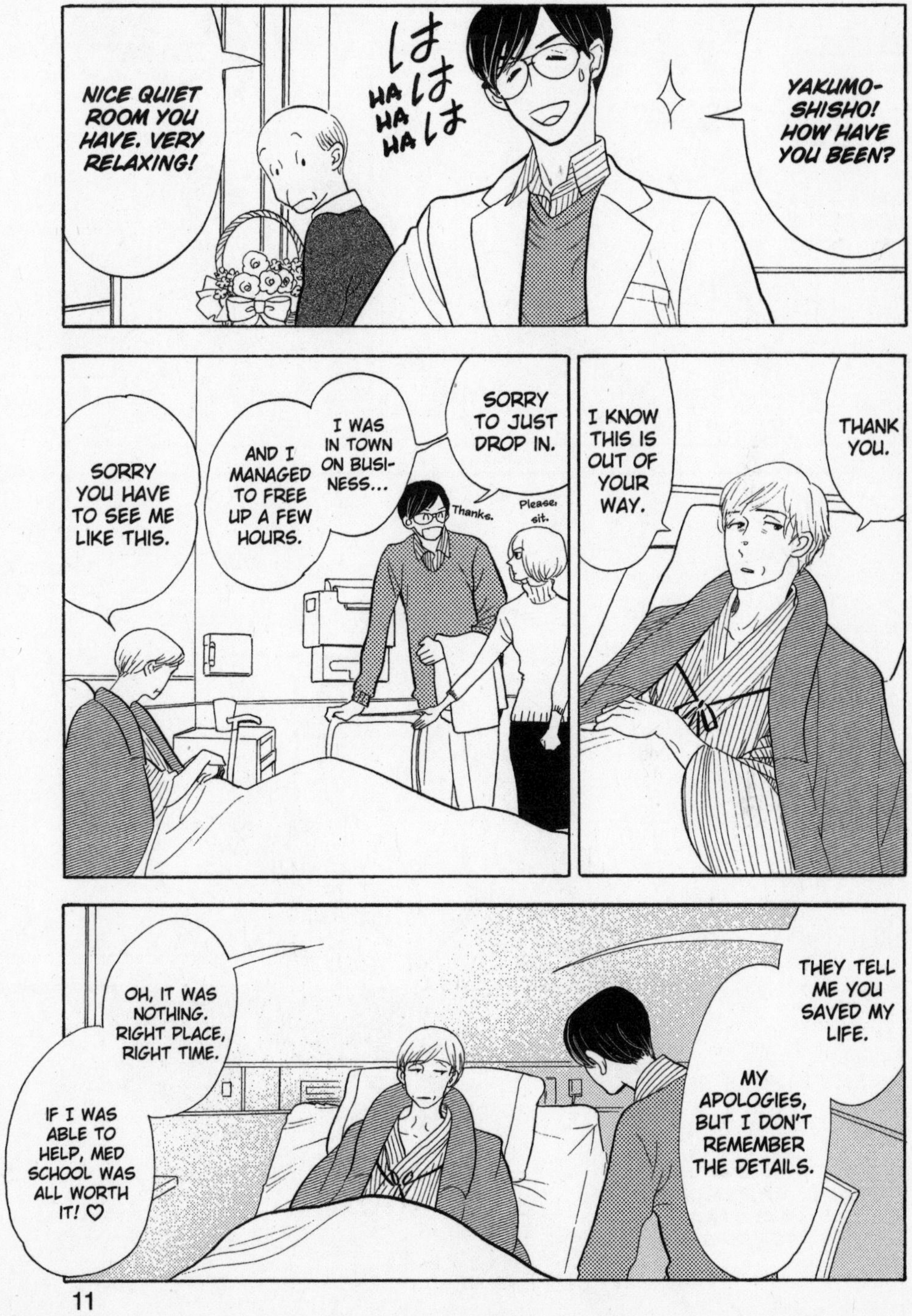
YAKUMO-SHISHO! HOW HAVE YOU BEEN?
ははは
HA HA HA
NICE QUIET ROOM YOU HAVE. VERY RELAXING!
THANK YOU.
I KNOW THIS IS OUT OF YOUR WAY.
SORRY TO JUST DROP IN.
Please, sit.
Thanks.
I WAS IN TOWN ON BUSINESS...
AND I MANAGED TO FREE UP A FEW HOURS.
SORRY YOU HAVE TO SEE ME LIKE THIS.
THEY TELL ME YOU SAVED MY LIFE.
MY APOLOGIES, BUT I DON'T REMEMBER THE DETAILS.
OH, IT WAS NOTHING. RIGHT PLACE, RIGHT TIME.
IF I WAS ABLE TO HELP, MED SCHOOL WAS ALL WORTH IT! ♡

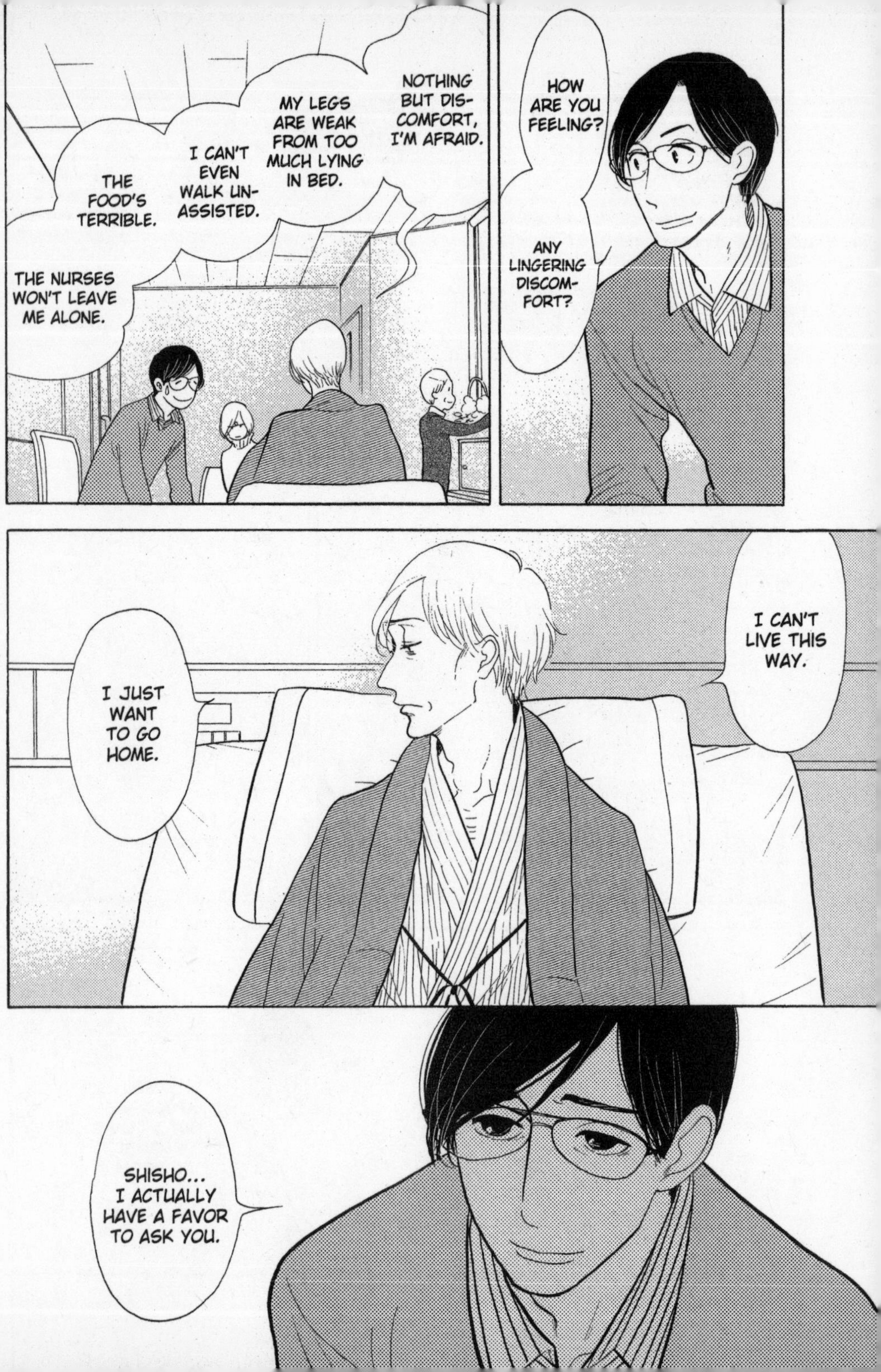
HOW ARE YOU FEELING?
ANY LINGERING DISCOMFORT?
NOTHING BUT DIS-COMFORT, I'M AFRAID.
MY LEGS ARE WEAK FROM TOO MUCH LYING IN BED.
I CAN'T EVEN WALK UN-ASSISTED.
THE FOOD'S TERRIBLE.
THE NURSES WON'T LEAVE ME ALONE.
I CAN'T LIVE THIS WAY.
I JUST WANT TO GO HOME.
SHISHO... I ACTUALLY HAVE A FAVOR TO ASK YOU.

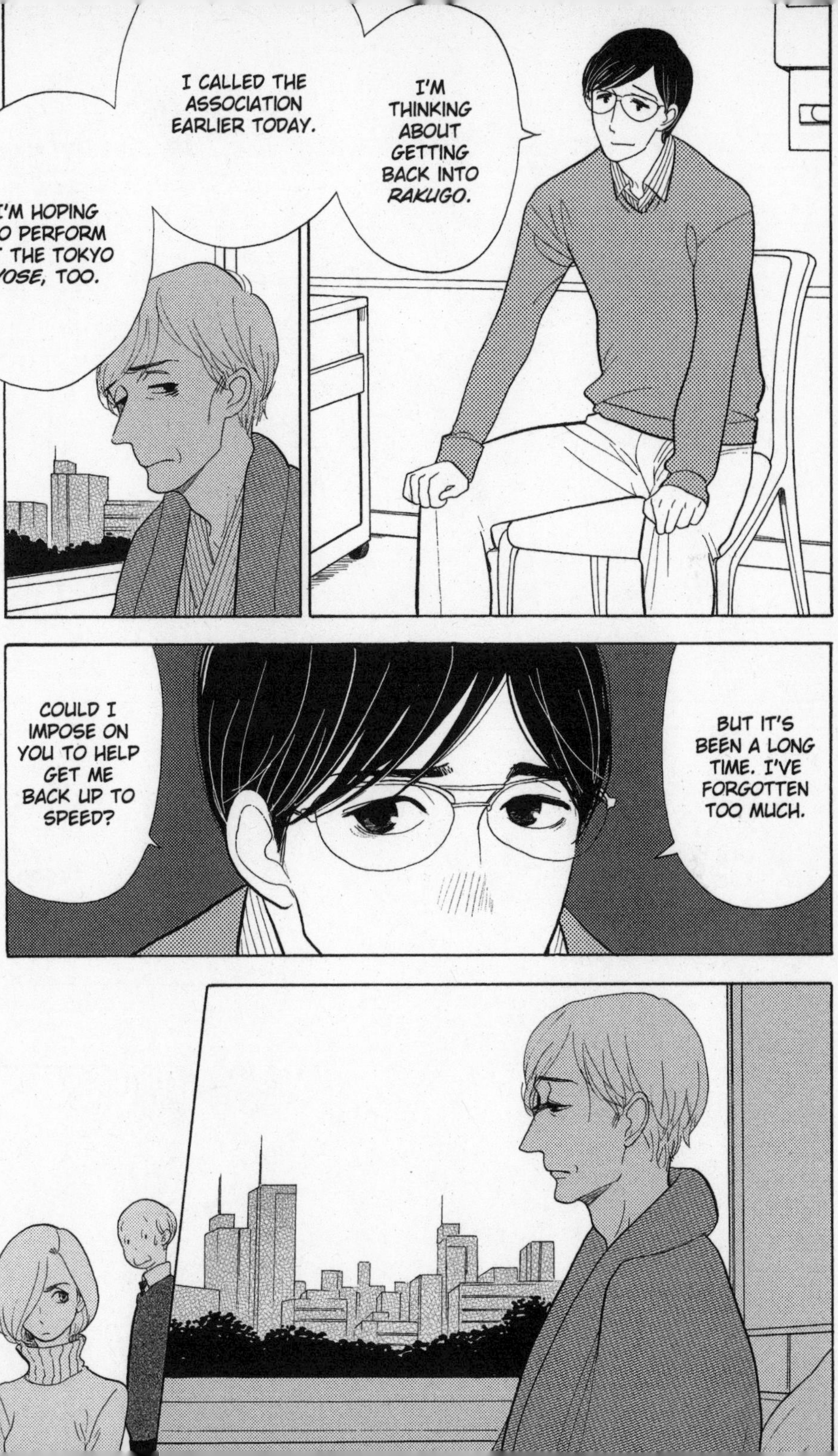
I'M THINKING ABOUT GETTING BACK INTO *RAKUGO*.
I CALLED THE ASSOCIATION EARLIER TODAY.
I'M HOPING TO PERFORM AT THE TOKYO *YOSE*, TOO.
BUT IT'S BEEN A LONG TIME. I'VE FORGOTTEN TOO MUCH.
COULD I IMPOSE ON YOU TO HELP GET ME BACK UP TO SPEED?

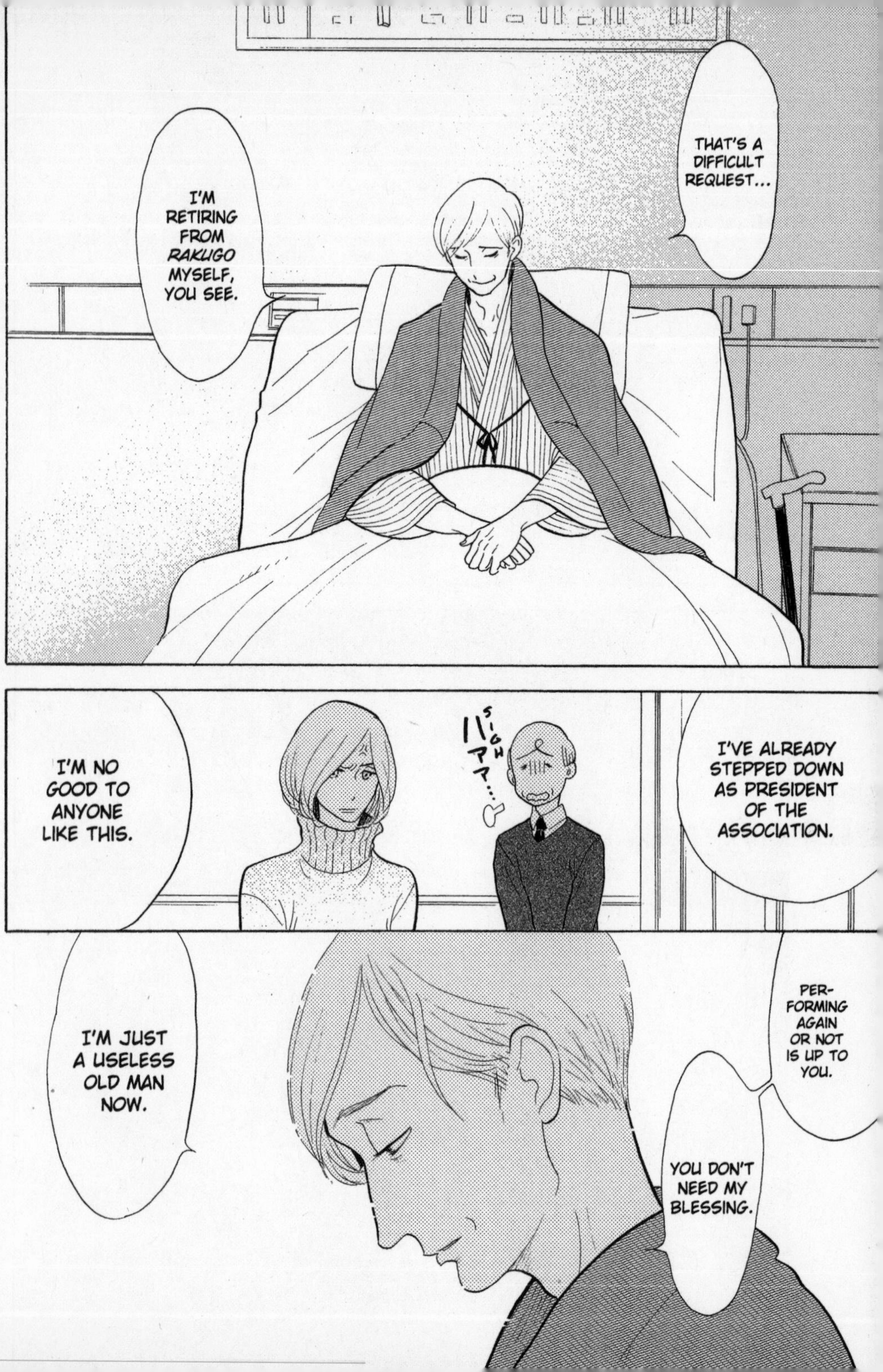
THAT'S A DIFFICULT REQUEST...
I'M RETIRING FROM *RAKUGO* MYSELF, YOU SEE.
I'VE ALREADY STEPPED DOWN AS PRESIDENT OF THE ASSOCIATION.
SIGH
I'M NO GOOD TO ANYONE LIKE THIS.
PER-FORMING AGAIN OR NOT IS UP TO YOU.
YOU DON'T NEED MY BLESSING.
I'M JUST A USELESS OLD MAN NOW.

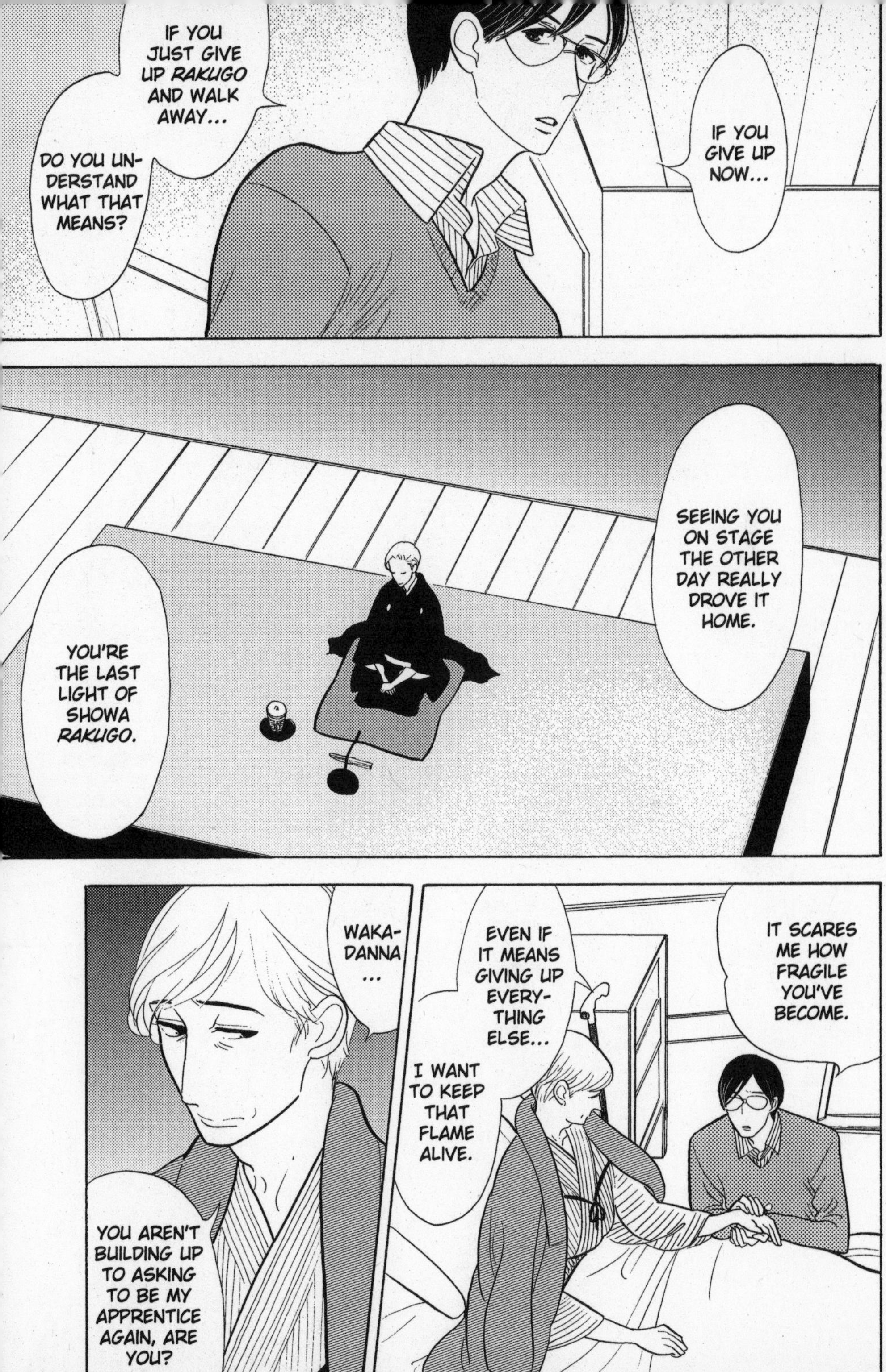
IF YOU GIVE UP NOW...
IF YOU JUST GIVE UP *RAKUGO* AND WALK AWAY...
DO YOU UNDERSTAND WHAT THAT MEANS?
SEEING YOU ON STAGE THE OTHER DAY REALLY DROVE IT HOME.
YOU'RE THE LAST LIGHT OF SHOWA *RAKUGO*.
IT SCARES ME HOW FRAGILE YOU'VE BECOME.
EVEN IF IT MEANS GIVING UP EVERYTHING ELSE...
I WANT TO KEEP THAT FLAME ALIVE.
WAKADANNA...
YOU AREN'T BUILDING UP TO ASKING TO BE MY APPRENTICE AGAIN, ARE YOU?

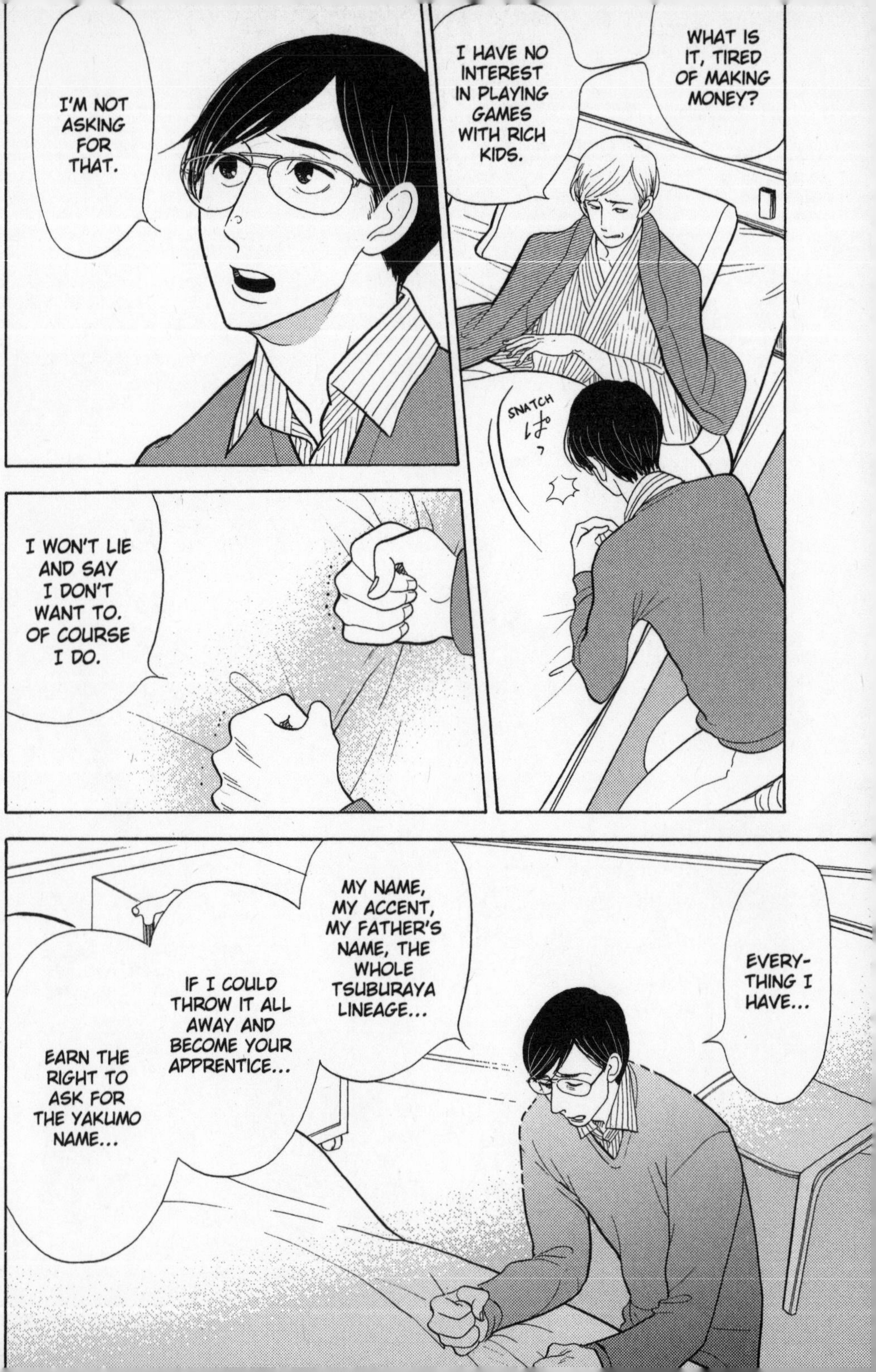
WHAT IS IT, TIRED OF MAKING MONEY?
I HAVE NO INTEREST IN PLAYING GAMES WITH RICH KIDS.
SNATCH
ぱっ
I'M NOT ASKING FOR THAT.
I WON'T LIE AND SAY I DON'T WANT TO. OF COURSE I DO.
EVERY-THING I HAVE...
MY NAME, MY ACCENT, MY FATHER'S NAME, THE WHOLE TSUBURAYA LINEAGE...
IF I COULD THROW IT ALL AWAY AND BECOME YOUR APPRENTICE...
EARN THE RIGHT TO ASK FOR THE YAKUMO NAME...

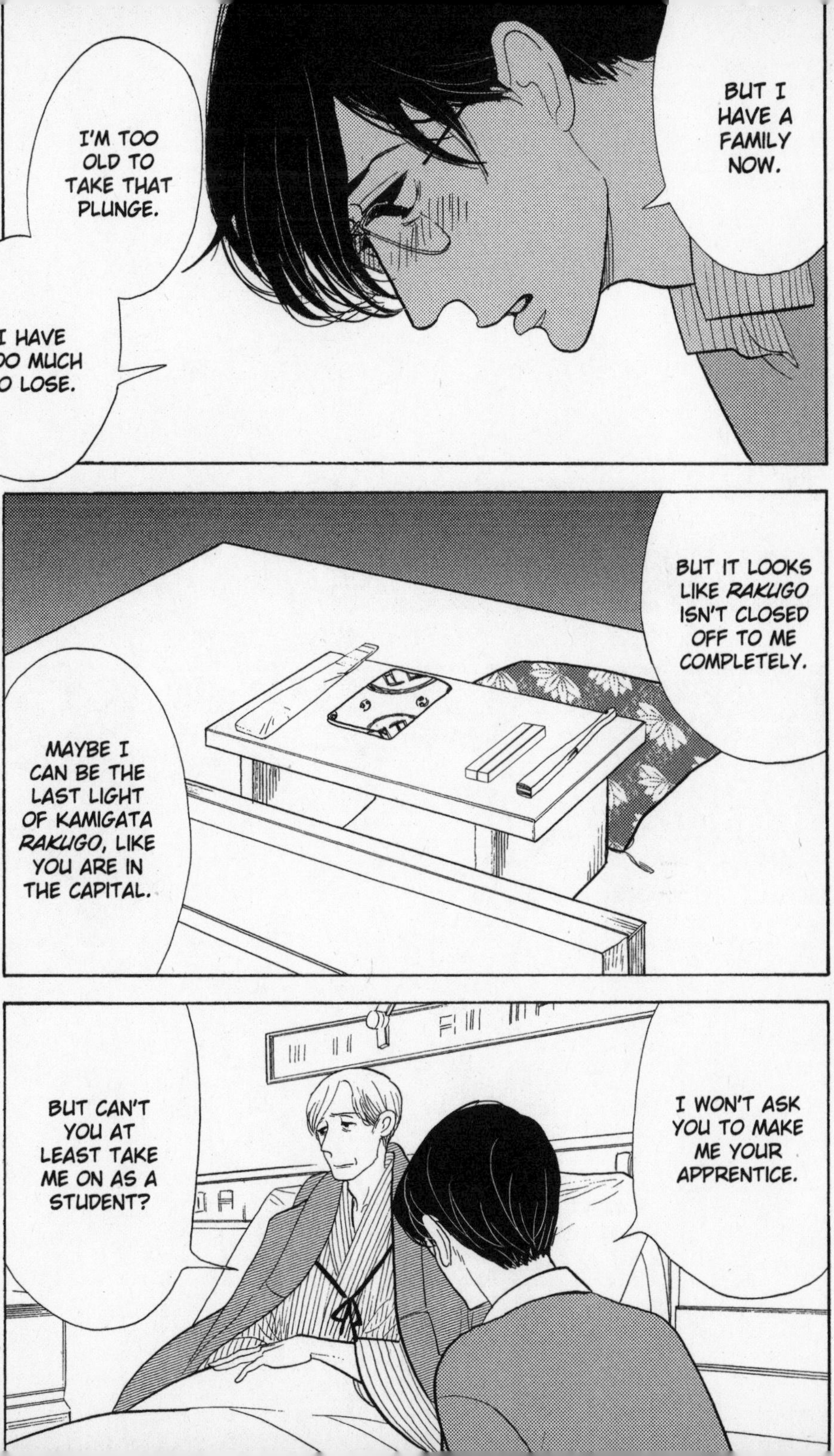
BUT I HAVE A FAMILY NOW.
I'M TOO OLD TO TAKE THAT PLUNGE.
I HAVE TOO MUCH TO LOSE.
BUT IT LOOKS LIKE *RAKUGO* ISN'T CLOSED OFF TO ME COMPLETELY.
MAYBE I CAN BE THE LAST LIGHT OF KAMIGATA *RAKUGO*, LIKE YOU ARE IN THE CAPITAL.
I WON'T ASK YOU TO MAKE ME YOUR APPRENTICE.
BUT CAN'T YOU AT LEAST TAKE ME ON AS A STUDENT?

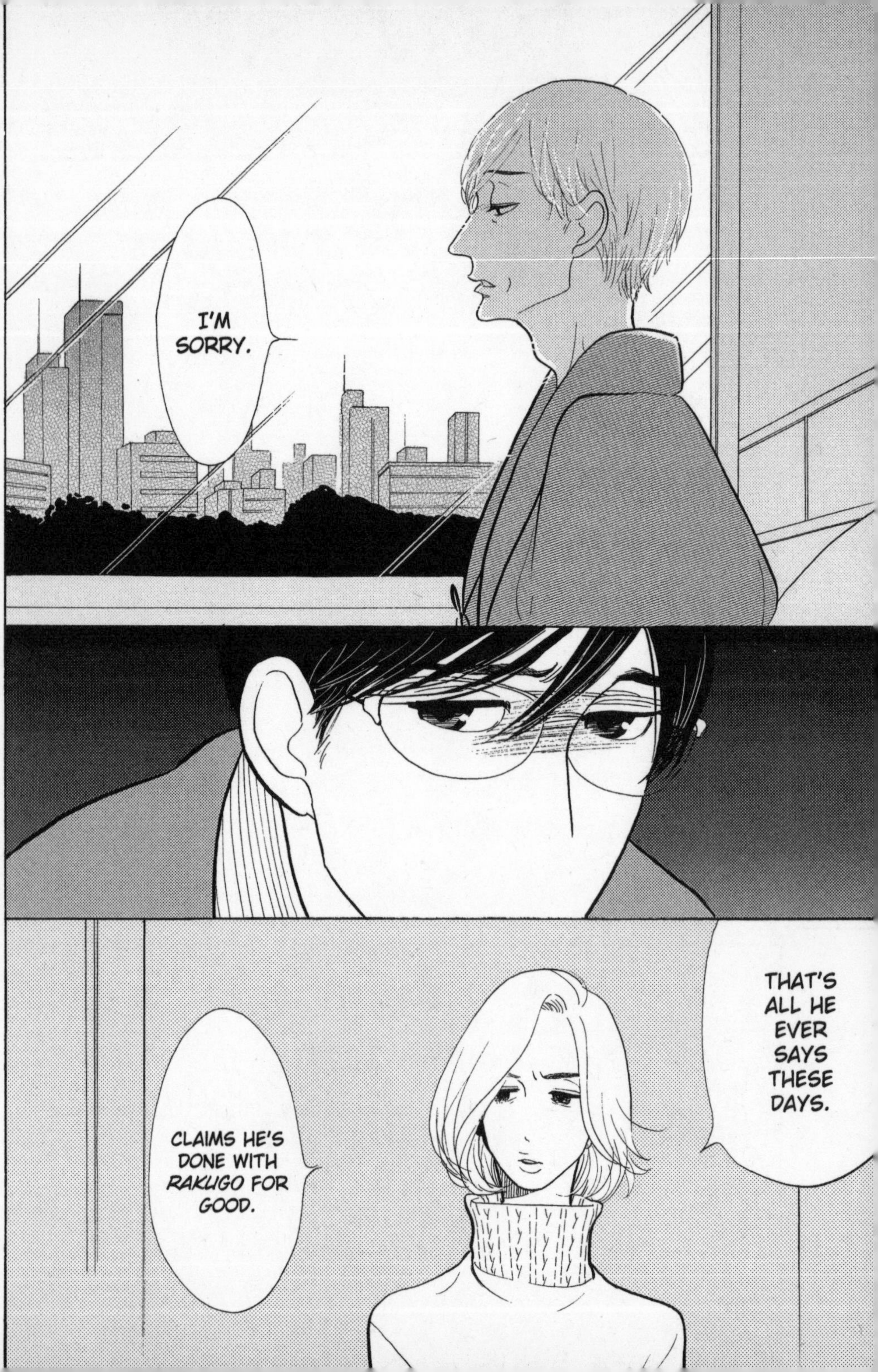
I'M SORRY.
THAT'S ALL HE EVER SAYS THESE DAYS.
CLAIMS HE'S DONE WITH *RAKUGO* FOR GOOD.

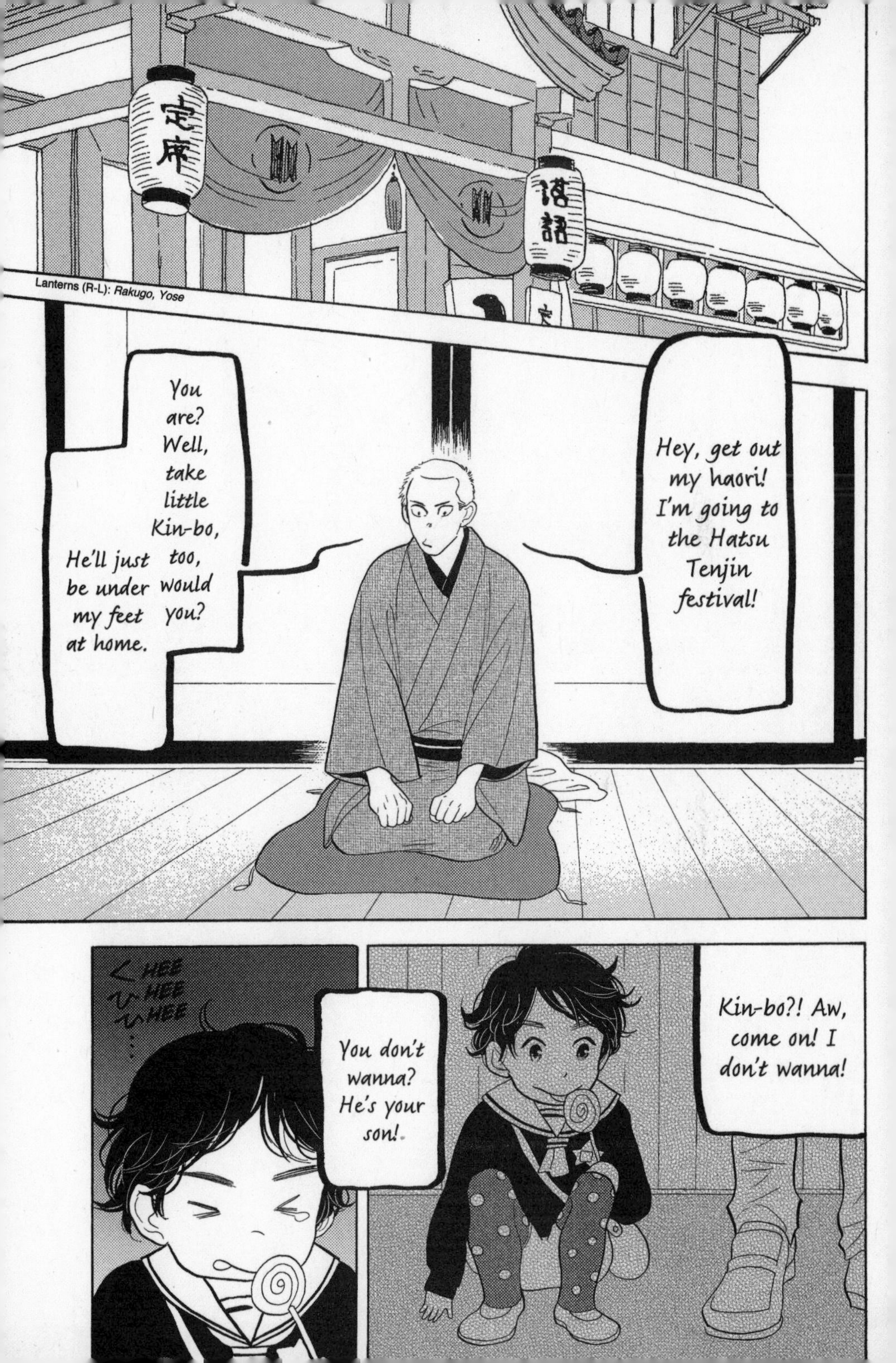
落語
定席
Lanterns (R-L): *Rakugo, Yose*
Hey, get out my haori! I'm going to the Hatsu Tenjin festival!
You are? Well, take little Kin-bo, too, would you? He'll just be under my feet at home.
Kin-bo?! Aw, come on! I don't wanna!
You don't wanna? He's your son!
HEE HEE HEE

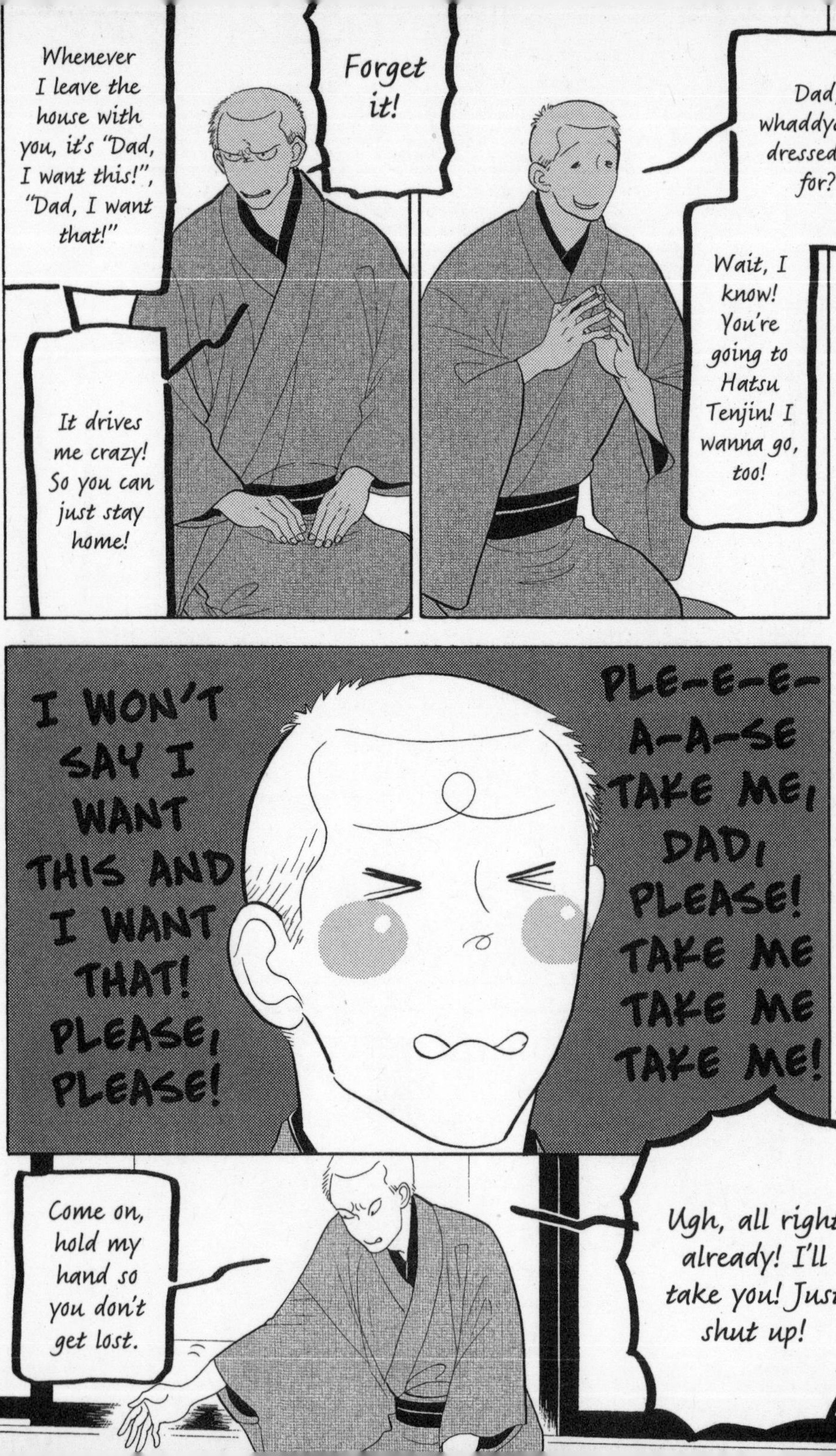
Dad, whaddya all dressed up for?
Wait, I know! You're going to Hatsu Tenjin! I wanna go, too!
Forget it!
Whenever I leave the house with you, it's "Dad, I want this!", "Dad, I want that!"
It drives me crazy! So you can just stay home!
PLE-E-E-A-A-SE TAKE ME, DAD, PLEASE! TAKE ME TAKE ME TAKE ME!
I WON'T SAY I WANT THIS AND I WANT THAT! PLEASE, PLEASE!
Ugh, all right already! I'll take you! Just shut up!
Come on, hold my hand so you don't get lost.

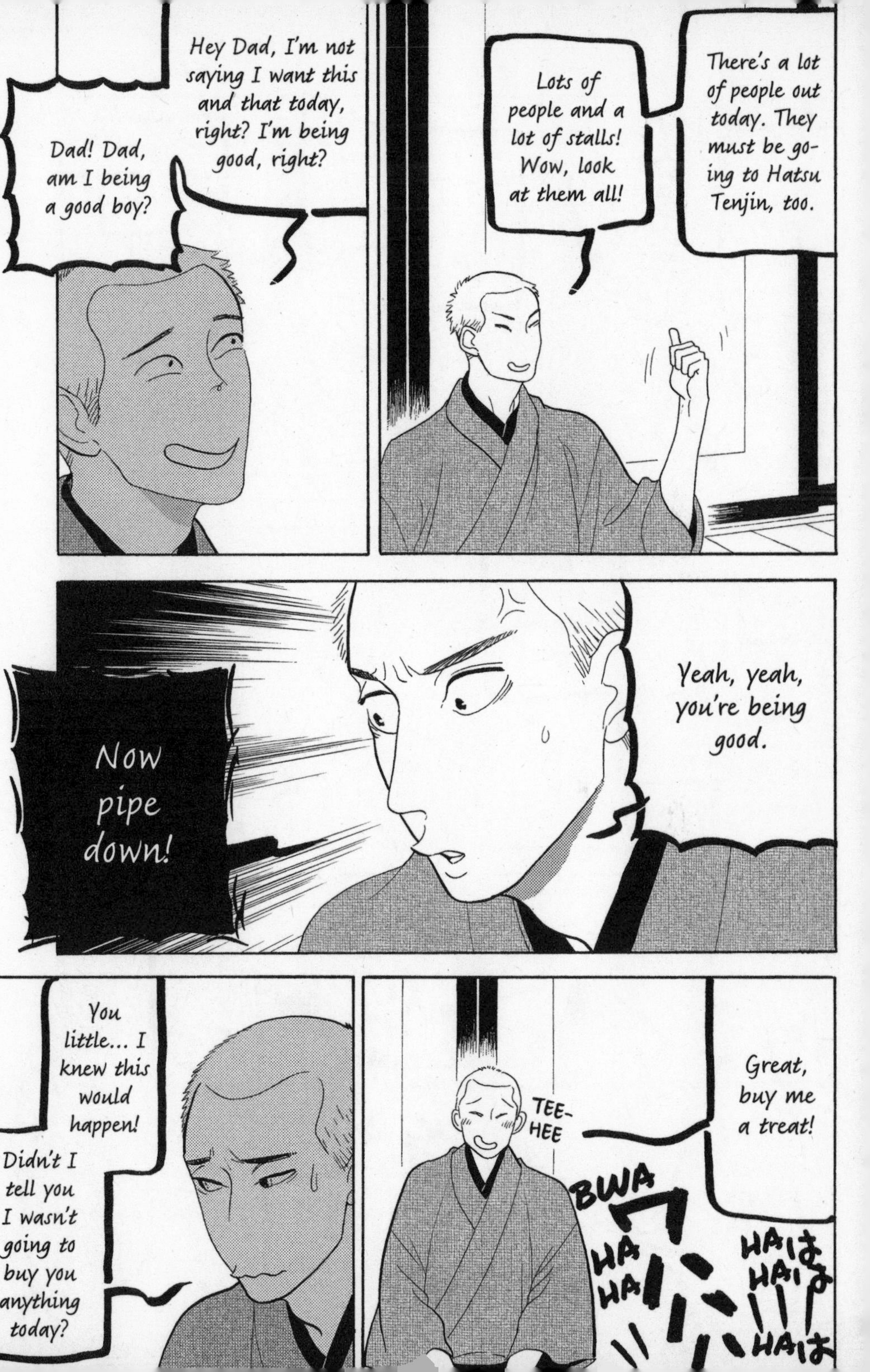

There's a lot of people out today. They must be going to Hatsu Tenjin, too.
Lots of people and a lot of stalls! Wow, look at them all!
Hey Dad, I'm not saying I want this and that today, right? I'm being good, right?
Dad! Dad, am I being a good boy?
Yeah, yeah, you're being good.
Now pipe down!
Great, buy me a treat!
TEE-HEE
HAは HAは HAは
BWA HA HA
You little... I knew this would happen!
Didn't I tell you I wasn't going to buy you anything today?

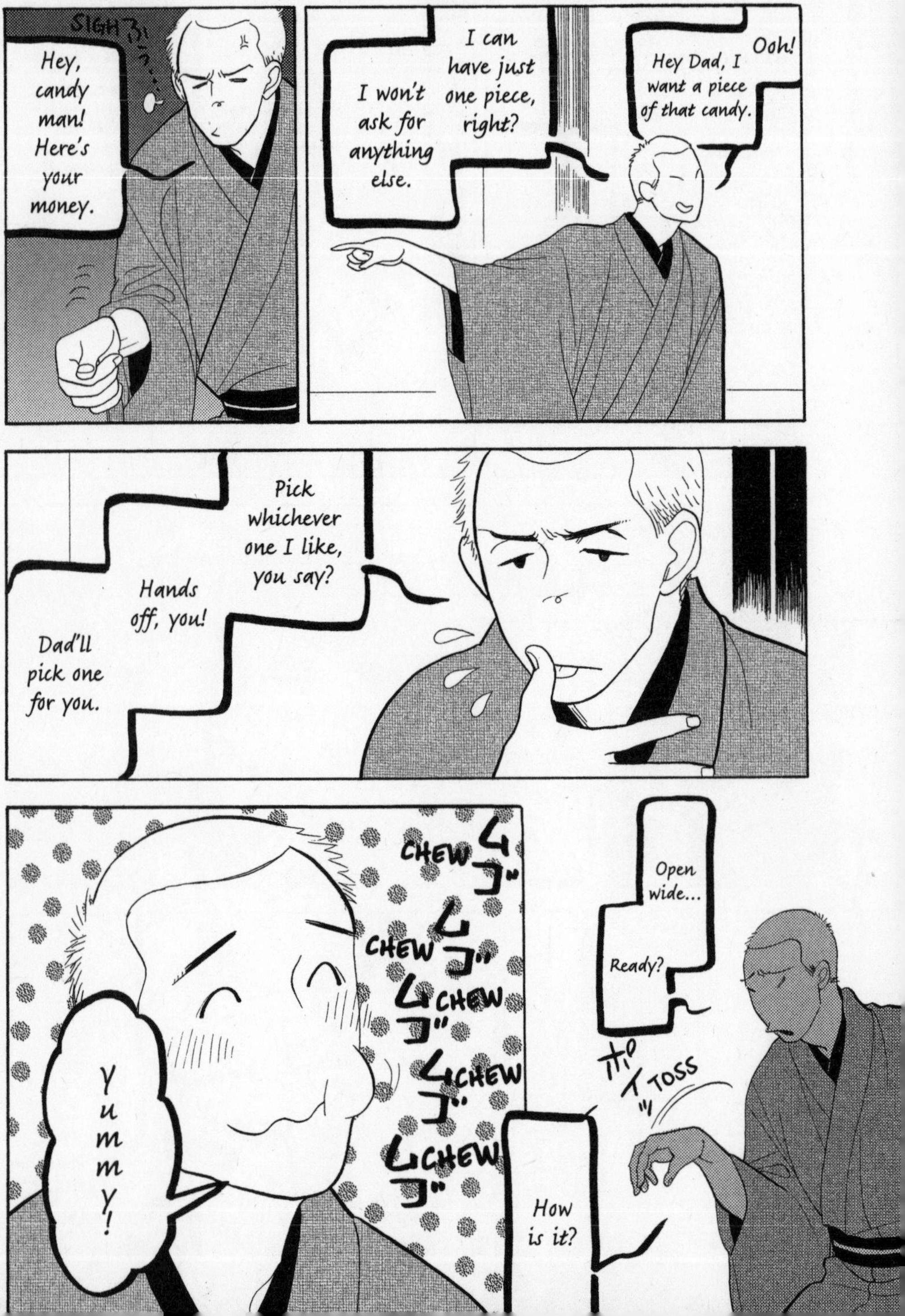
Ooh!
Hey Dad, I want a piece of that candy.
I can have just one piece, right?
I won't ask for anything else.
SIGH
Hey, candy man! Here's your money.
Pick whichever one I like, you say?
Hands off, you!
Dad'll pick one for you.
Open wide...
Ready?
TOSS
How is it?
CHEW
CHEW
CHEW
CHEW
CHEW
Yummy!

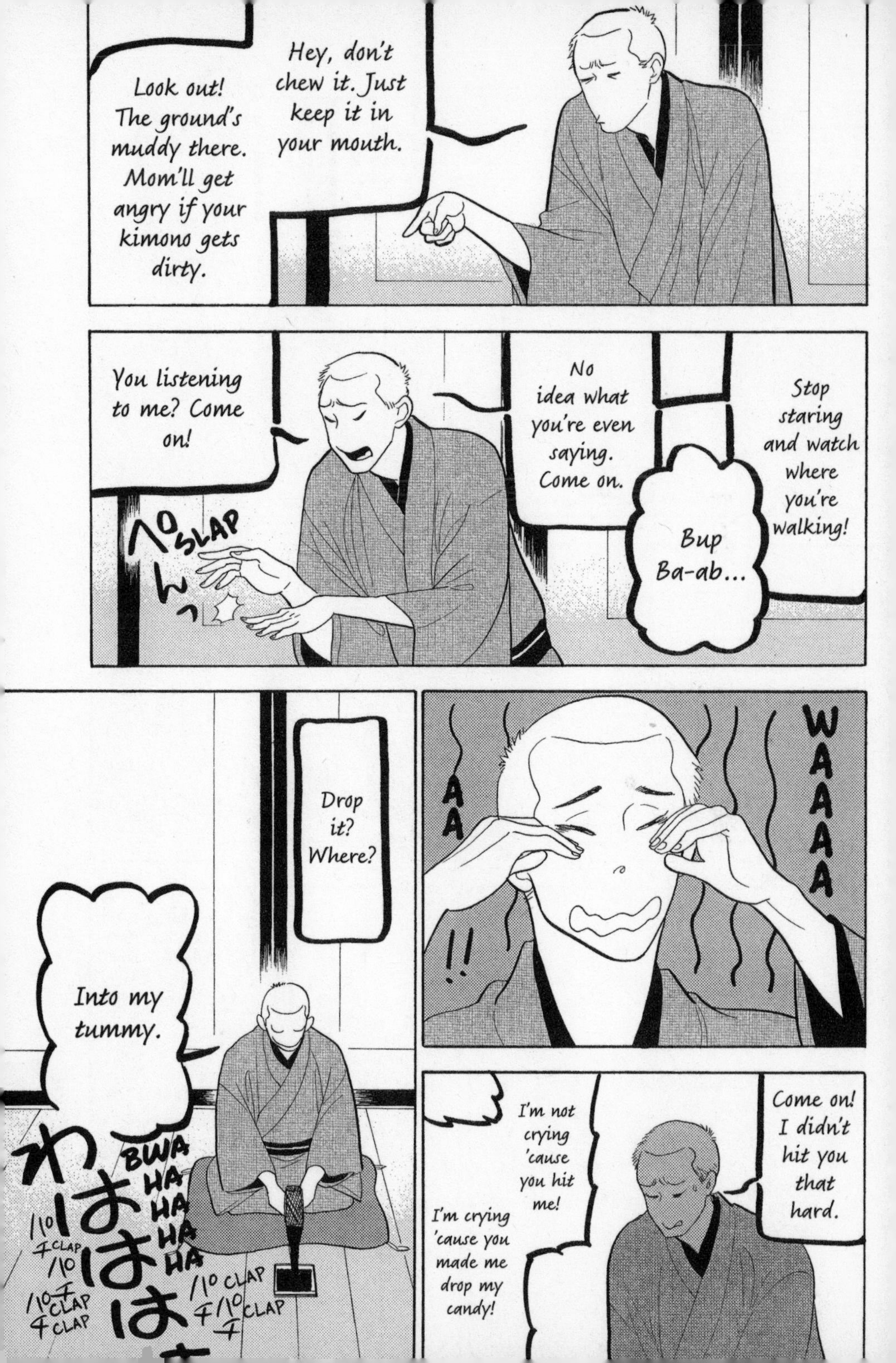
Hey, don't chew it. Just keep it in your mouth.
Look out! The ground's muddy there. Mom'll get angry if your kimono gets dirty.
Stop staring and watch where you're walking!
Bup Ba-ab...
No idea what you're even saying. Come on.
You listening to me? Come on!
SLAP
WAAAAA
AA
!!
Come on! I didn't hit you that hard.
I'm not crying 'cause you hit me!
I'm crying 'cause you made me drop my candy!
Drop it? Where?
Into my tummy.
BWA HA HA HA HA
CLAP CLAP CLAP CLAP CLAP

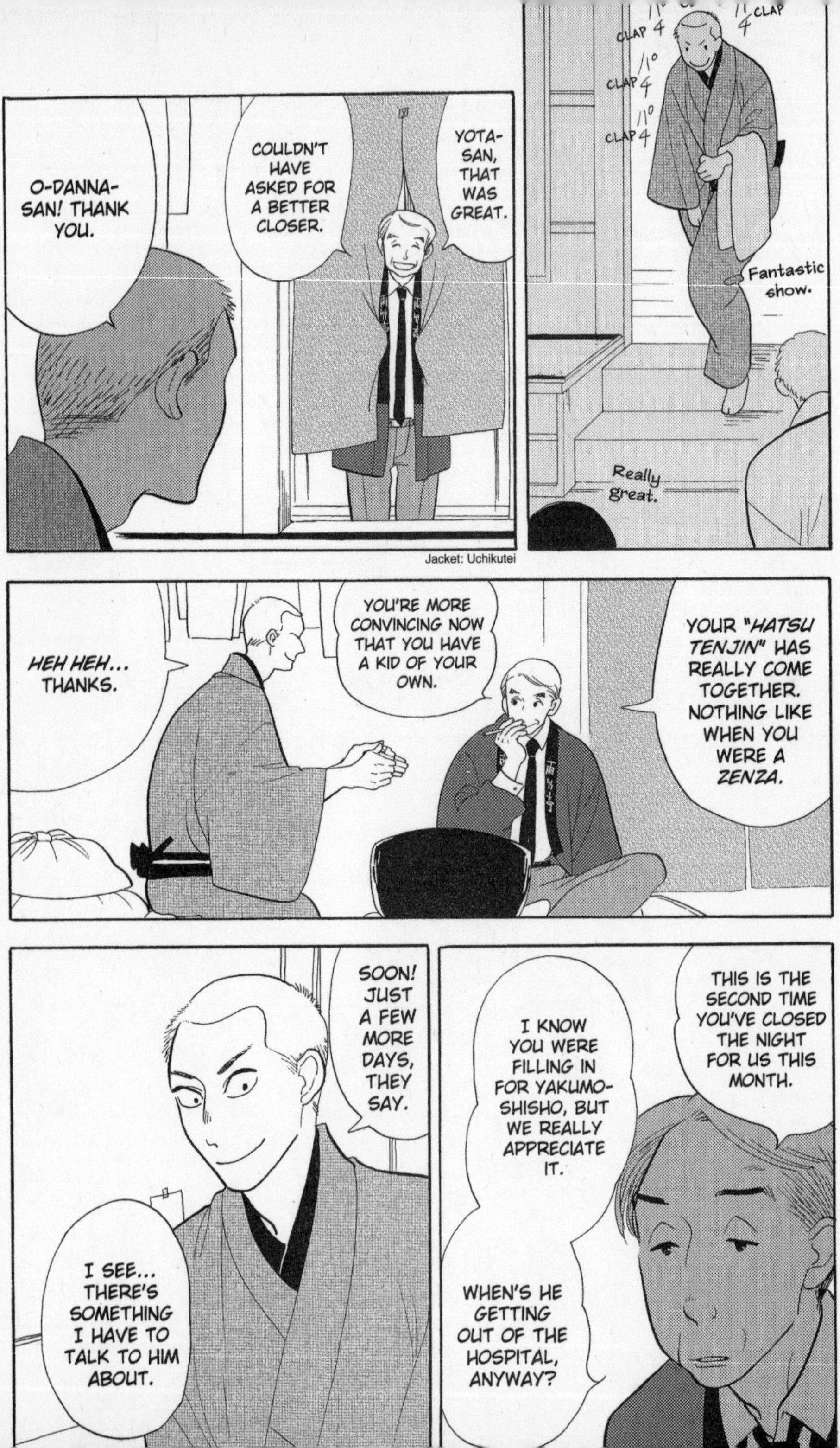
CLAP CLAP
CLAP
CLAP
Fantastic show.
Really great.
YOTA-SAN, THAT WAS GREAT.
COULDN'T HAVE ASKED FOR A BETTER CLOSER.
O-DANNA-SAN! THANK YOU.
Jacket: Uchikutei
YOUR "HATSU TENJIN" HAS REALLY COME TOGETHER. NOTHING LIKE WHEN YOU WERE A ZENZA.
YOU'RE MORE CONVINCING NOW THAT YOU HAVE A KID OF YOUR OWN.
HEH HEH... THANKS.
THIS IS THE SECOND TIME YOU'VE CLOSED THE NIGHT FOR US THIS MONTH.
I KNOW YOU WERE FILLING IN FOR YAKUMO-SHISHO, BUT WE REALLY APPRECIATE IT.
WHEN'S HE GETTING OUT OF THE HOSPITAL, ANYWAY?
SOON! JUST A FEW MORE DAYS, THEY SAY.
I SEE... THERE'S SOMETHING I HAVE TO TALK TO HIM ABOUT.

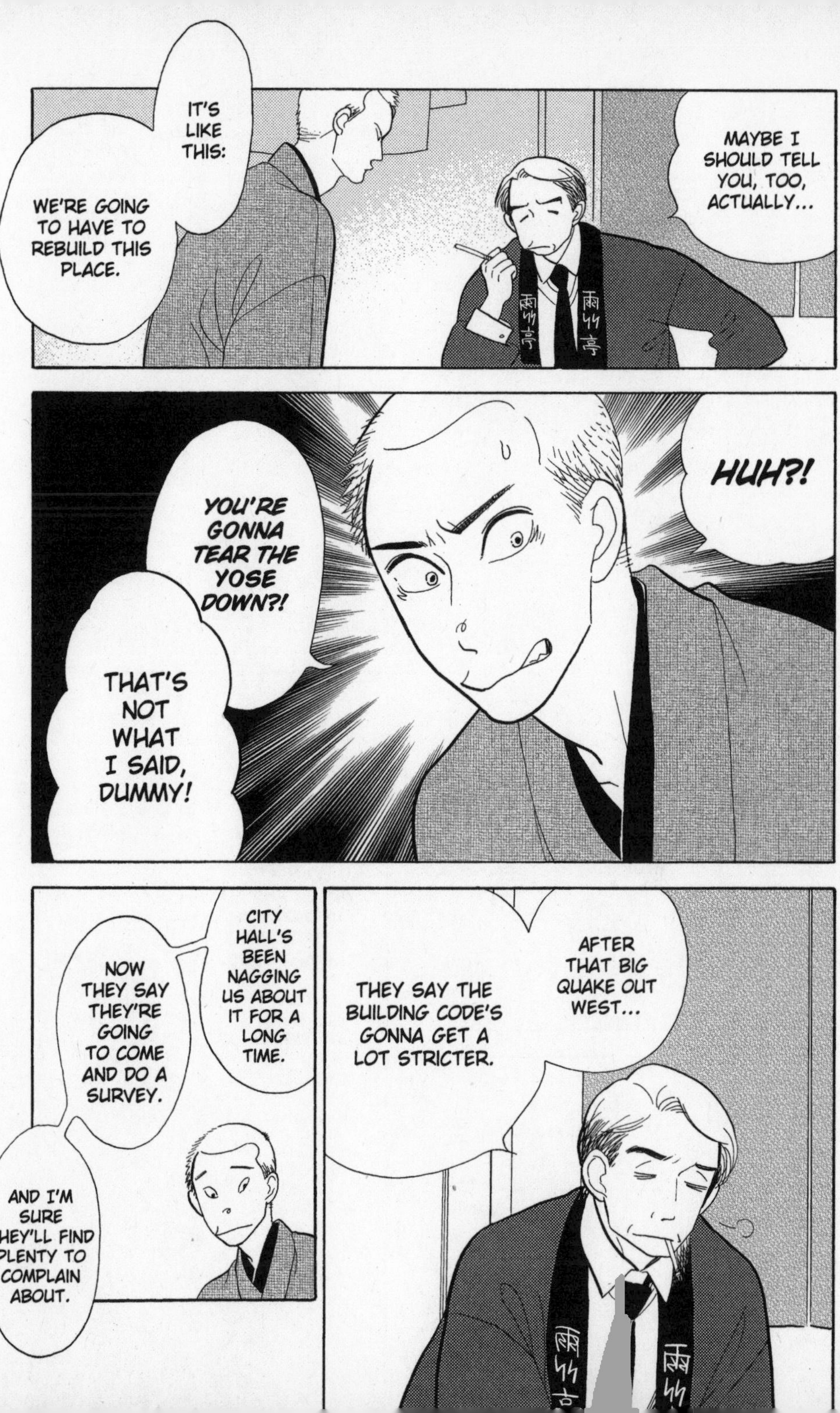
MAYBE I SHOULD TELL YOU, TOO, ACTUALLY...
IT'S LIKE THIS:
WE'RE GOING TO HAVE TO REBUILD THIS PLACE.
雨竹亭
HUH?!
YOU'RE GONNA TEAR THE YOSE DOWN?!
THAT'S NOT WHAT I SAID, DUMMY!
AFTER THAT BIG QUAKE OUT WEST...
THEY SAY THE BUILDING CODE'S GONNA GET A LOT STRICTER.
CITY HALL'S BEEN NAGGING US ABOUT IT FOR A LONG TIME.
NOW THEY SAY THEY'RE GOING TO COME AND DO A SURVEY.
AND I'M SURE THEY'LL FIND PLENTY TO COMPLAIN ABOUT.

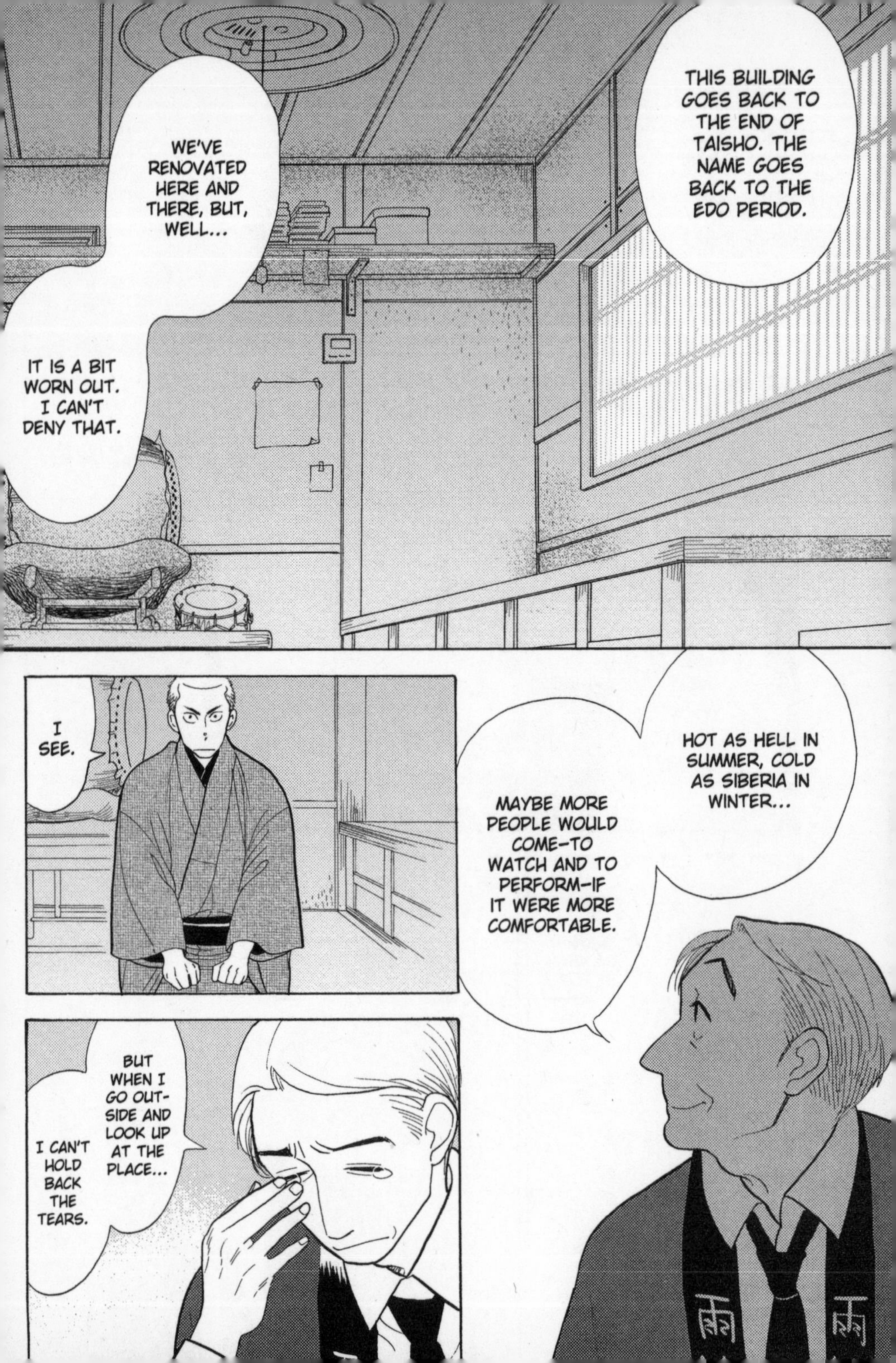
THIS BUILDING GOES BACK TO THE END OF TAISHO. THE NAME GOES BACK TO THE EDO PERIOD.
WE'VE RENOVATED HERE AND THERE, BUT, WELL...
IT IS A BIT WORN OUT. I CAN'T DENY THAT.
HOT AS HELL IN SUMMER, COLD AS SIBERIA IN WINTER...
MAYBE MORE PEOPLE WOULD COME—TO WATCH AND TO PERFORM—IF IT WERE MORE COMFORTABLE.
I SEE.
BUT WHEN I GO OUT-SIDE AND LOOK UP AT THE PLACE...
I CAN'T HOLD BACK THE TEARS.

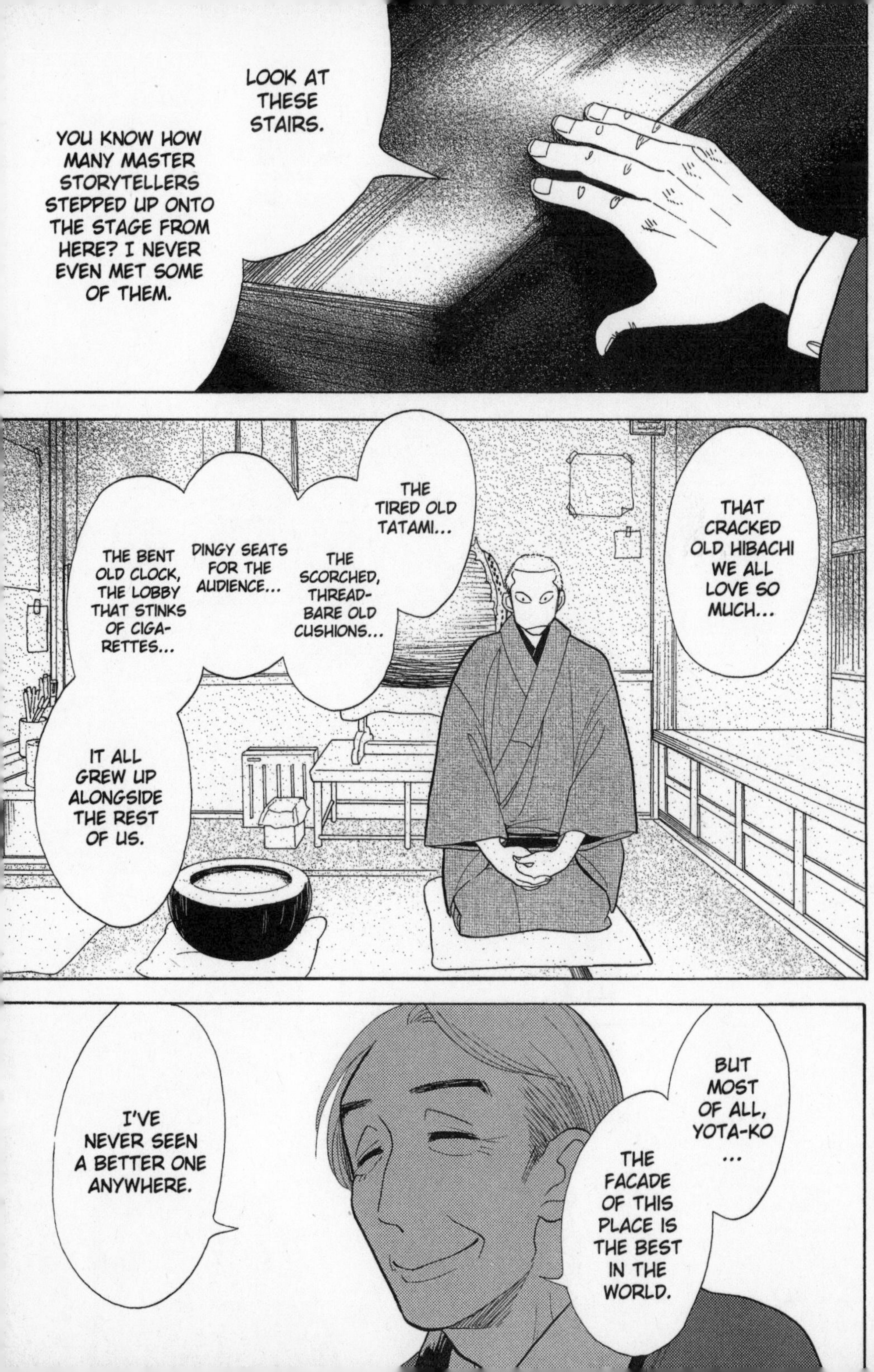
LOOK AT THESE STAIRS.
YOU KNOW HOW MANY MASTER STORYTELLERS STEPPED UP ONTO THE STAGE FROM HERE? I NEVER EVEN MET SOME OF THEM.
THAT CRACKED OLD HIBACHI WE ALL LOVE SO MUCH...
THE TIRED OLD TATAMI...
THE SCORCHED, THREAD-BARE OLD CUSHIONS...
DINGY SEATS FOR THE AUDIENCE...
THE BENT OLD CLOCK, THE LOBBY THAT STINKS OF CIGA-RETTES...
IT ALL GREW UP ALONGSIDE THE REST OF US.
BUT MOST OF ALL, YOTA-KO ...
THE FACADE OF THIS PLACE IS THE BEST IN THE WORLD.
I'VE NEVER SEEN A BETTER ONE ANYWHERE.

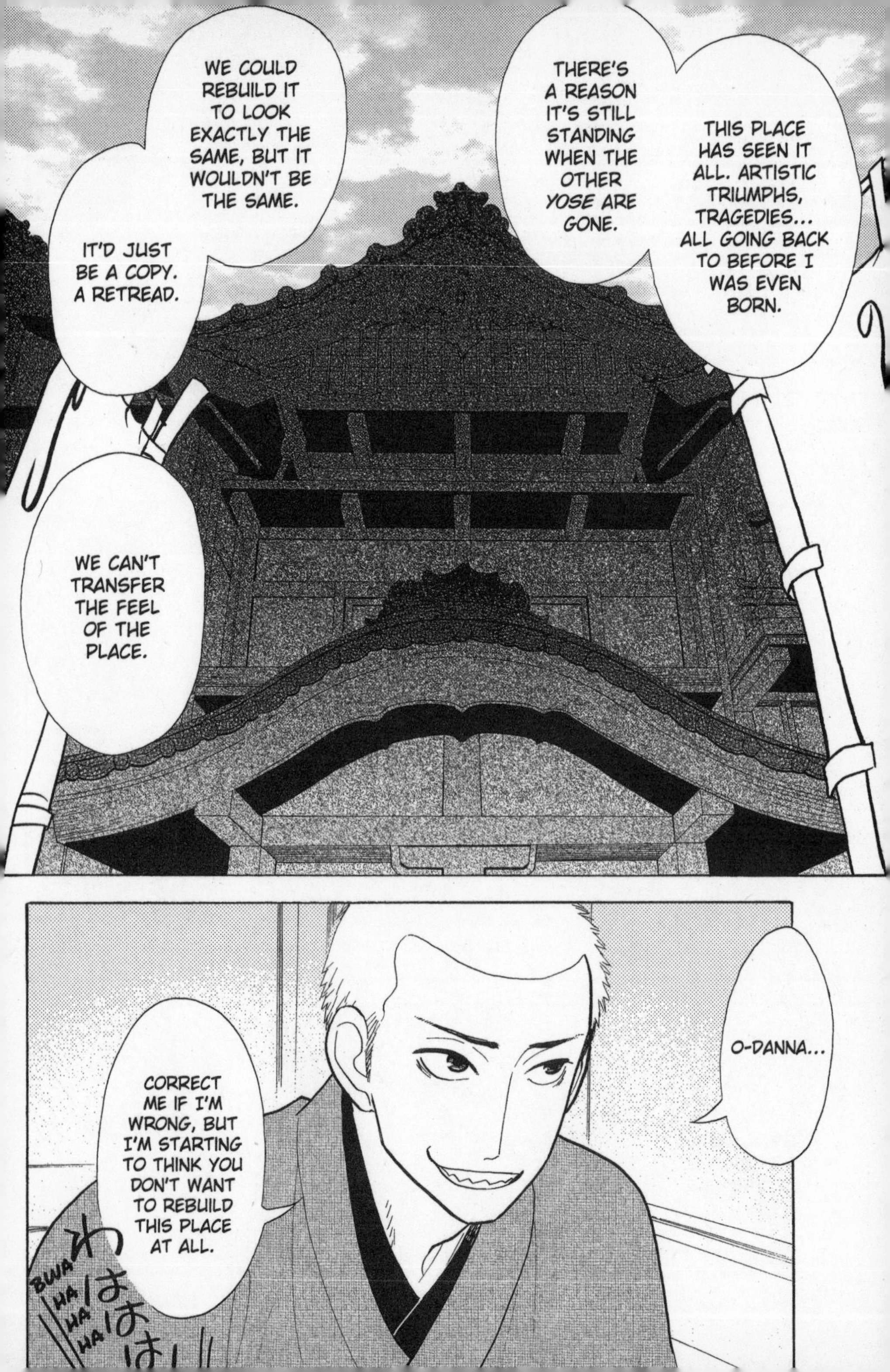
THIS PLACE HAS SEEN IT ALL. ARTISTIC TRIUMPHS, TRAGEDIES... ALL GOING BACK TO BEFORE I WAS EVEN BORN.
THERE'S A REASON IT'S STILL STANDING WHEN THE OTHER *YOSE* ARE GONE.
WE COULD REBUILD IT TO LOOK EXACTLY THE SAME, BUT IT WOULDN'T BE THE SAME.
IT'D JUST BE A COPY. A RETREAD.
WE CAN'T TRANSFER THE FEEL OF THE PLACE.
O-DANNA...
CORRECT ME IF I'M WRONG, BUT I'M STARTING TO THINK YOU DON'T WANT TO REBUILD THIS PLACE AT ALL.
わははは
BWA HA HA HA

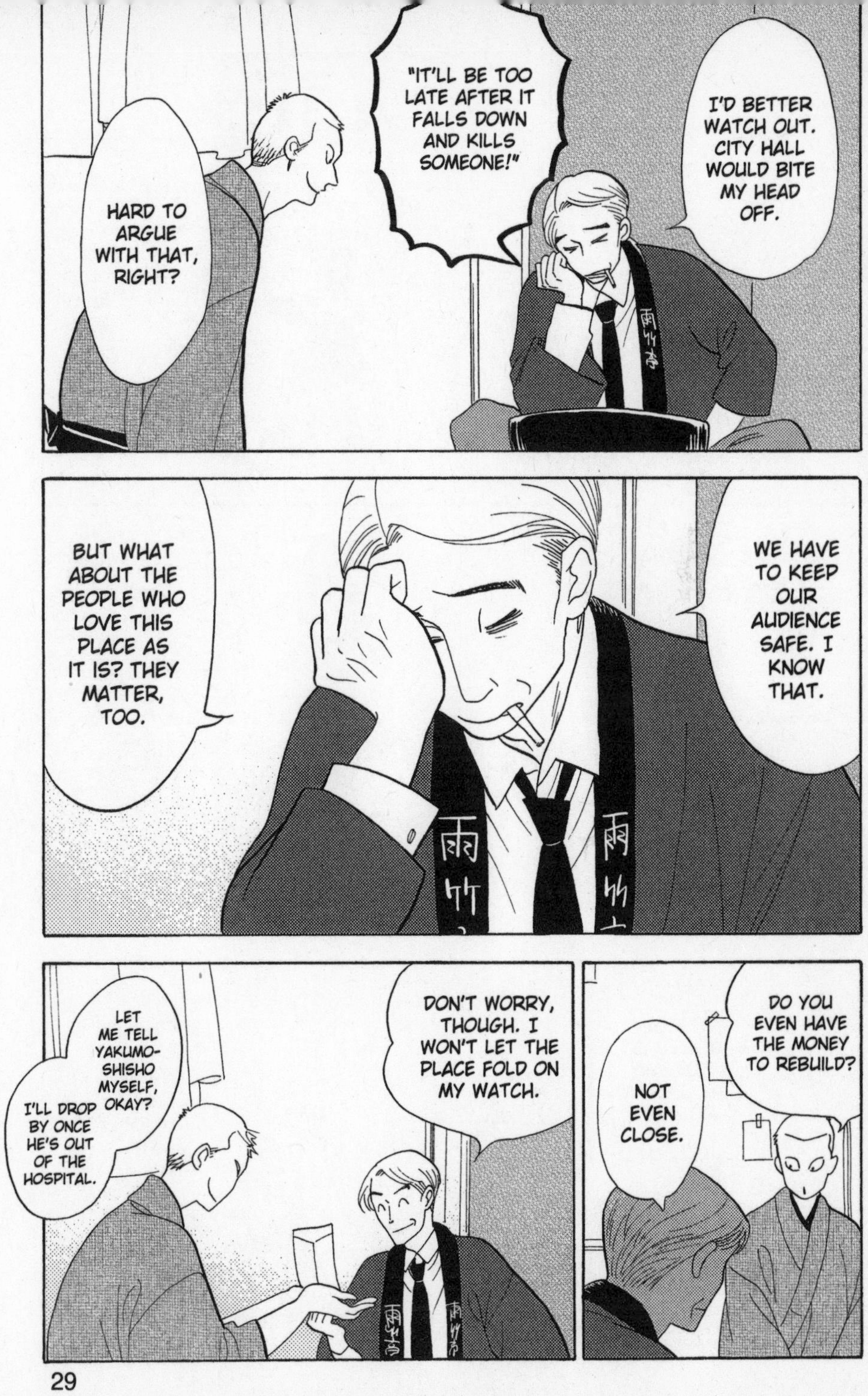
I'D BETTER WATCH OUT. CITY HALL WOULD BITE MY HEAD OFF.
"IT'LL BE TOO LATE AFTER IT FALLS DOWN AND KILLS SOMEONE!"
HARD TO ARGUE WITH THAT, RIGHT?
WE HAVE TO KEEP OUR AUDIENCE SAFE. I KNOW THAT.
BUT WHAT ABOUT THE PEOPLE WHO LOVE THIS PLACE AS IT IS? THEY MATTER, TOO.
DO YOU EVEN HAVE THE MONEY TO REBUILD?
NOT EVEN CLOSE.
DON'T WORRY, THOUGH. I WON'T LET THE PLACE FOLD ON MY WATCH.
LET ME TELL YAKUMO-SHISHO MYSELF, OKAY?
I'LL DROP BY ONCE HE'S OUT OF THE HOSPITAL.

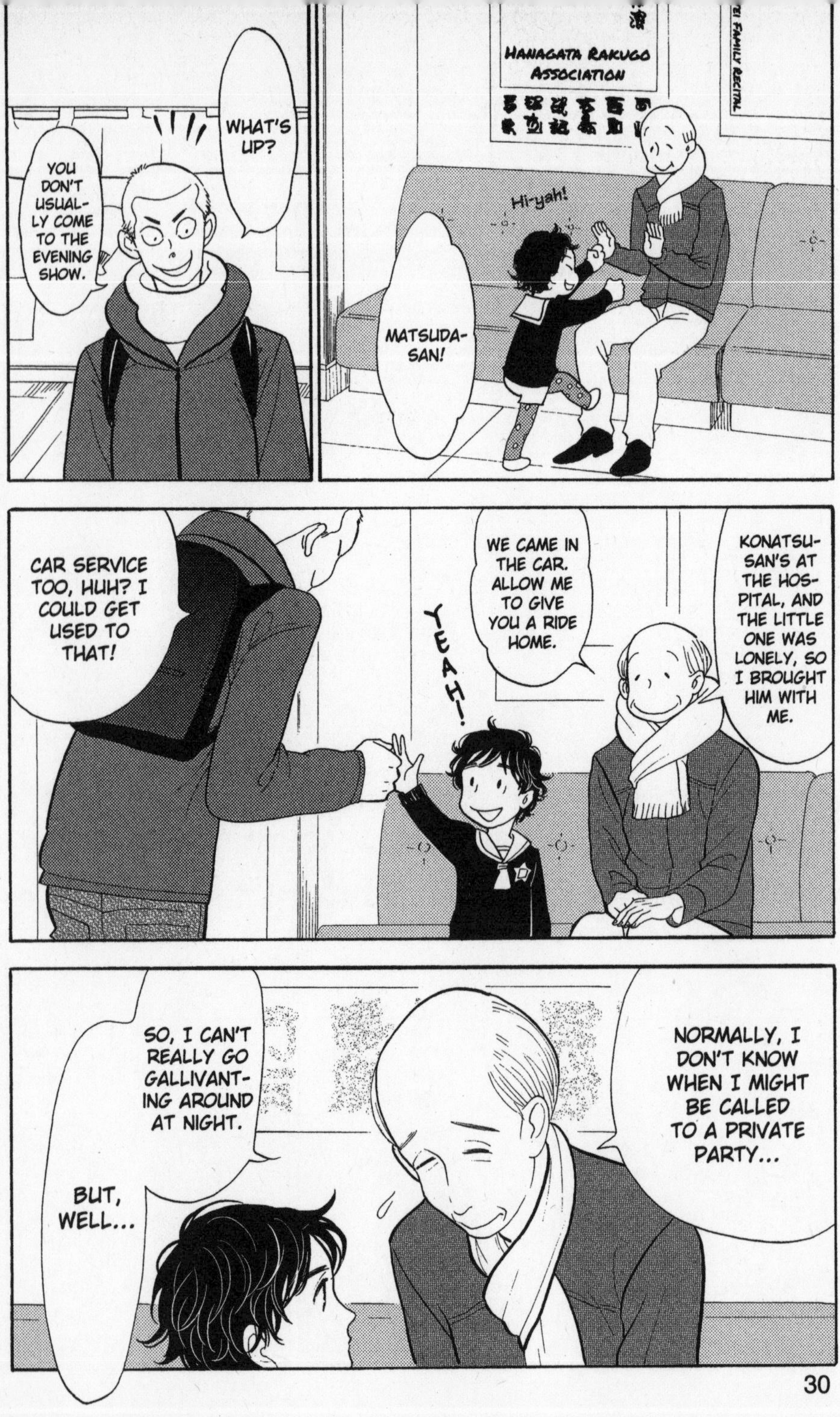

HANAGATA RAKUGO ASSOCIATION
FAMILY RECITAL
Hi-yah!
MATSUDA-SAN!
WHAT'S UP?
YOU DON'T USUALLY COME TO THE EVENING SHOW.
KONATSU-SAN'S AT THE HOSPITAL, AND THE LITTLE ONE WAS LONELY, SO I BROUGHT HIM WITH ME.
WE CAME IN THE CAR. ALLOW ME TO GIVE YOU A RIDE HOME.
YEAH!
CAR SERVICE TOO, HUH? I COULD GET USED TO THAT!
NORMALLY, I DON'T KNOW WHEN I MIGHT BE CALLED TO A PRIVATE PARTY...
SO, I CAN'T REALLY GO GALLIVANTING AROUND AT NIGHT.
BUT, WELL...

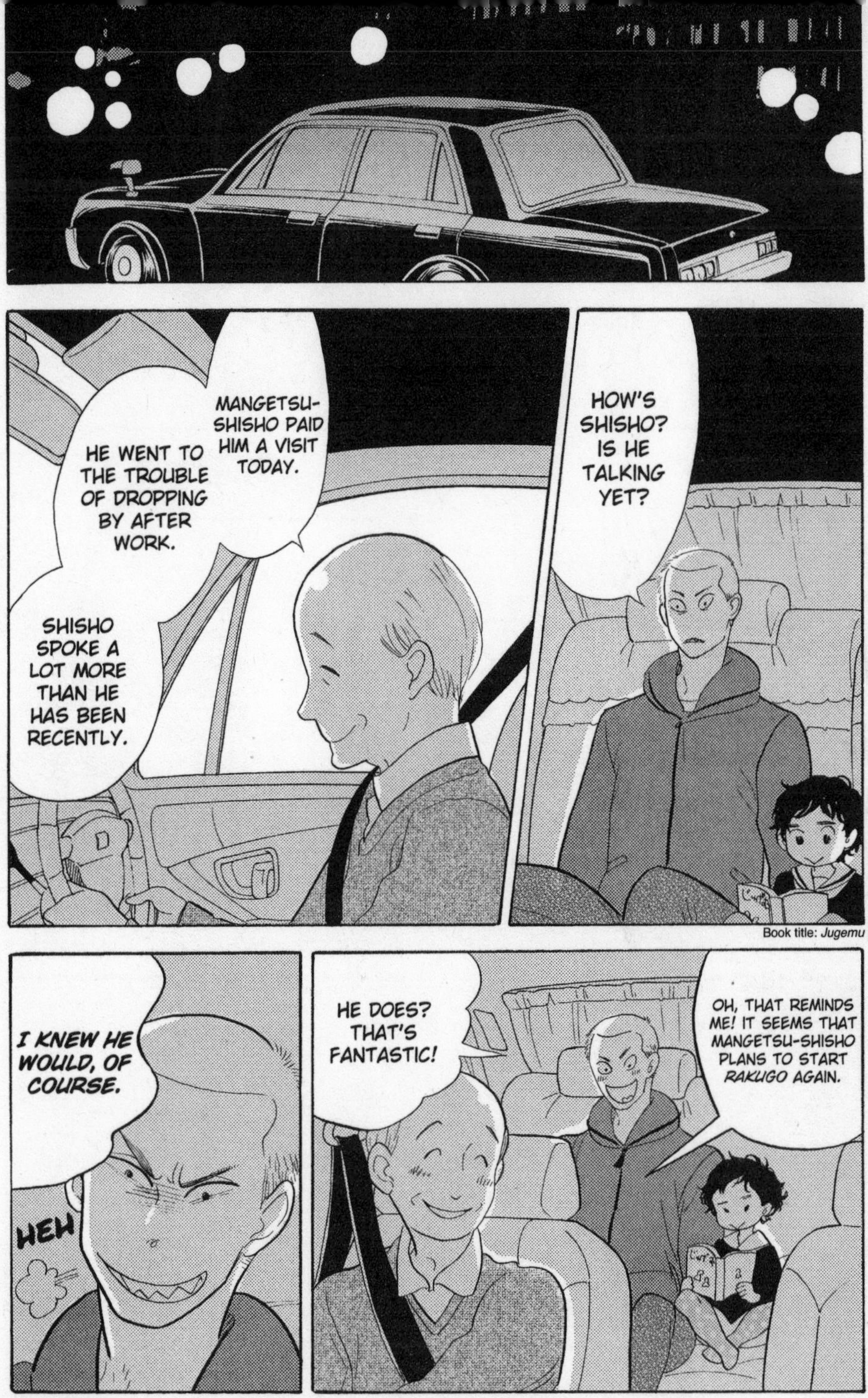
HOW'S SHISHO? IS HE TALKING YET?
MANGETSU-SHISHO PAID HIM A VISIT TODAY.
HE WENT TO THE TROUBLE OF DROPPING BY AFTER WORK.
SHISHO SPOKE A LOT MORE THAN HE HAS BEEN RECENTLY.
OH, THAT REMINDS ME! IT SEEMS THAT MANGETSU-SHISHO PLANS TO START *RAKUGO* AGAIN.
HE DOES? THAT'S FANTASTIC!
I KNEW HE WOULD, OF COURSE.
HEH
Book title: *Jugemu*

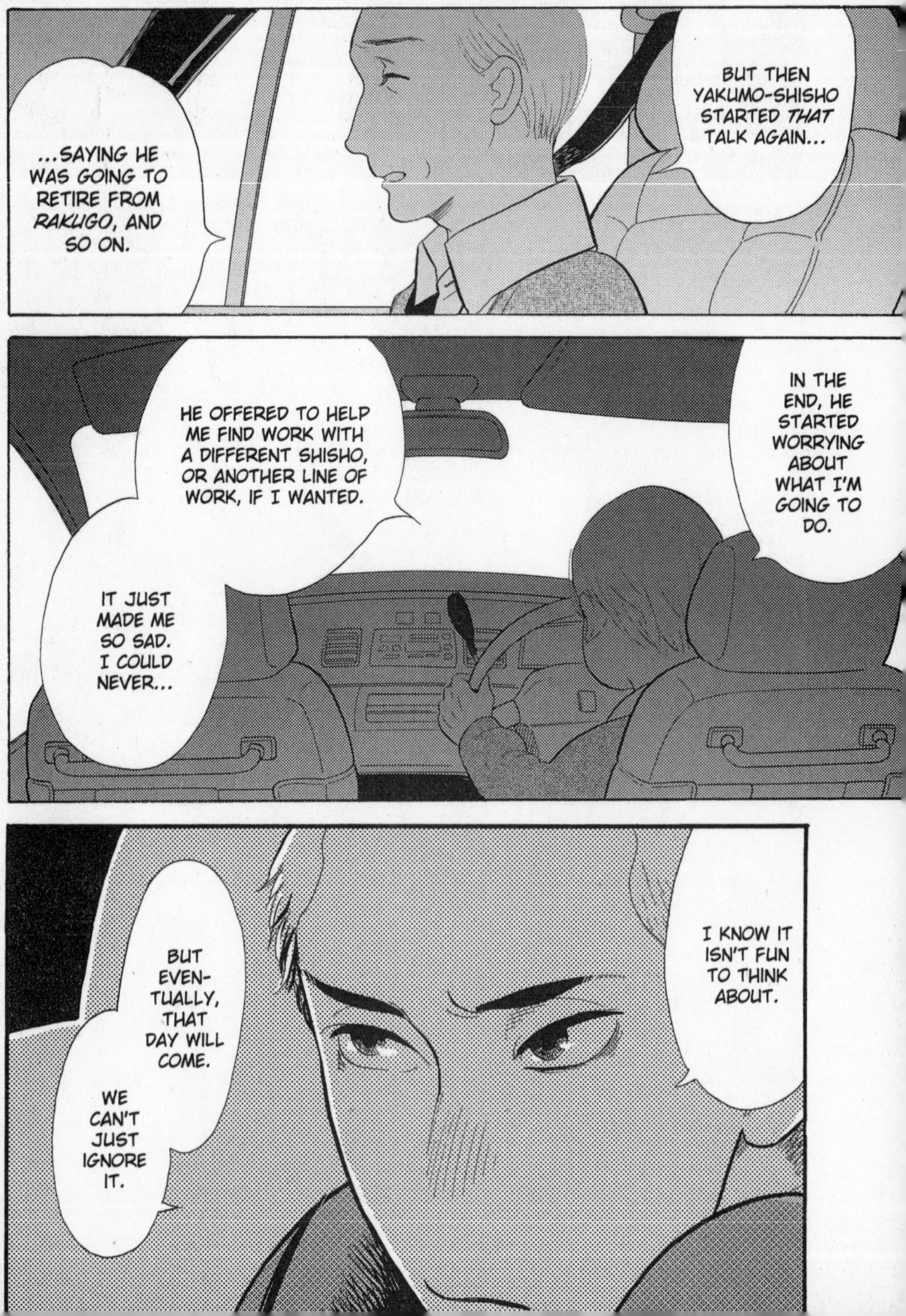
BUT THEN YAKUMO-SHISHO STARTED *THAT* TALK AGAIN...
...SAYING HE WAS GOING TO RETIRE FROM *RAKUGO*, AND SO ON.
IN THE END, HE STARTED WORRYING ABOUT WHAT I'M GOING TO DO.
HE OFFERED TO HELP ME FIND WORK WITH A DIFFERENT SHISHO, OR ANOTHER LINE OF WORK, IF I WANTED.
IT JUST MADE ME SO SAD. I COULD NEVER...
I KNOW IT ISN'T FUN TO THINK ABOUT.
BUT EVEN-TUALLY, THAT DAY WILL COME.
WE CAN'T JUST IGNORE IT.

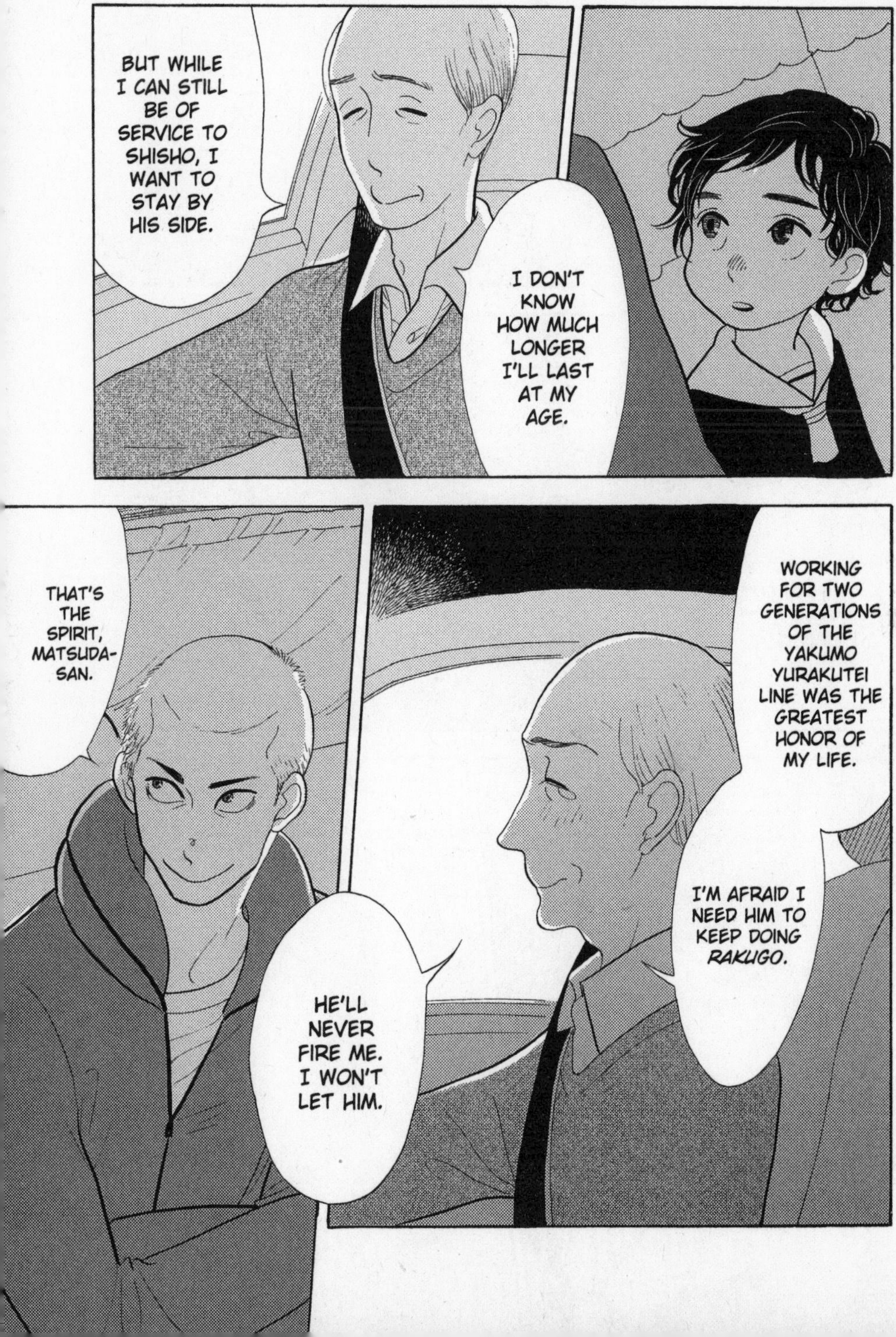
I DON'T KNOW HOW MUCH LONGER I'LL LAST AT MY AGE.
BUT WHILE I CAN STILL BE OF SERVICE TO SHISHO, I WANT TO STAY BY HIS SIDE.
WORKING FOR TWO GENERATIONS OF THE YAKUMO YURAKUTEI LINE WAS THE GREATEST HONOR OF MY LIFE.
I'M AFRAID I NEED HIM TO KEEP DOING *RAKUGO*.
HE'LL NEVER FIRE ME. I WON'T LET HIM.
THAT'S THE SPIRIT, MATSUDA-SAN.

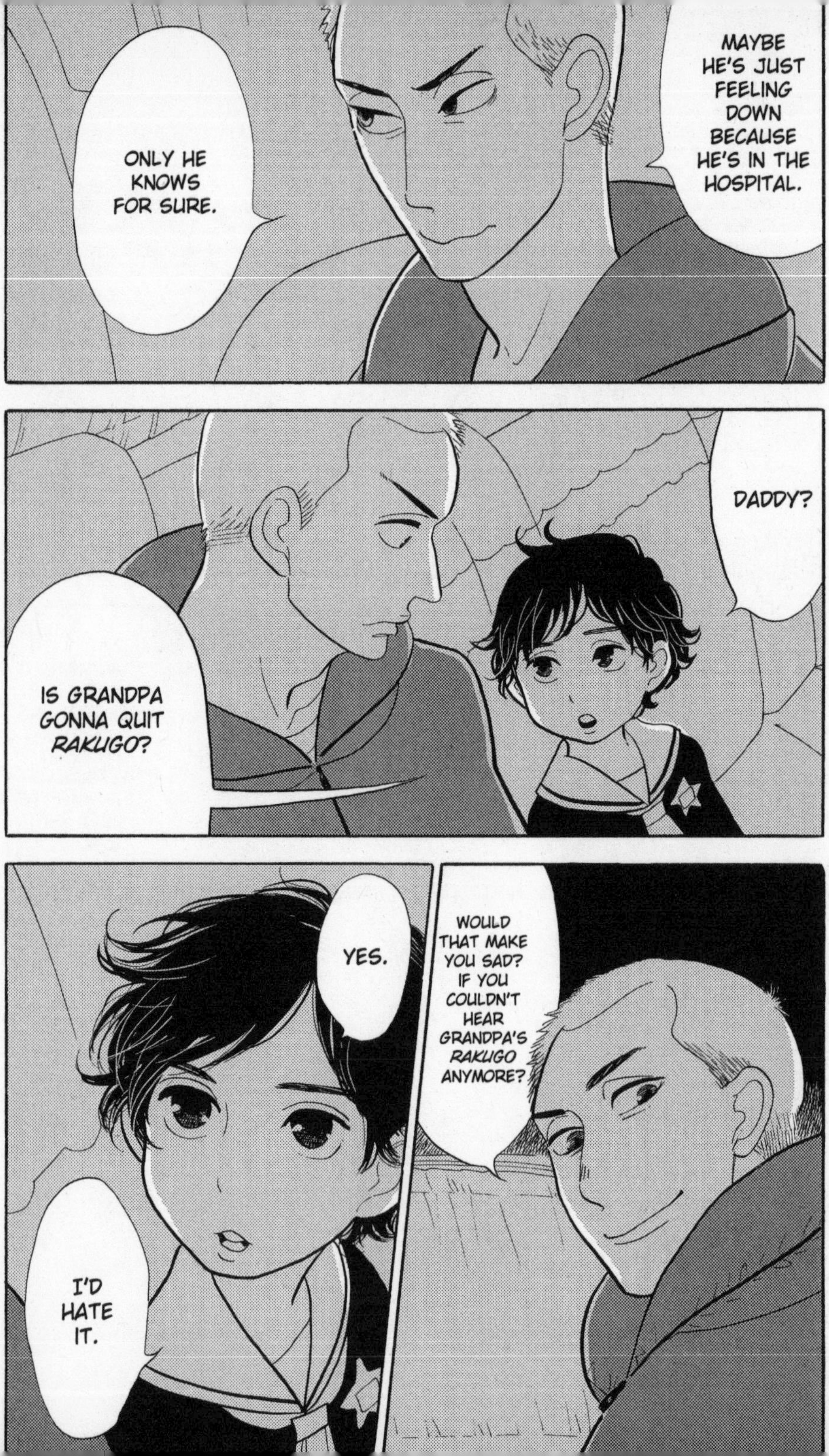
MAYBE HE'S JUST FEELING DOWN BECAUSE HE'S IN THE HOSPITAL.
ONLY HE KNOWS FOR SURE.
DADDY?
IS GRANDPA GONNA QUIT *RAKUGO*?
WOULD THAT MAKE YOU SAD? IF YOU COULDN'T HEAR GRANDPA'S *RAKUGO* ANYMORE?
YES.
I'D HATE IT.

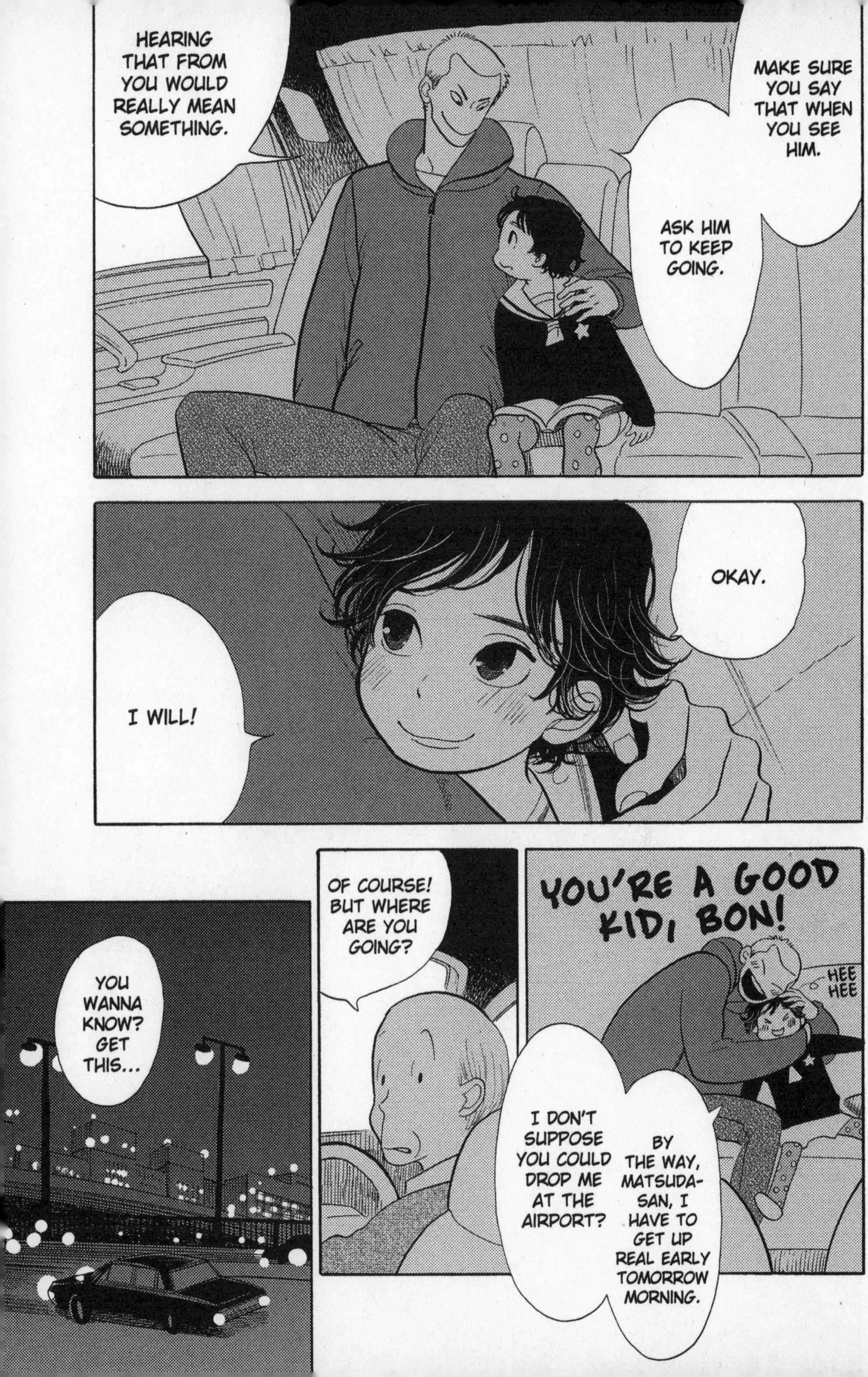
MAKE SURE YOU SAY THAT WHEN YOU SEE HIM.
ASK HIM TO KEEP GOING.
HEARING THAT FROM YOU WOULD REALLY MEAN SOMETHING.
OKAY.
I WILL!
YOU'RE A GOOD KID, BON!
HEE HEE
BY THE WAY, MATSUDA-SAN, I HAVE TO GET UP REAL EARLY TOMORROW MORNING.
I DON'T SUPPOSE YOU COULD DROP ME AT THE AIRPORT?
OF COURSE! BUT WHERE ARE YOU GOING?
YOU WANNA KNOW? GET THIS...

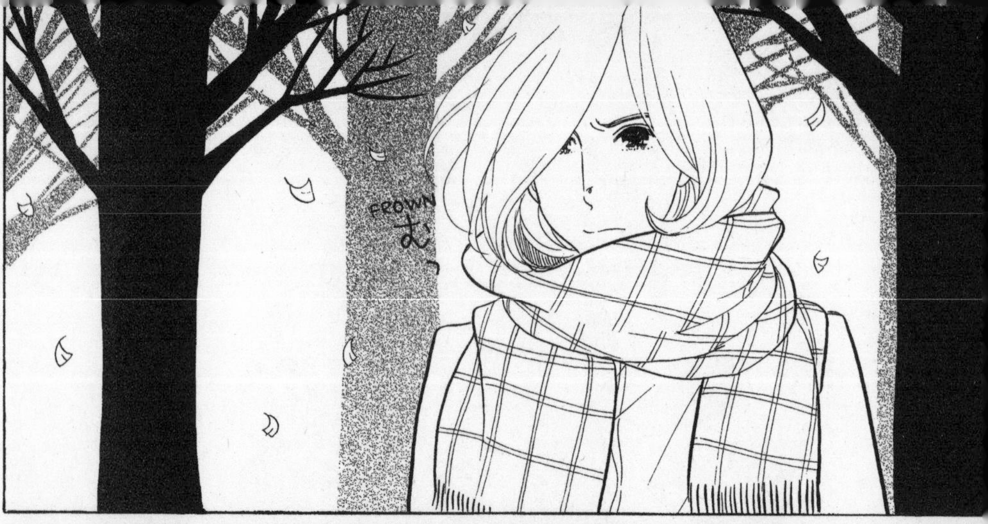
FROWN
むっ

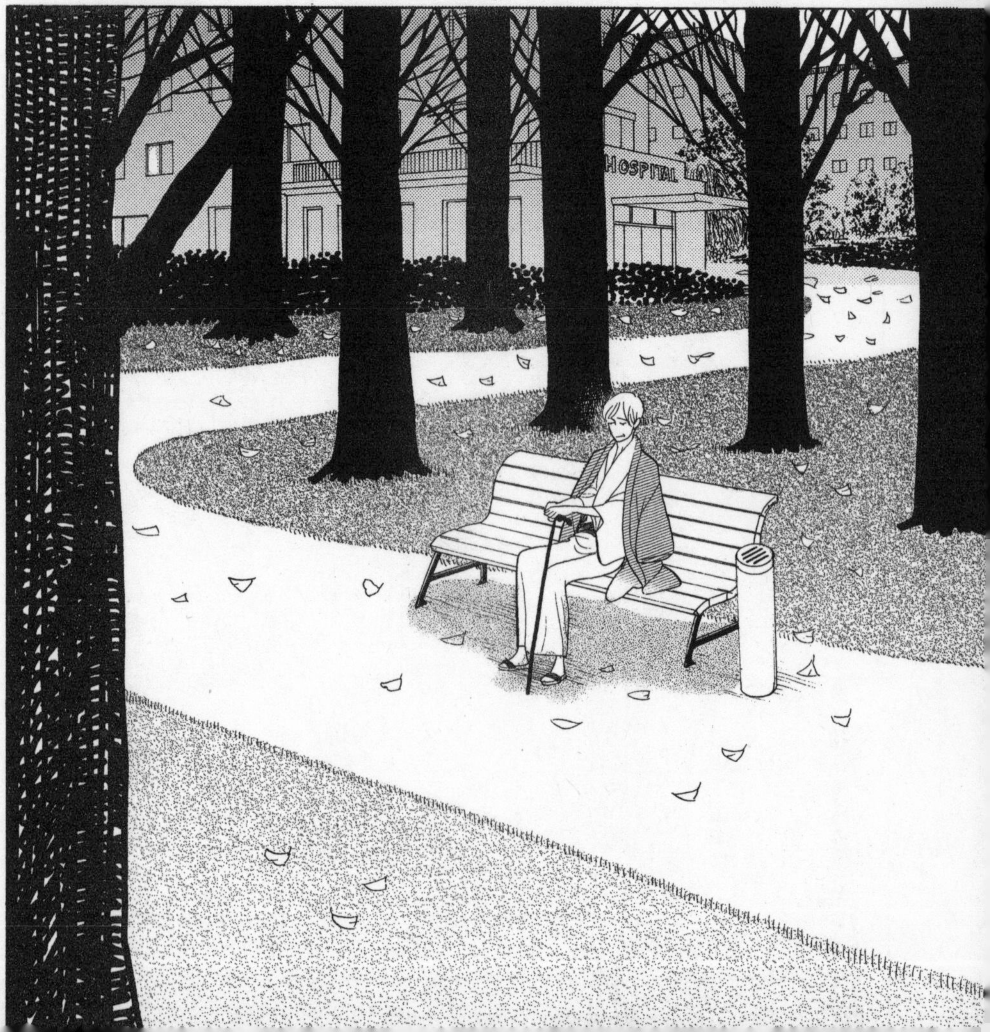
HOSPITAL

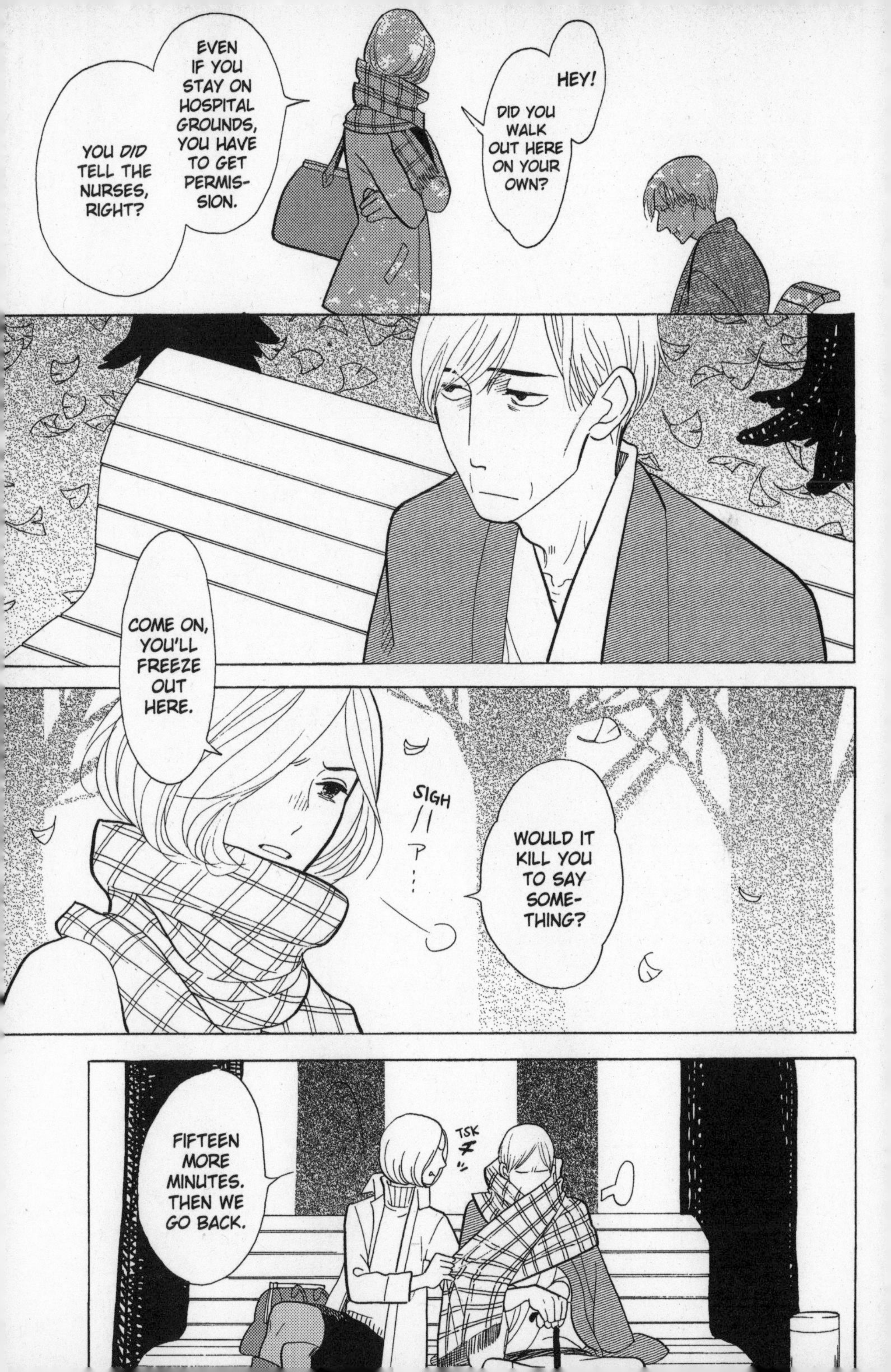
HEY! DID YOU WALK OUT HERE ON YOUR OWN?
EVEN IF YOU STAY ON HOSPITAL GROUNDS, YOU HAVE TO GET PERMIS-SION.
YOU *DID* TELL THE NURSES, RIGHT?
COME ON, YOU'LL FREEZE OUT HERE.
WOULD IT KILL YOU TO SAY SOME-THING?
SIGH
TSK
FIFTEEN MORE MINUTES. THEN WE GO BACK.

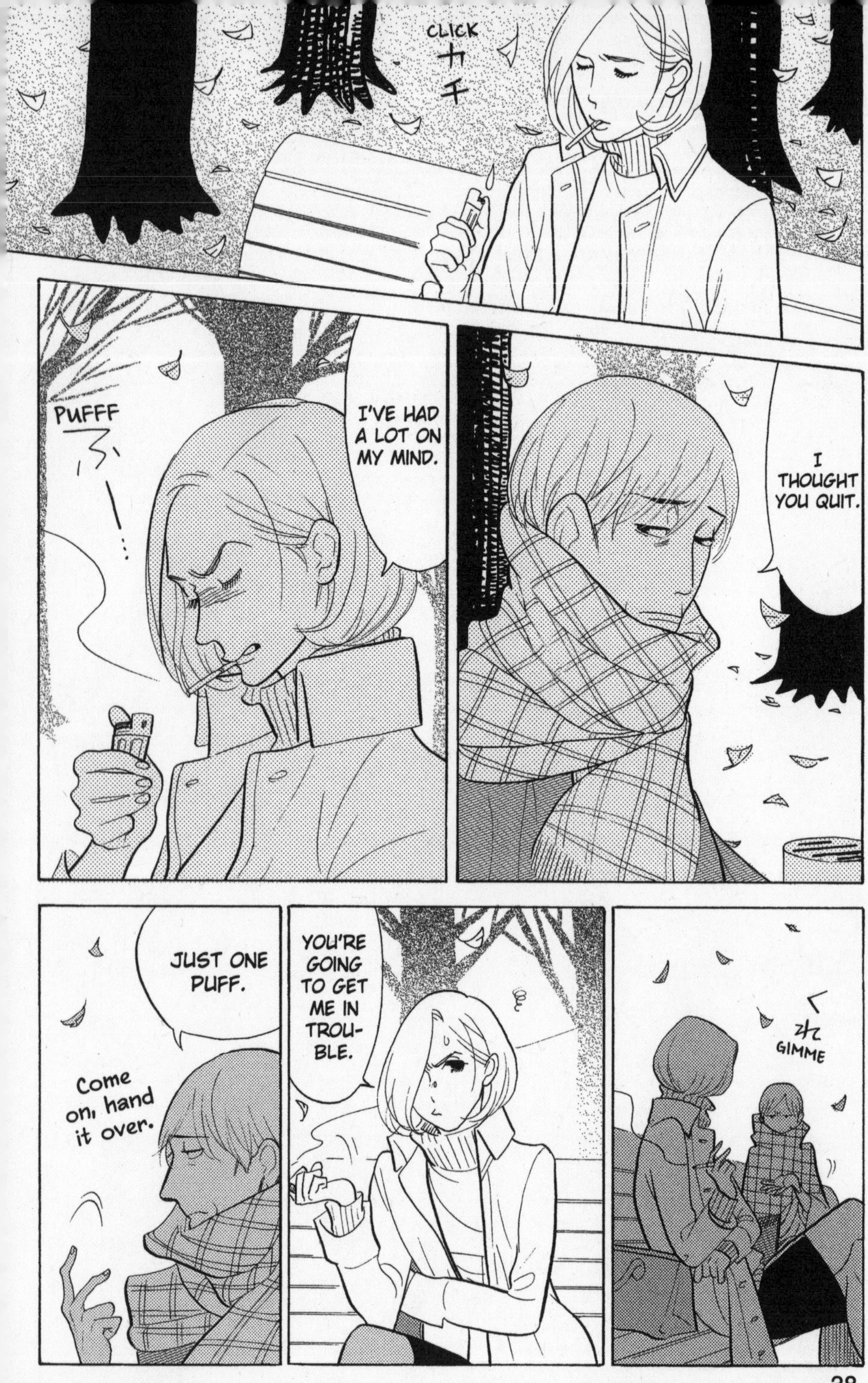
CLICK
カチ
I THOUGHT YOU QUIT.
I'VE HAD A LOT ON MY MIND.
PUFFF
ふ
くれ
GIMME
YOU'RE GOING TO GET ME IN TROUBLE.
JUST ONE PUFF.
Come on, hand it over.

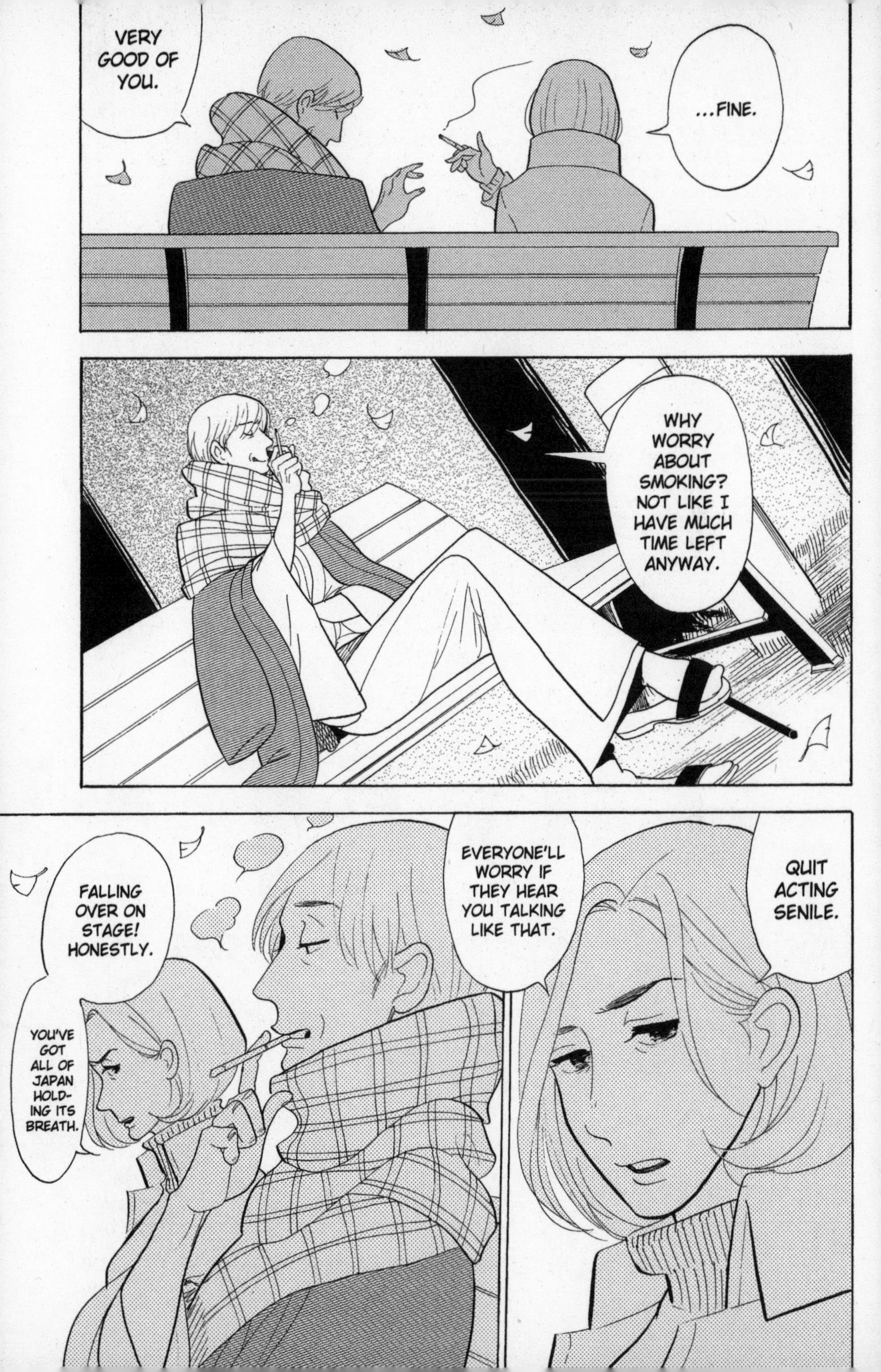
...FINE.
VERY GOOD OF YOU.
WHY WORRY ABOUT SMOKING? NOT LIKE I HAVE MUCH TIME LEFT ANYWAY.
QUIT ACTING SENILE.
EVERYONE'LL WORRY IF THEY HEAR YOU TALKING LIKE THAT.
FALLING OVER ON STAGE! HONESTLY.
YOU'VE GOT ALL OF JAPAN HOLDING ITS BREATH.

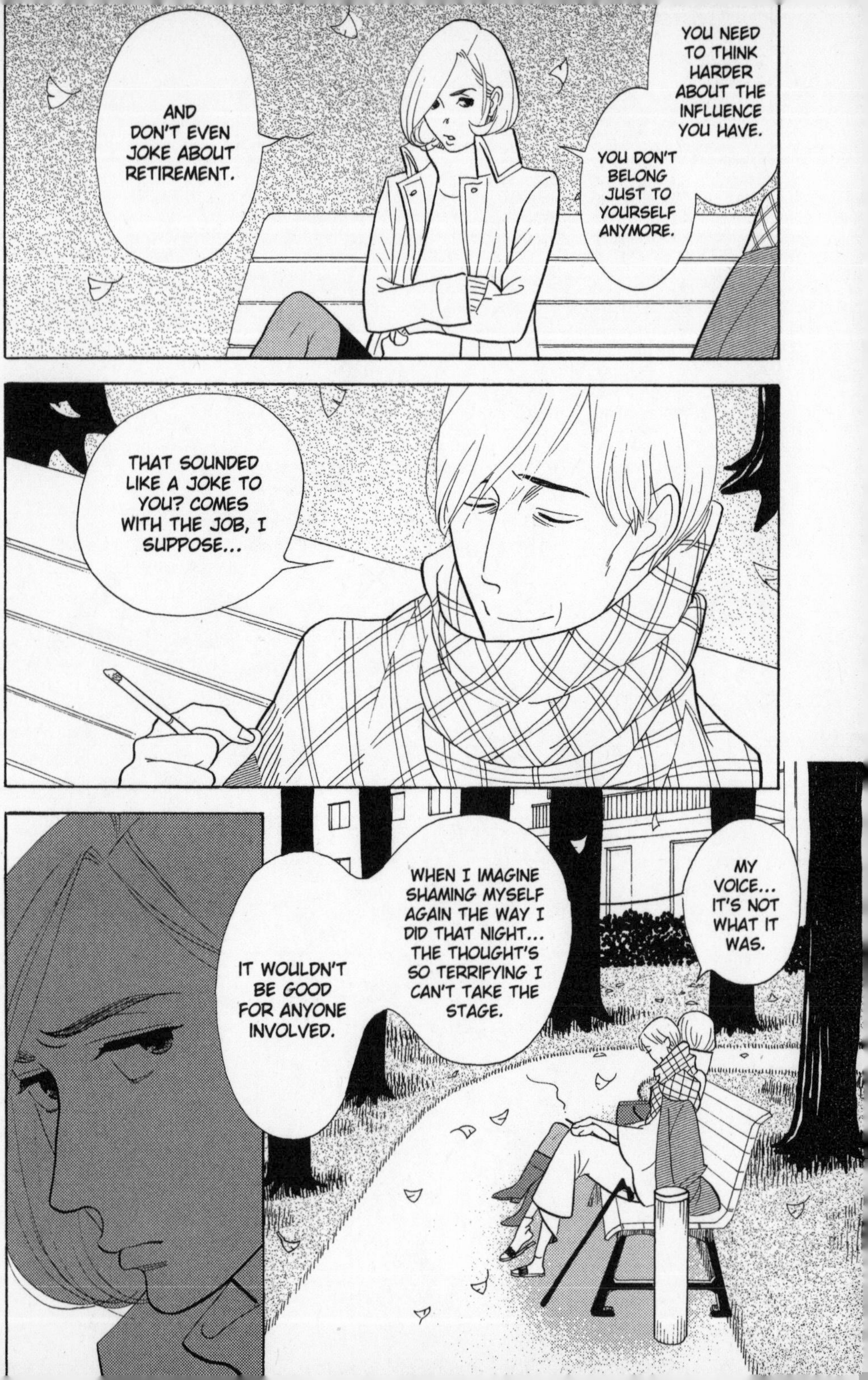
YOU NEED TO THINK HARDER ABOUT THE INFLUENCE YOU HAVE.
YOU DON'T BELONG JUST TO YOURSELF ANYMORE.
AND DON'T EVEN JOKE ABOUT RETIREMENT.
THAT SOUNDED LIKE A JOKE TO YOU? COMES WITH THE JOB, I SUPPOSE...
MY VOICE... IT'S NOT WHAT IT WAS.
WHEN I IMAGINE SHAMING MYSELF AGAIN THE WAY I DID THAT NIGHT... THE THOUGHT'S SO TERRIFYING I CAN'T TAKE THE STAGE.
IT WOULDN'T BE GOOD FOR ANYONE INVOLVED.

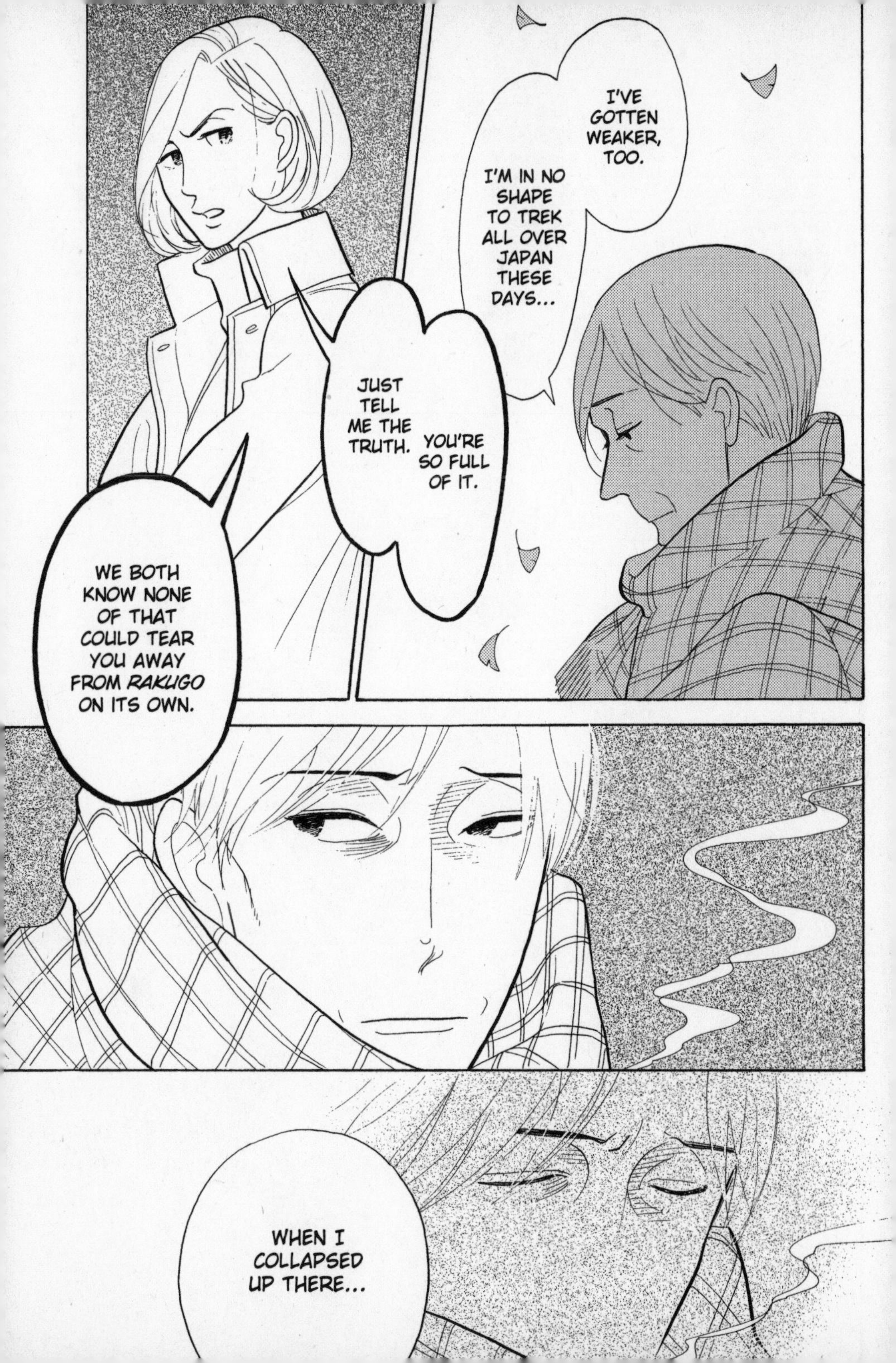
I'VE GOTTEN WEAKER, TOO.
I'M IN NO SHAPE TO TREK ALL OVER JAPAN THESE DAYS...
YOU'RE SO FULL OF IT.
JUST TELL ME THE TRUTH.
WE BOTH KNOW NONE OF THAT COULD TEAR YOU AWAY FROM *RAKUGO* ON ITS OWN.
WHEN I COLLAPSED UP THERE...

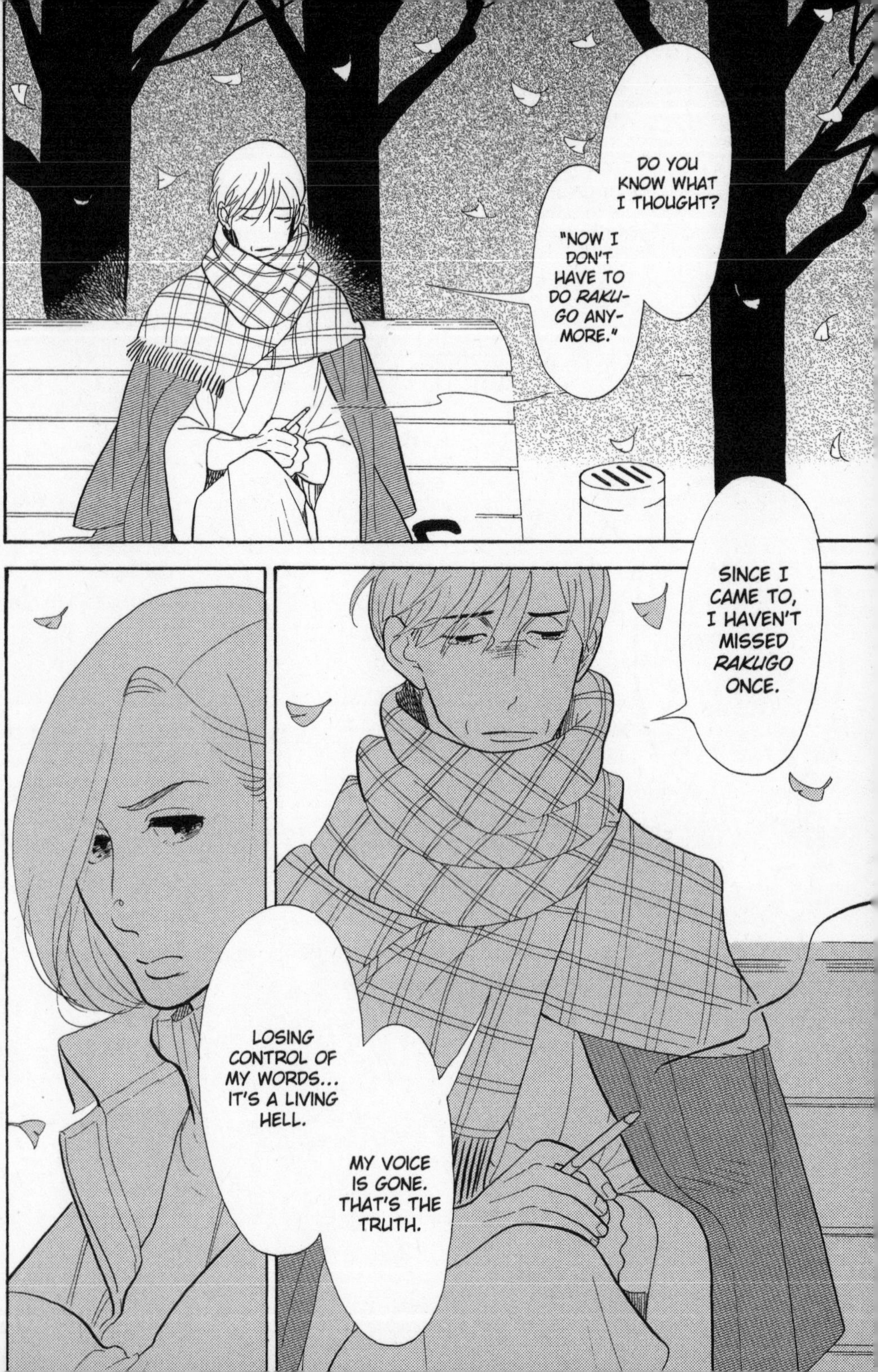
DO YOU KNOW WHAT I THOUGHT?
"NOW I DON'T HAVE TO DO *RAKUGO* ANYMORE."
SINCE I CAME TO, I HAVEN'T MISSED *RAKUGO* ONCE.
LOSING CONTROL OF MY WORDS... IT'S A LIVING HELL.
MY VOICE IS GONE. THAT'S THE TRUTH.

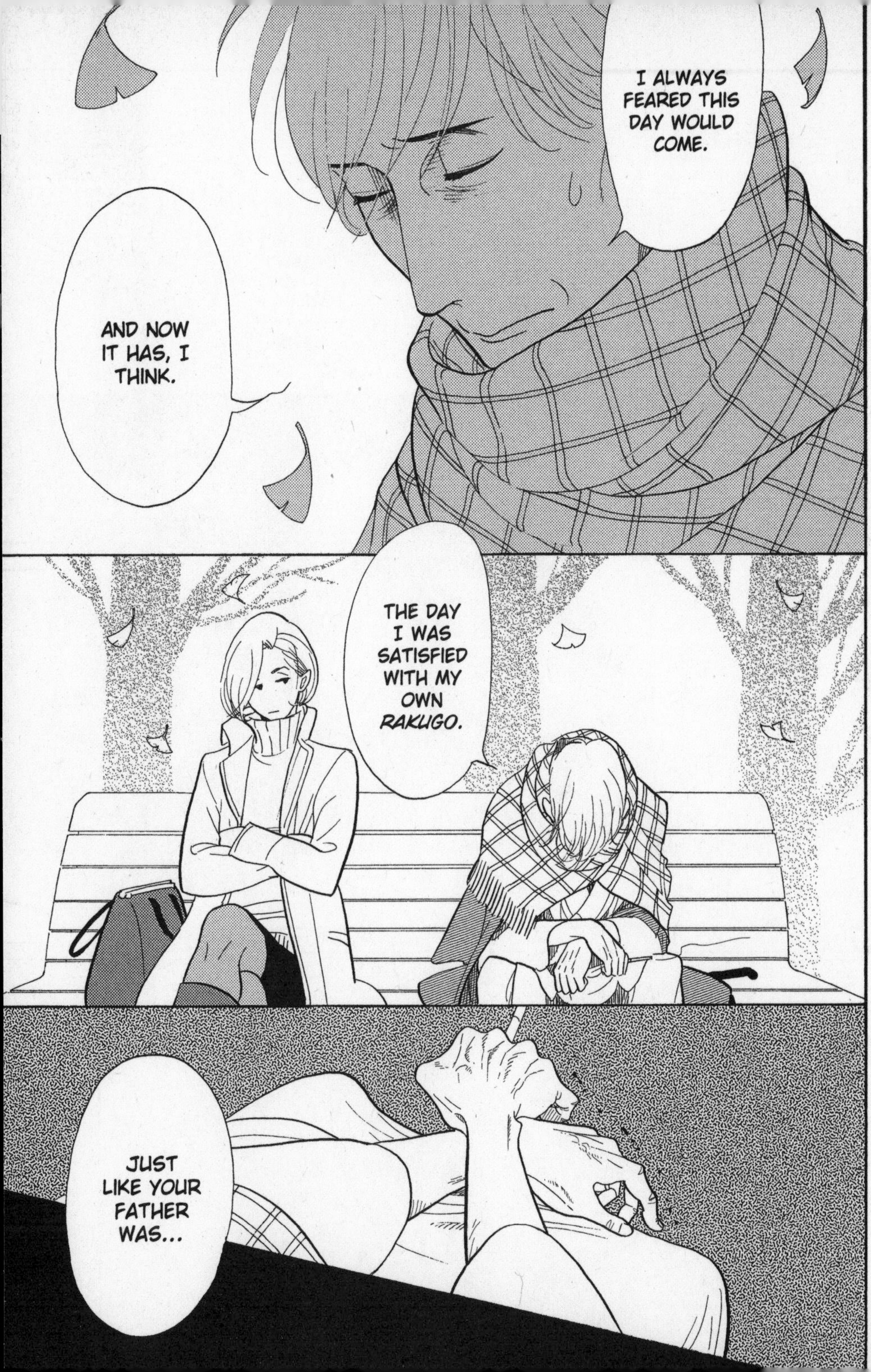
I ALWAYS FEARED THIS DAY WOULD COME.
AND NOW IT HAS, I THINK.
THE DAY I WAS SATISFIED WITH MY OWN *RAKUGO*.
JUST LIKE YOUR FATHER WAS...

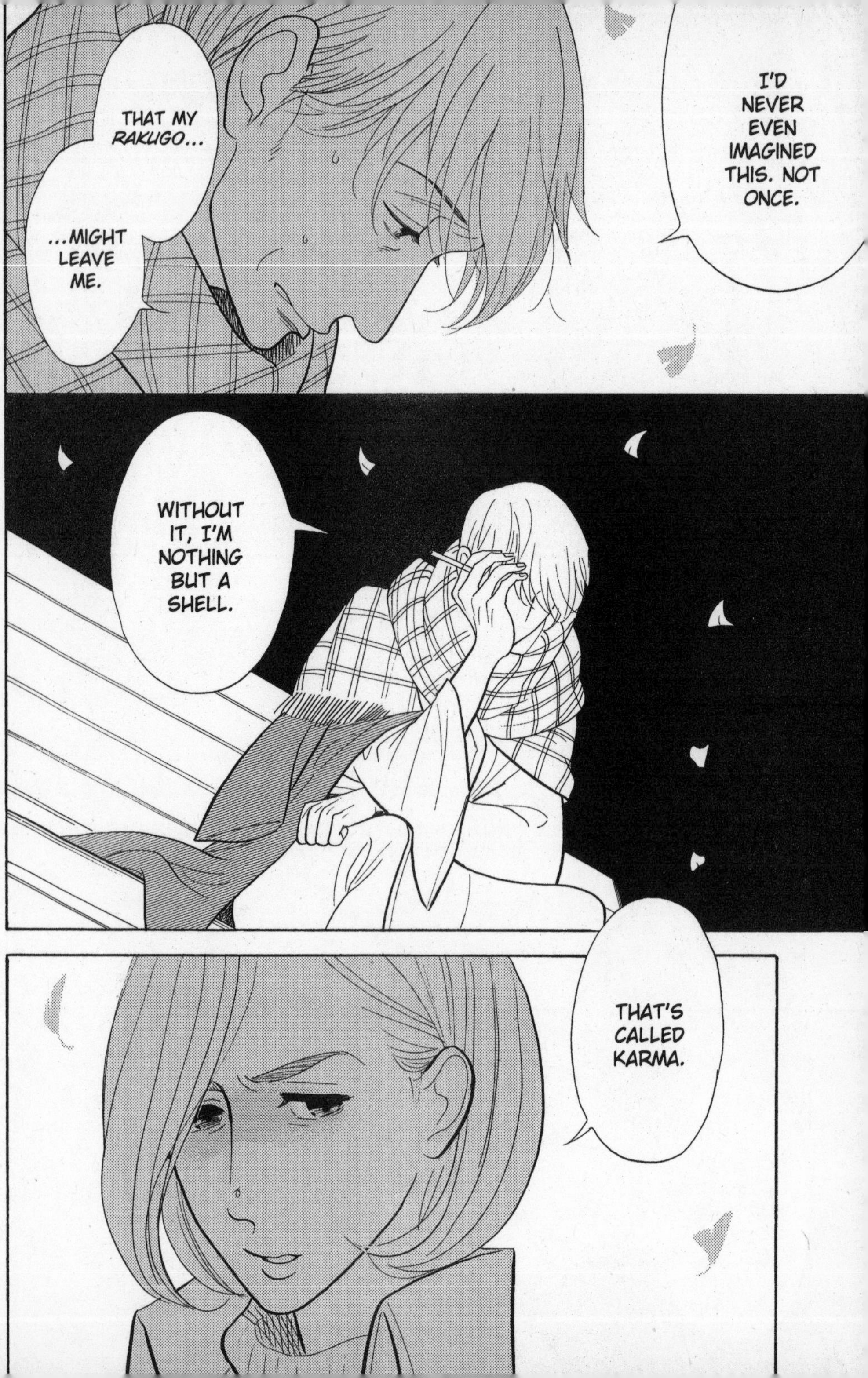
I'D NEVER EVEN IMAGINED THIS. NOT ONCE.
THAT MY *RAKUGO*...
...MIGHT LEAVE ME.
WITHOUT IT, I'M NOTHING BUT A SHELL.
THAT'S CALLED KARMA.

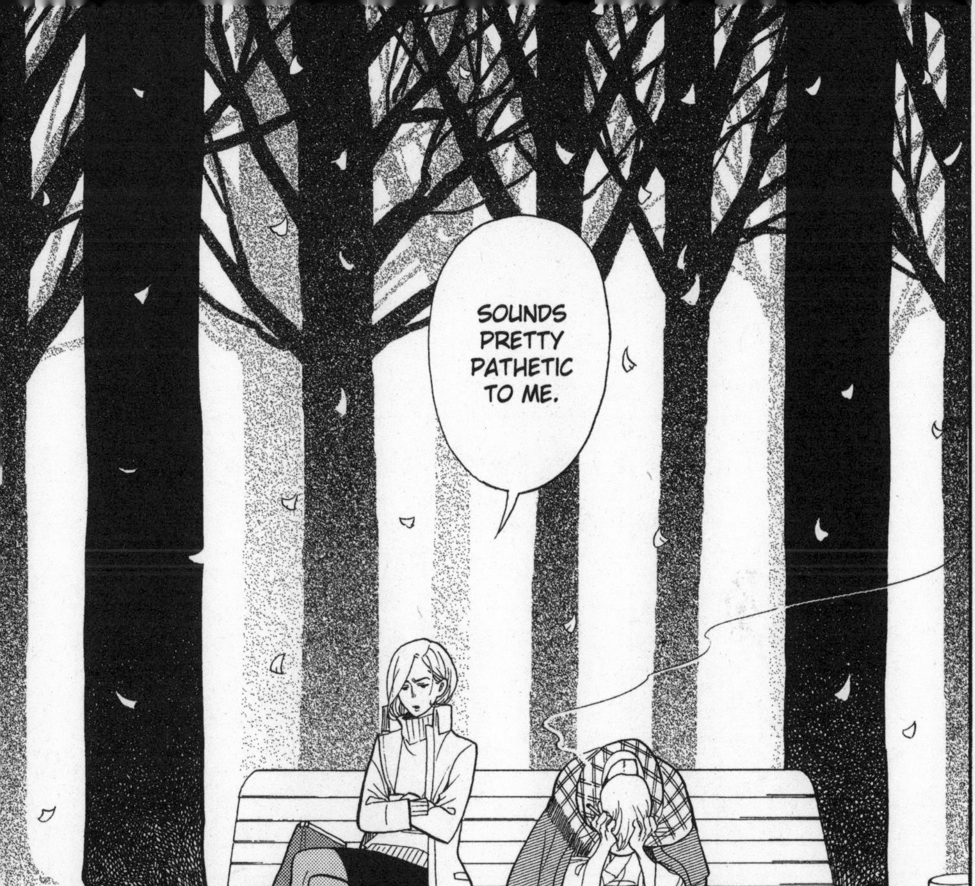
SOUNDS PRETTY PATHETIC TO ME.
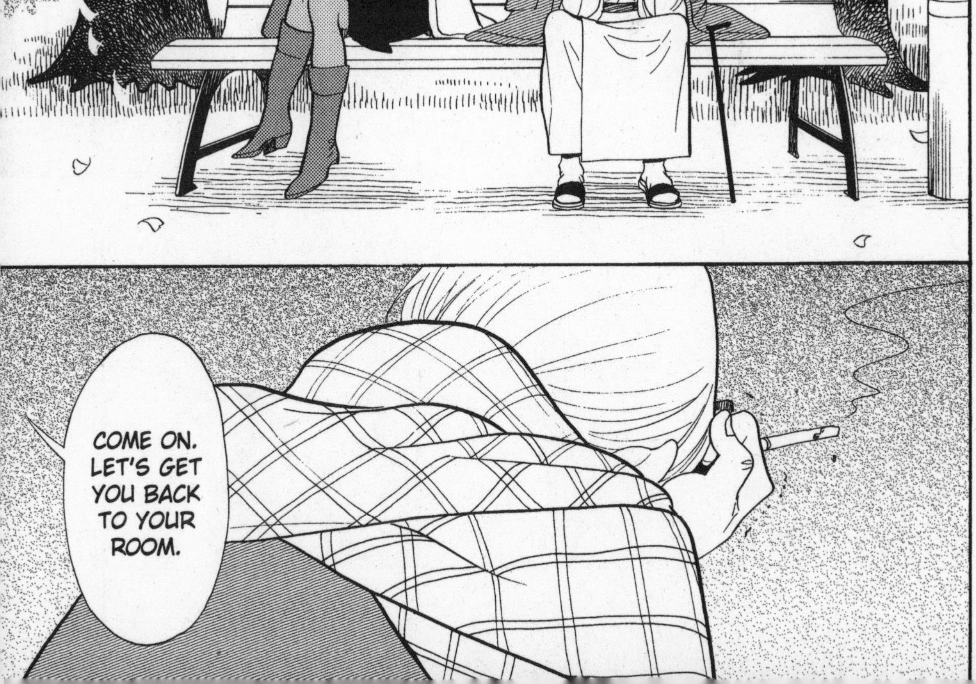
COME ON. LET'S GET YOU BACK TO YOUR ROOM.

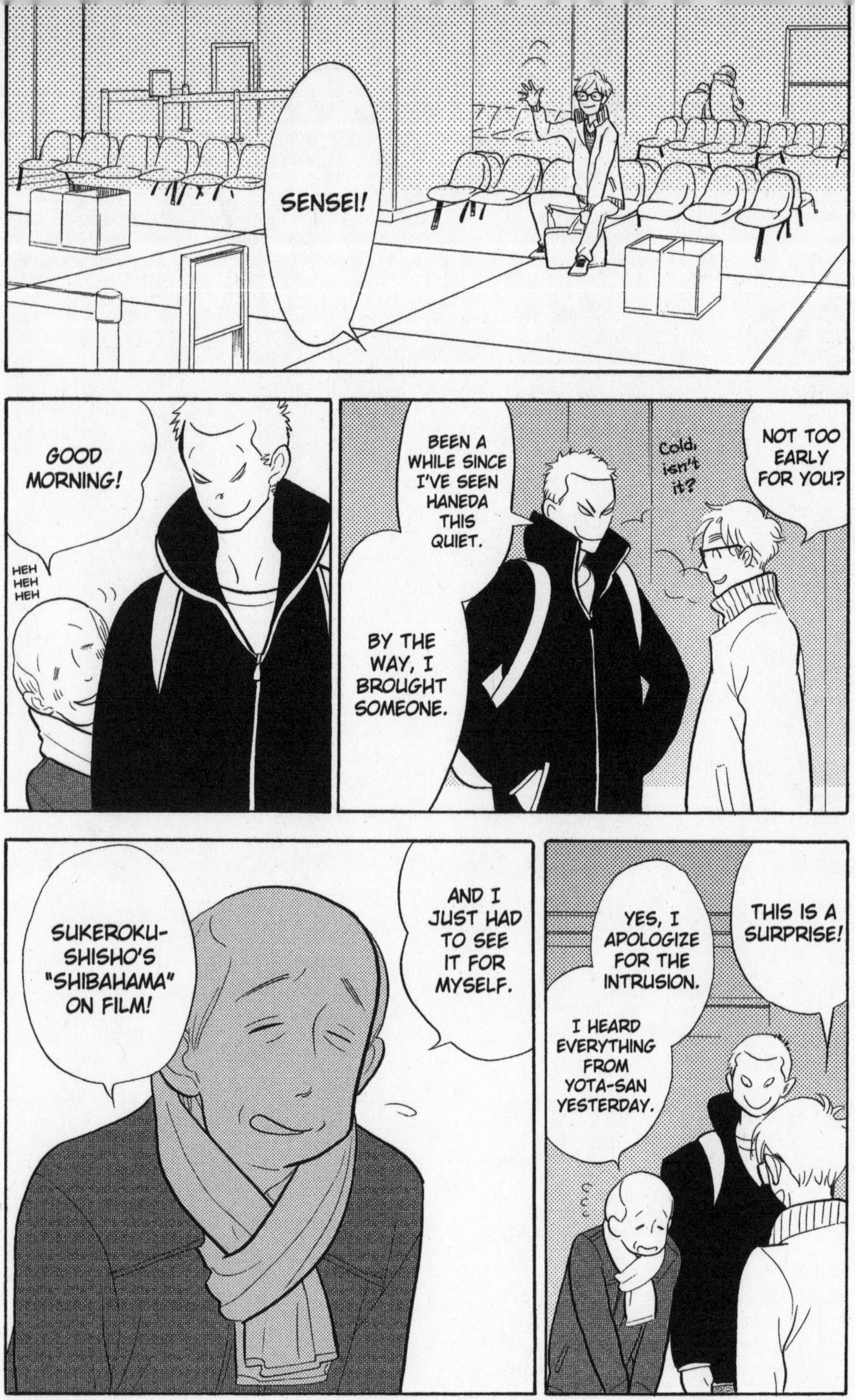
SENSEI!
NOT TOO EARLY FOR YOU?
Cold, isn't it?
BEEN A WHILE SINCE I'VE SEEN HANEDA THIS QUIET.
BY THE WAY, I BROUGHT SOMEONE.
GOOD MORNING!
HEH HEH HEH
THIS IS A SURPRISE!
YES, I APOLOGIZE FOR THE INTRUSION.
I HEARD EVERYTHING FROM YOTA-SAN YESTERDAY.
AND I JUST HAD TO SEE IT FOR MYSELF.
SUKEROKU-SHISHO'S "SHIBAHAMA" ON FILM!

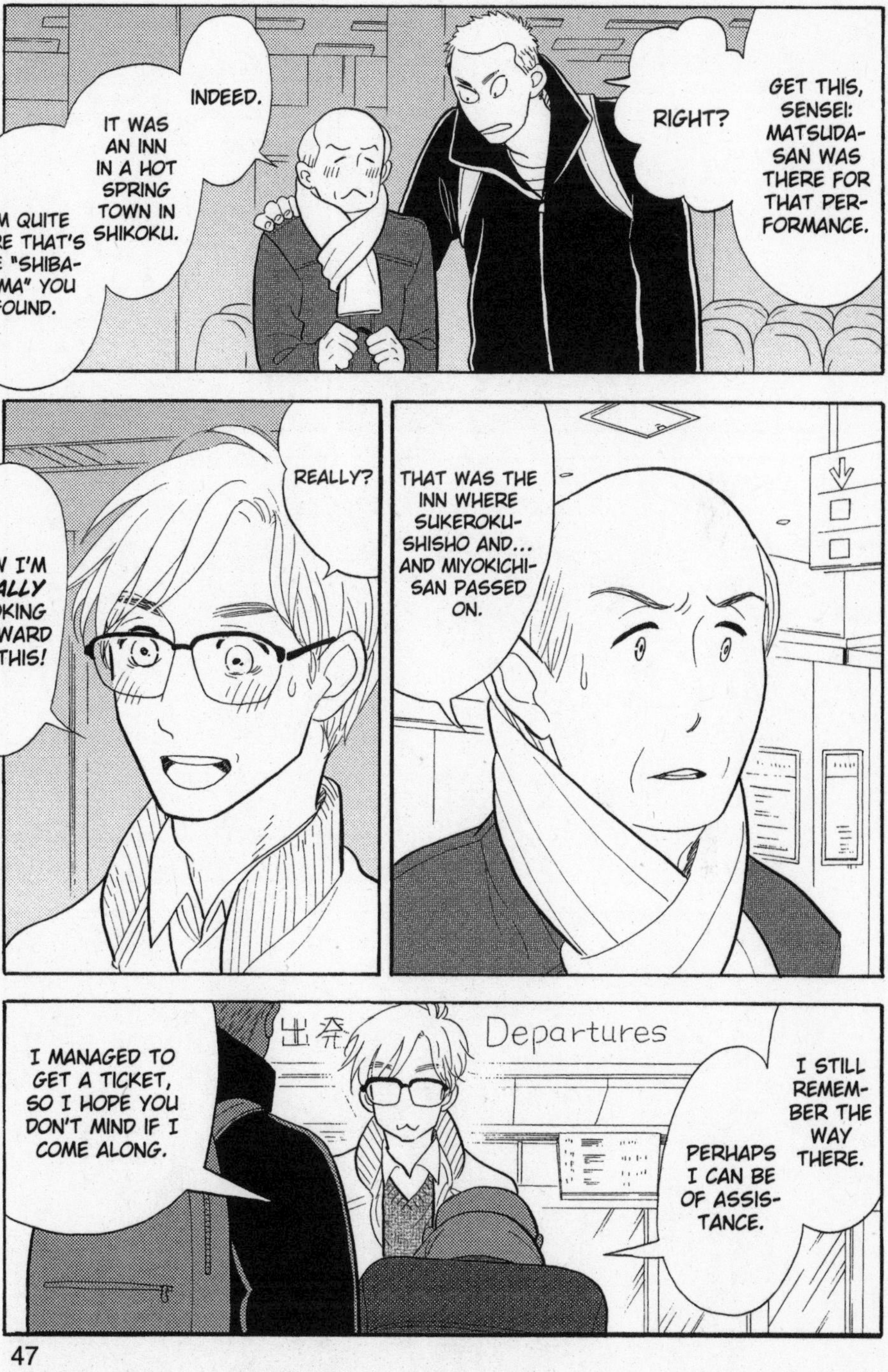
GET THIS, SENSEI: MATSUDA-SAN WAS THERE FOR THAT PERFORMANCE.
RIGHT?
INDEED.
IT WAS AN INN IN A HOT SPRING TOWN IN SHIKOKU.
I'M QUITE SURE THAT'S THE "SHIBA-HAMA" YOU FOUND.
THAT WAS THE INN WHERE SUKEROKU-SHISHO AND... AND MIYOKICHI-SAN PASSED ON.
REALLY?
NOW I'M *REALLY* LOOKING FORWARD TO THIS!
I STILL REMEMBER THE WAY THERE.
PERHAPS I CAN BE OF ASSISTANCE.
出発 Departures
I MANAGED TO GET A TICKET, SO I HOPE YOU DON'T MIND IF I COME ALONG.

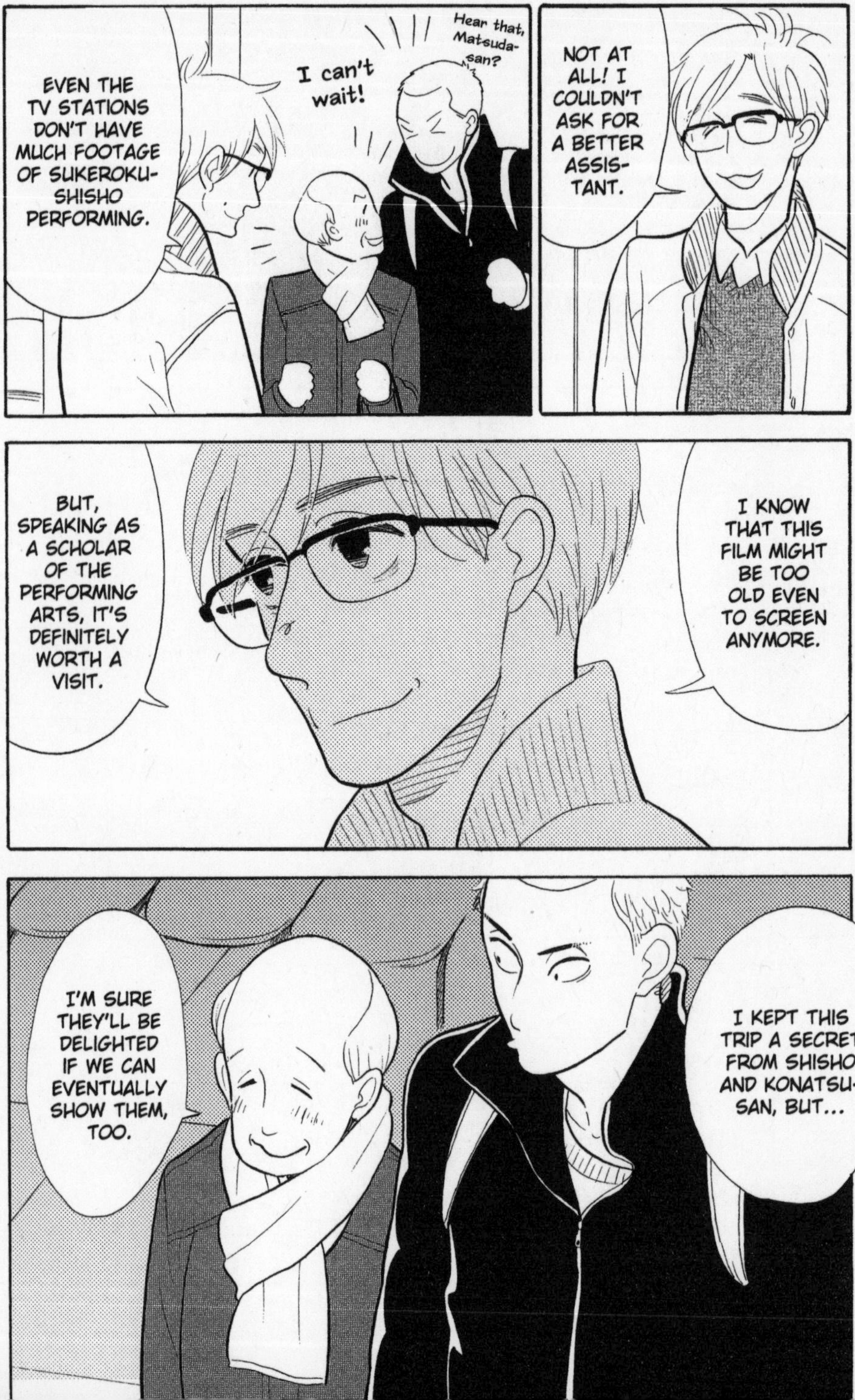
NOT AT ALL! I COULDN'T ASK FOR A BETTER ASSIS-TANT.
Hear that, Matsuda-san?
I can't wait!
EVEN THE TV STATIONS DON'T HAVE MUCH FOOTAGE OF SUKEROKU-SHISHO PERFORMING.
I KNOW THAT THIS FILM MIGHT BE TOO OLD EVEN TO SCREEN ANYMORE.
BUT, SPEAKING AS A SCHOLAR OF THE PERFORMING ARTS, IT'S DEFINITELY WORTH A VISIT.
I KEPT THIS TRIP A SECRET FROM SHISHO AND KONATSU-SAN, BUT...
I'M SURE THEY'LL BE DELIGHTED IF WE CAN EVENTUALLY SHOW THEM, TOO.

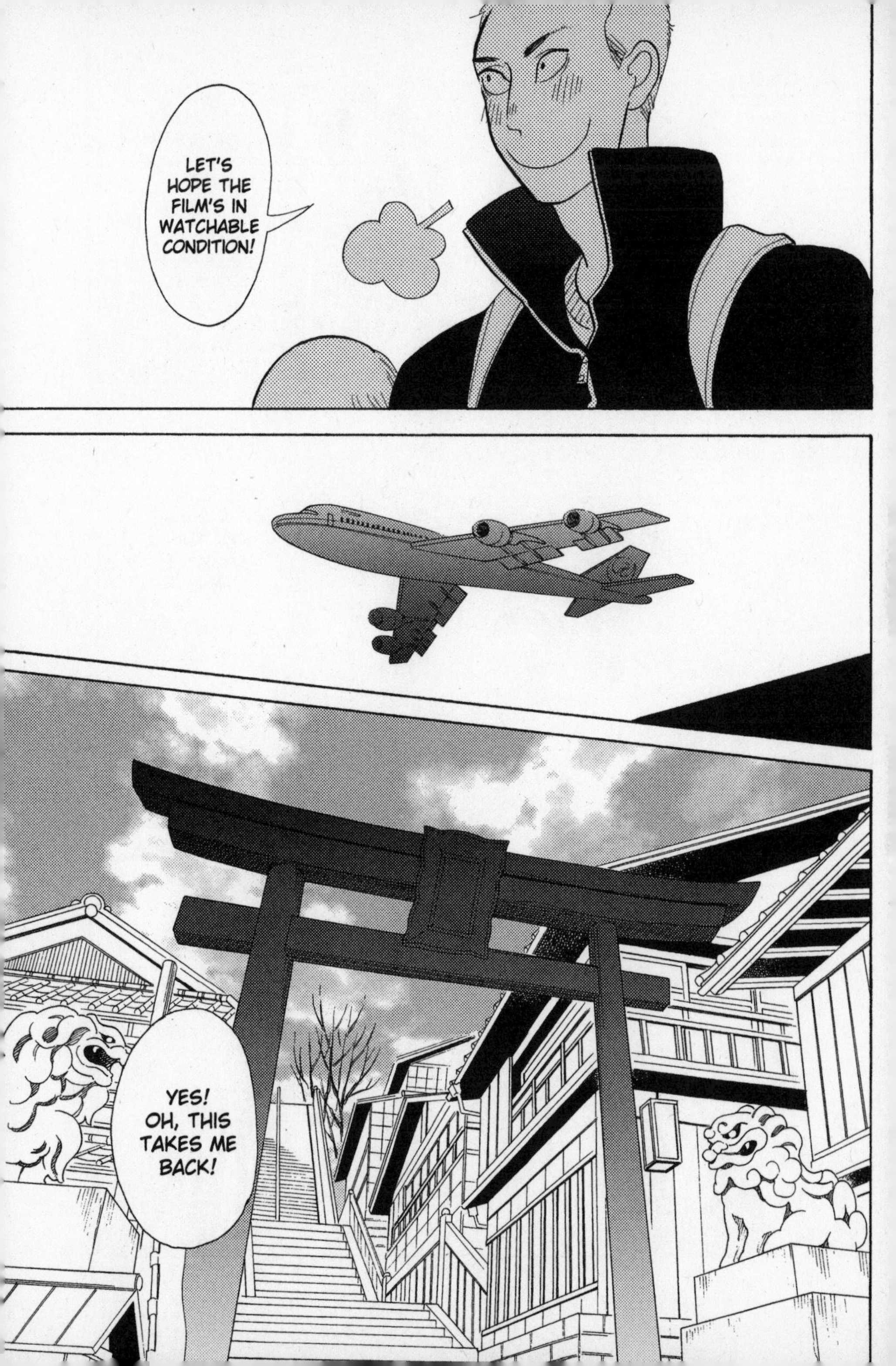
LET'S HOPE THE FILM'S IN WATCHABLE CONDITION!
YES! OH, THIS TAKES ME BACK!

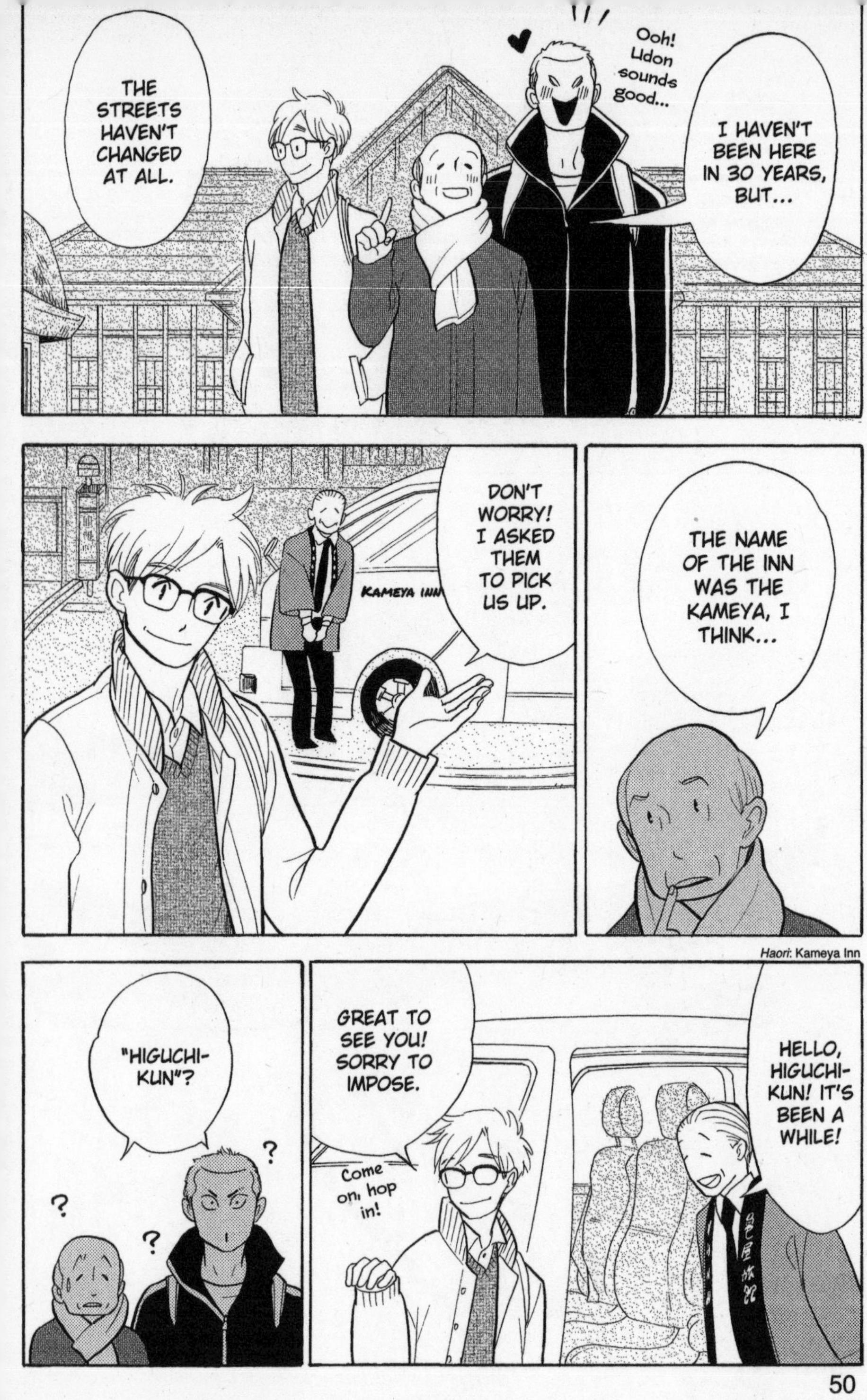
I HAVEN'T BEEN HERE IN 30 YEARS, BUT...
Ooh! Udon sounds good...
THE STREETS HAVEN'T CHANGED AT ALL.
THE NAME OF THE INN WAS THE KAMEYA, I THINK...
DON'T WORRY! I ASKED THEM TO PICK US UP.
KAMEYA INN
HELLO, HIGUCHI-KUN! IT'S BEEN A WHILE!
GREAT TO SEE YOU! SORRY TO IMPOSE.
Come on, hop in!
"HIGUCHI-KUN"?

Haori: Kameya Inn

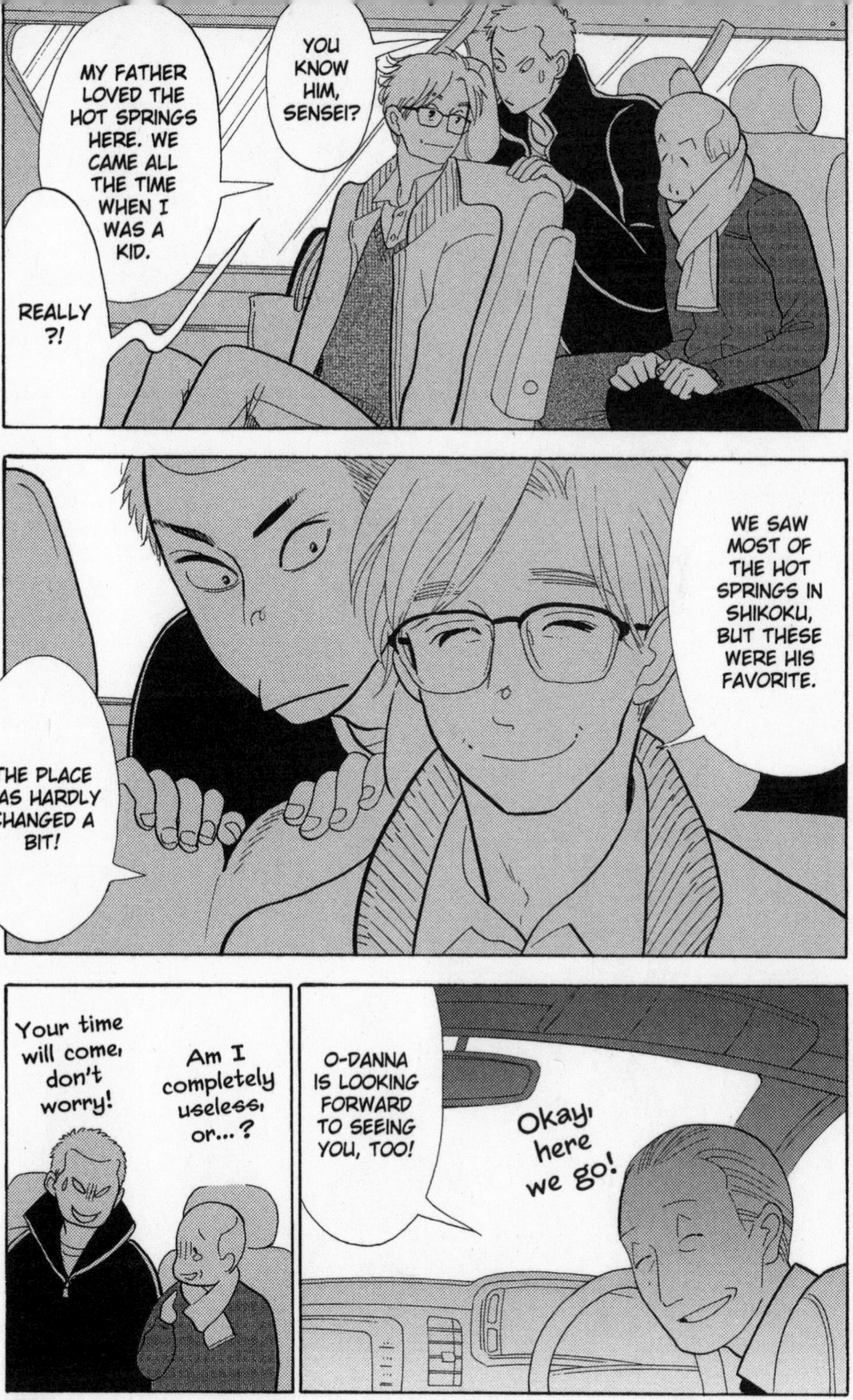

YOU KNOW HIM, SENSEI?
MY FATHER LOVED THE HOT SPRINGS HERE. WE CAME ALL THE TIME WHEN I WAS A KID.
REALLY ?!
WE SAW MOST OF THE HOT SPRINGS IN SHIKOKU, BUT THESE WERE HIS FAVORITE.
THE PLACE HAS HARDLY CHANGED A BIT!
O-DANNA IS LOOKING FORWARD TO SEEING YOU, TOO!
Okay, here we go!
Am I completely useless, or...?
Your time will come, don't worry!

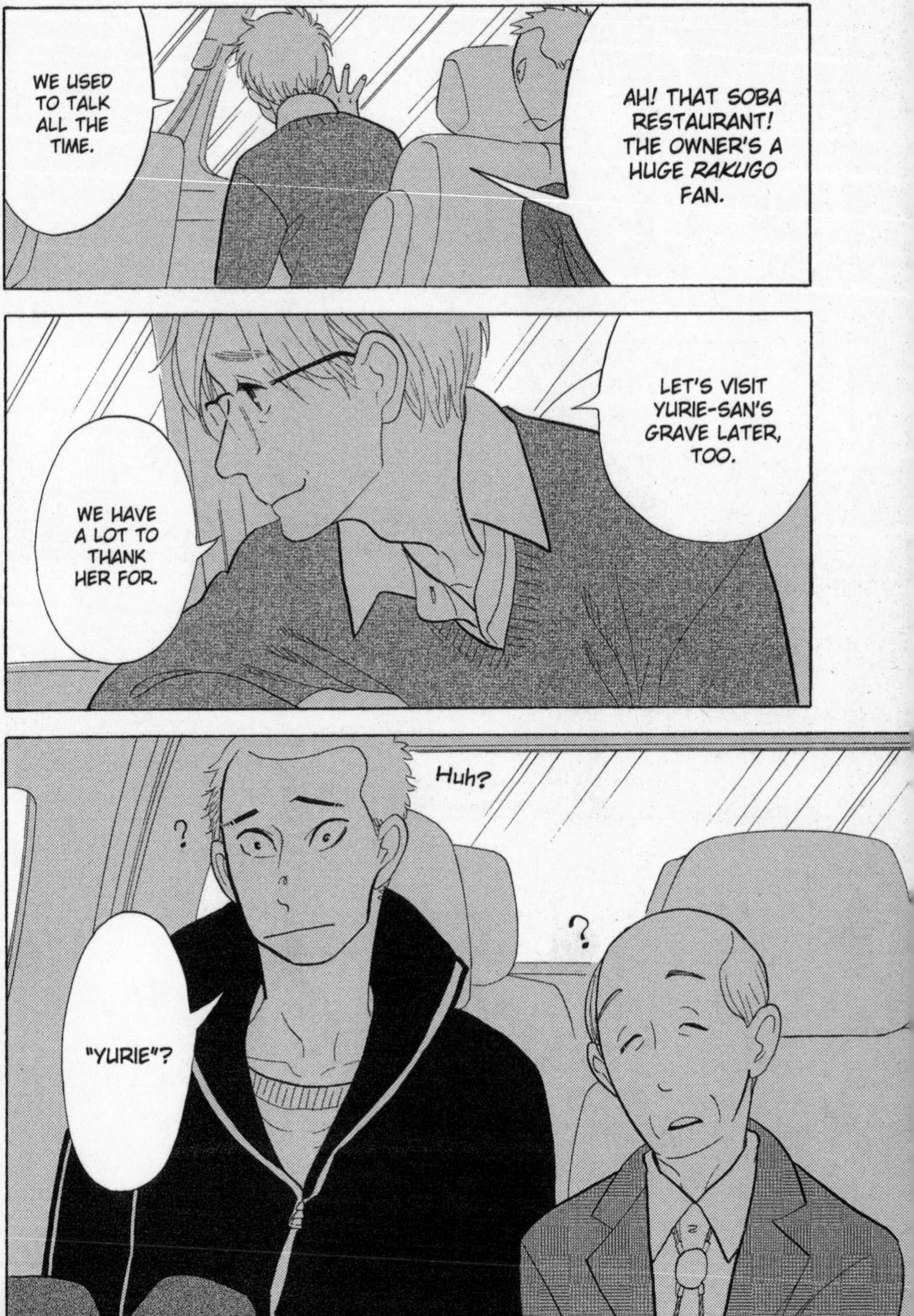
AH! THAT SOBA RESTAURANT! THE OWNER'S A HUGE *RAKUGO* FAN.
WE USED TO TALK ALL THE TIME.
LET'S VISIT YURIE-SAN'S GRAVE LATER, TOO.
WE HAVE A LOT TO THANK HER FOR.
Huh?
?
?
"YURIE"?

DESCENDING STORIES

SHOWA GENROKU RAKUGO SHINJU

HARUKO KUMOTA

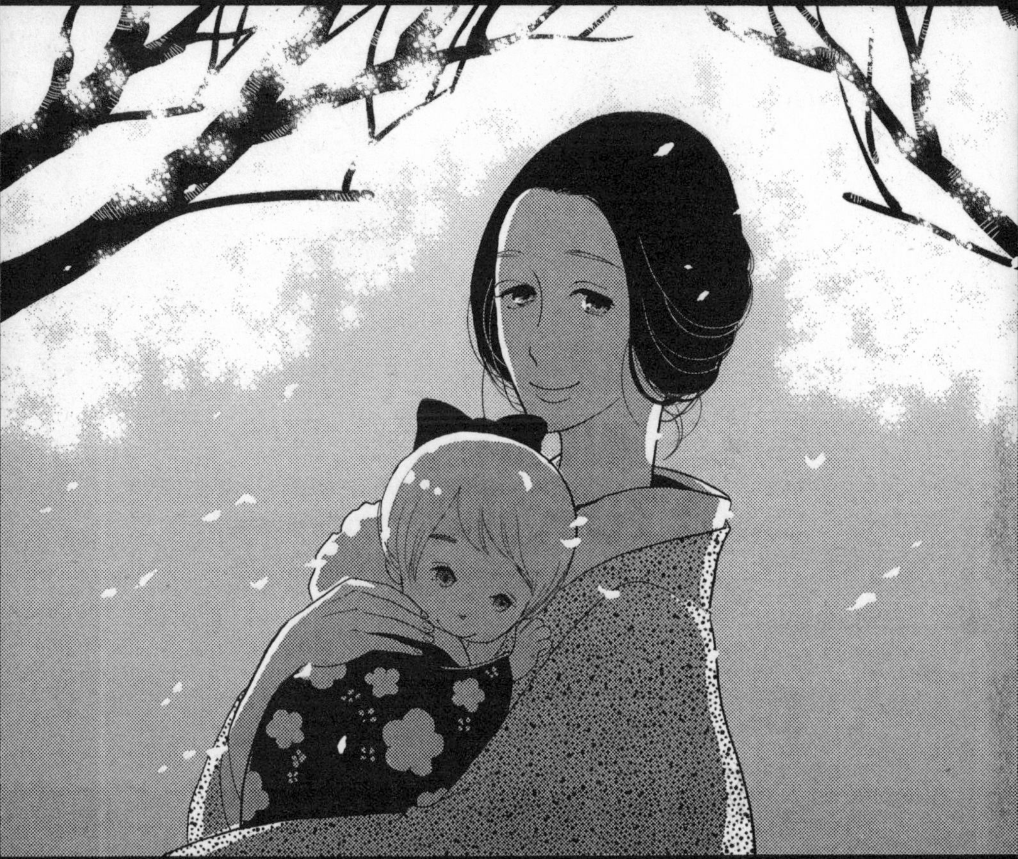

DESCENDING STORIES

SHOWA GENROKU RAKUGO SHINJU

SUKEROKU AGAIN: 10

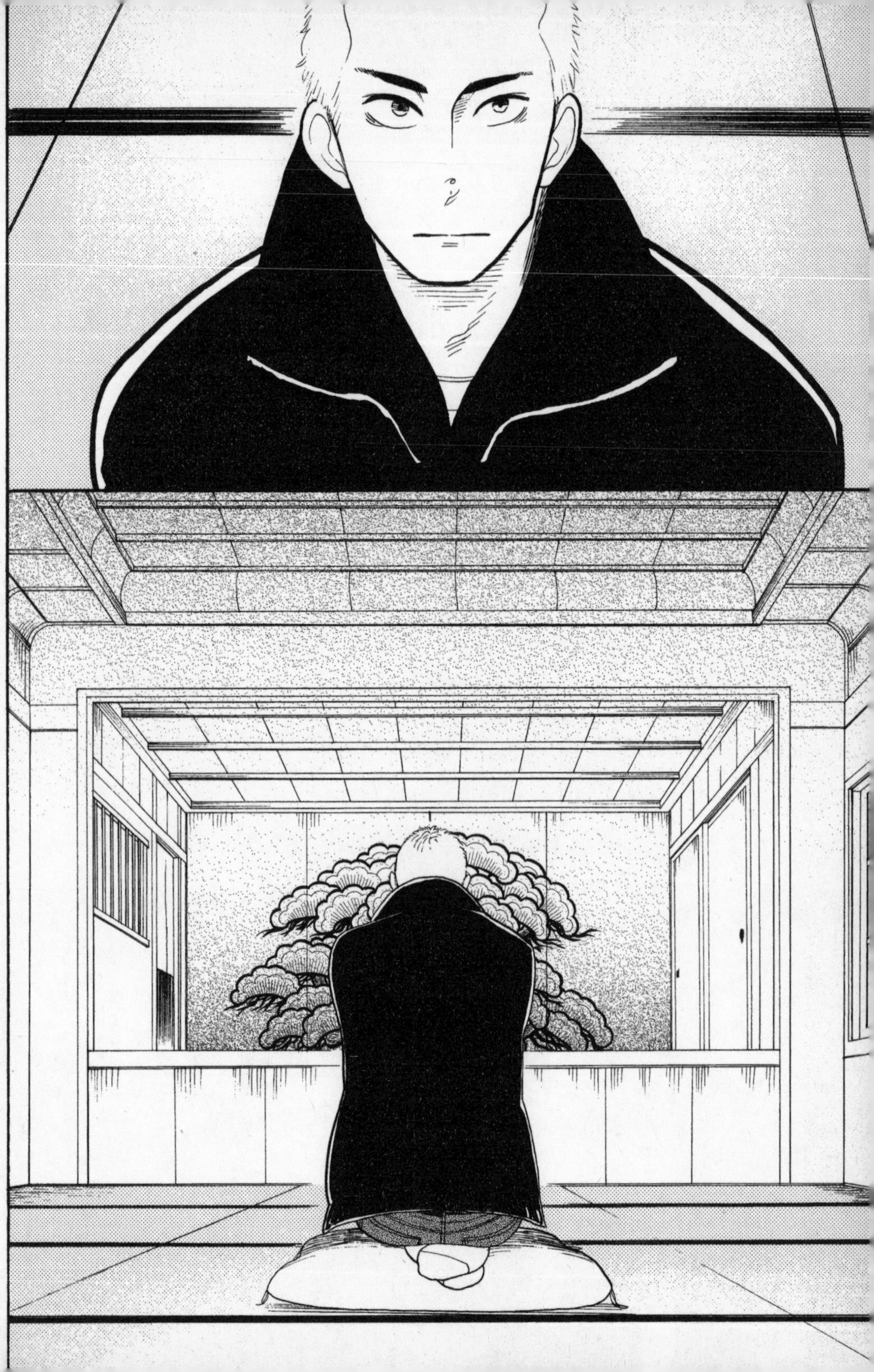

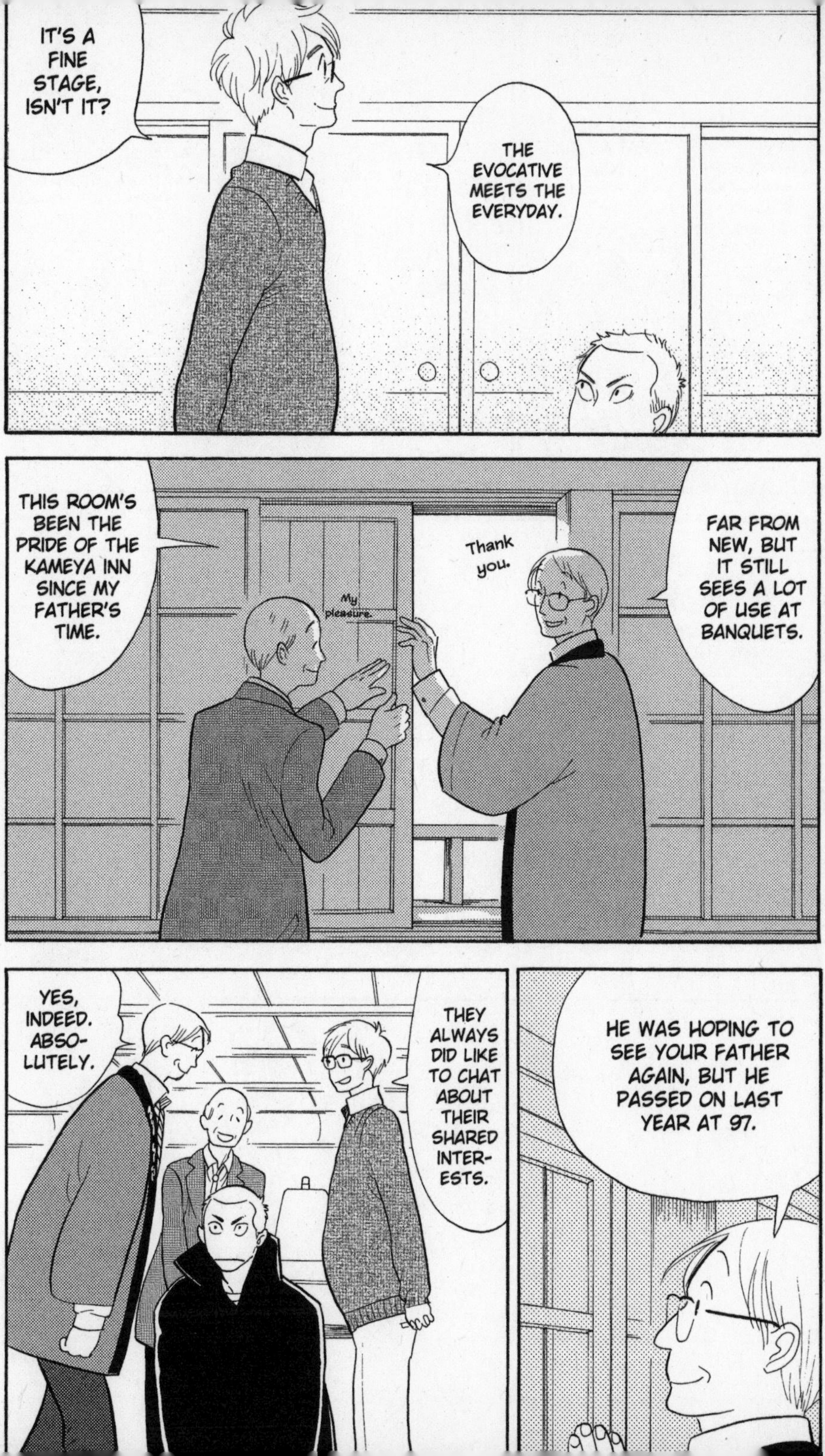
IT'S A FINE STAGE, ISN'T IT?
THE EVOCATIVE MEETS THE EVERYDAY.
FAR FROM NEW, BUT IT STILL SEES A LOT OF USE AT BANQUETS.
Thank you.
My pleasure.
THIS ROOM'S BEEN THE PRIDE OF THE KAMEYA INN SINCE MY FATHER'S TIME.
HE WAS HOPING TO SEE YOUR FATHER AGAIN, BUT HE PASSED ON LAST YEAR AT 97.
THEY ALWAYS DID LIKE TO CHAT ABOUT THEIR SHARED INTER-ESTS.
YES, INDEED. ABSO-LUTELY.

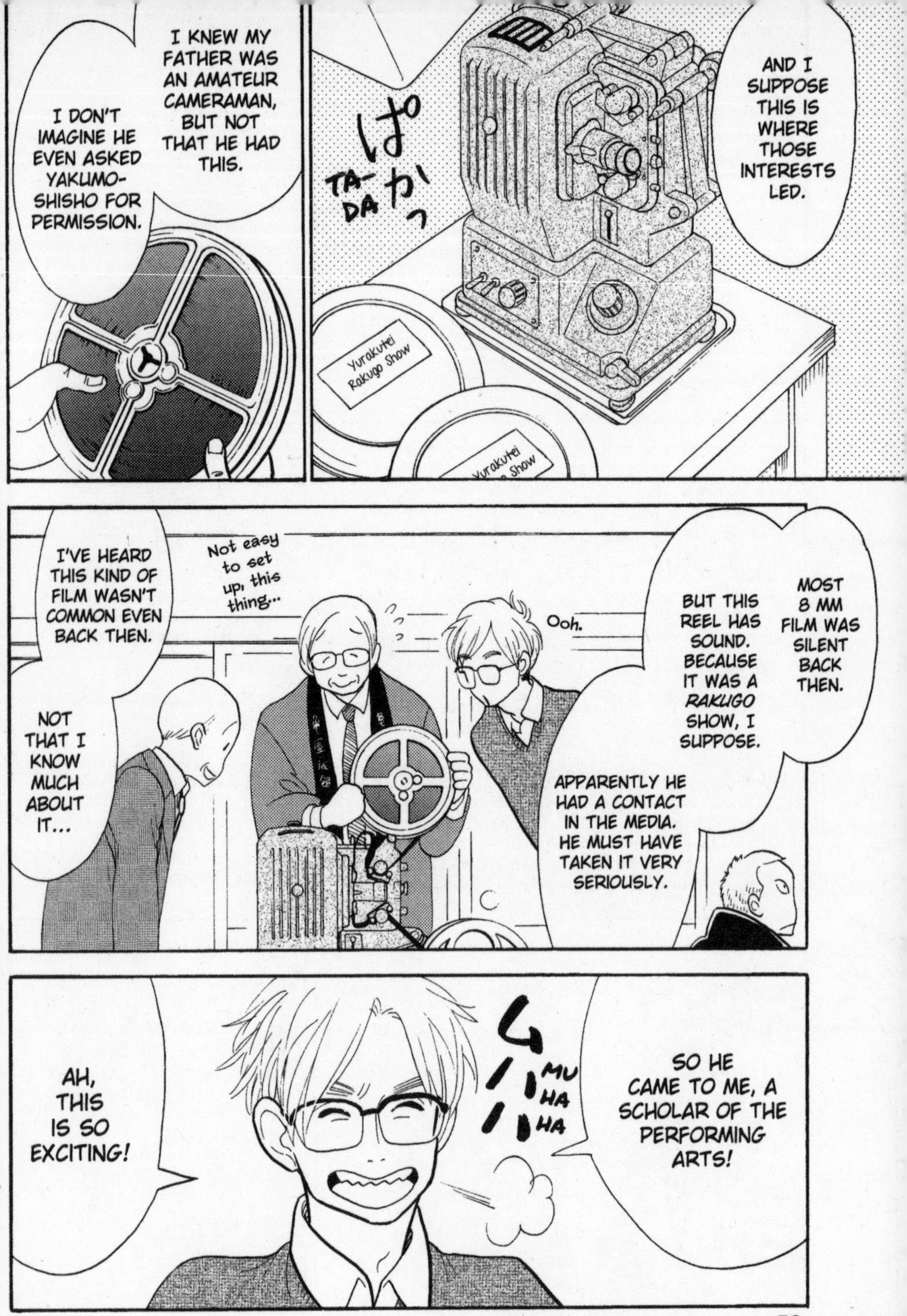
AND I SUPPOSE THIS IS WHERE THOSE INTERESTS LED.
ぱかっ
TA-DA
Yurakutei Rakugo Show
Yurakutei
I KNEW MY FATHER WAS AN AMATEUR CAMERAMAN, BUT NOT THAT HE HAD THIS.
I DON'T IMAGINE HE EVEN ASKED YAKUMO-SHISHO FOR PERMISSION.
MOST 8 MM FILM WAS SILENT BACK THEN.
BUT THIS REEL HAS SOUND. BECAUSE IT WAS A *RAKUGO* SHOW, I SUPPOSE.
Ooh.
APPARENTLY HE HAD A CONTACT IN THE MEDIA. HE MUST HAVE TAKEN IT VERY SERIOUSLY.
Not easy to set up, this thing...
I'VE HEARD THIS KIND OF FILM WASN'T COMMON EVEN BACK THEN.
NOT THAT I KNOW MUCH ABOUT IT...
SO HE CAME TO ME, A SCHOLAR OF THE PERFORMING ARTS!
ムハハ
MU HA HA
AH, THIS IS SO EXCITING!

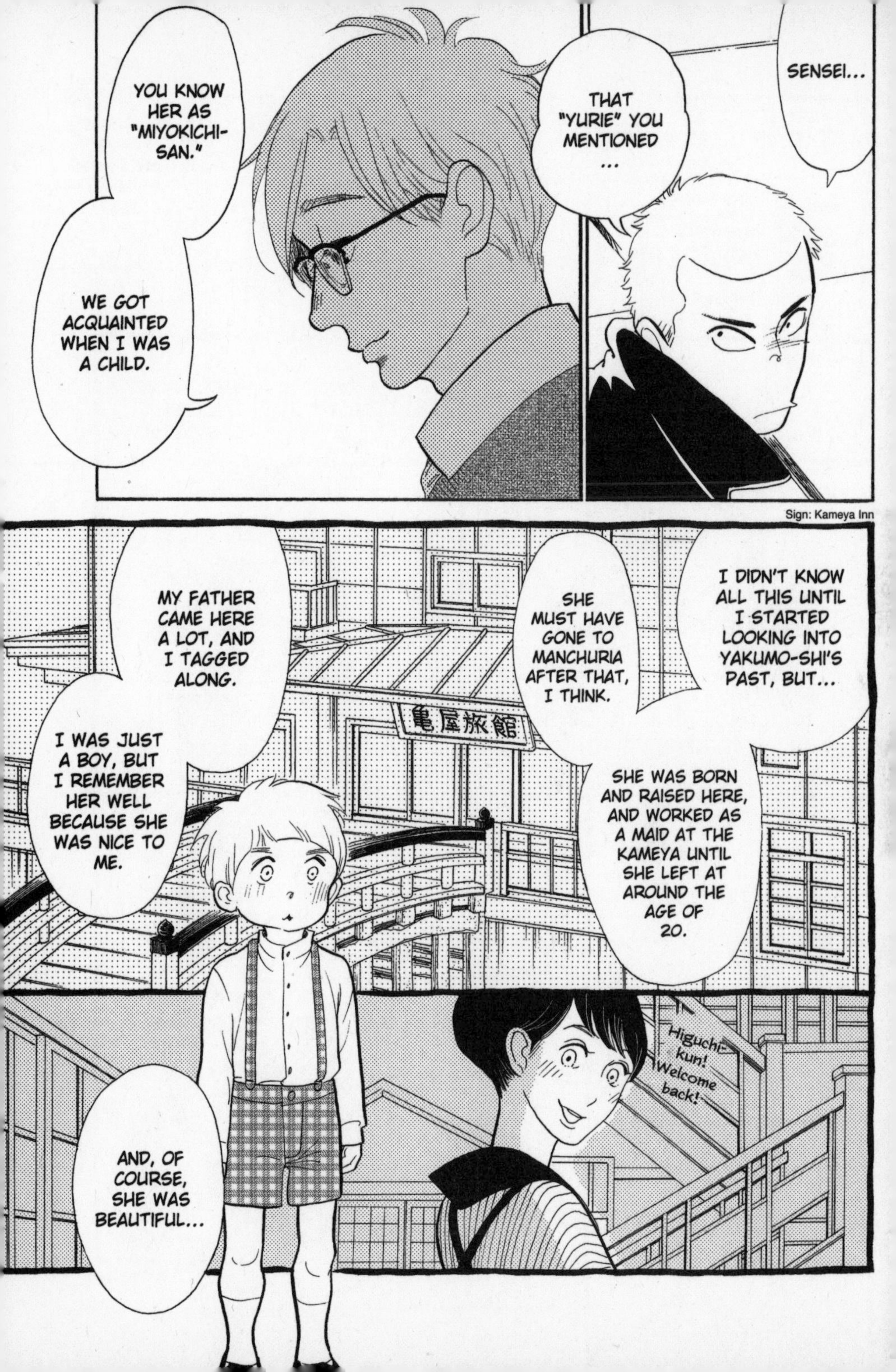
SENSEI...
THAT "YURIE" YOU MENTIONED ...
YOU KNOW HER AS "MIYOKICHI-SAN."
WE GOT ACQUAINTED WHEN I WAS A CHILD.
Sign: Kameya Inn
I DIDN'T KNOW ALL THIS UNTIL I STARTED LOOKING INTO YAKUMO-SHI'S PAST, BUT...
SHE WAS BORN AND RAISED HERE, AND WORKED AS A MAID AT THE KAMEYA UNTIL SHE LEFT AT AROUND THE AGE OF 20.
SHE MUST HAVE GONE TO MANCHURIA AFTER THAT, I THINK.
亀屋旅館
MY FATHER CAME HERE A LOT, AND I TAGGED ALONG.
I WAS JUST A BOY, BUT I REMEMBER HER WELL BECAUSE SHE WAS NICE TO ME.
Higuchi-kun! Welcome back!
AND, OF COURSE, SHE WAS BEAUTIFUL...

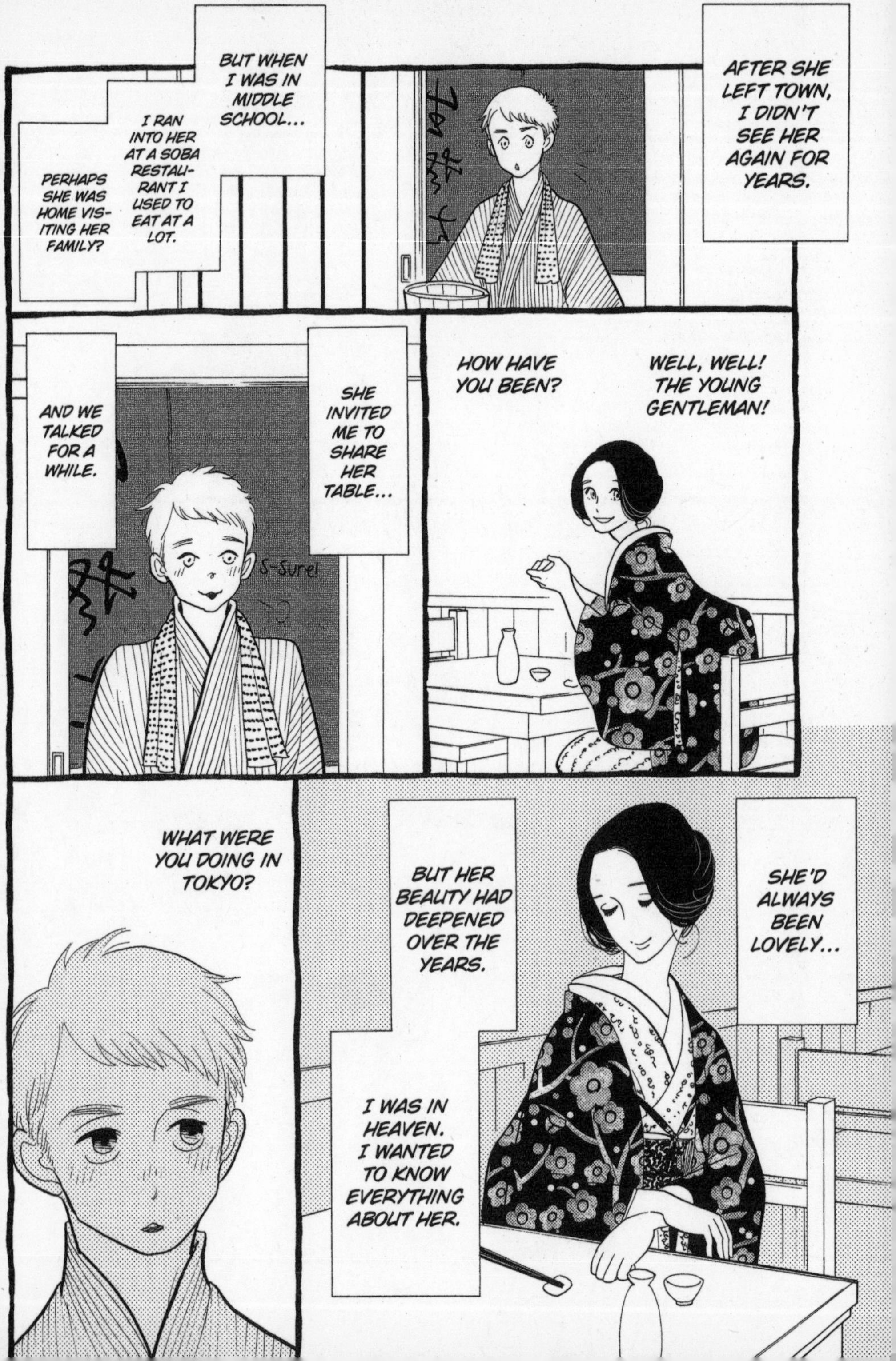
AFTER SHE LEFT TOWN, I DIDN'T SEE HER AGAIN FOR YEARS.
BUT WHEN I WAS IN MIDDLE SCHOOL...
I RAN INTO HER AT A SOBA RESTAU-RANT I USED TO EAT AT A LOT.
PERHAPS SHE WAS HOME VIS-ITING HER FAMILY?
WELL, WELL! THE YOUNG GENTLEMAN!
HOW HAVE YOU BEEN?
SHE INVITED ME TO SHARE HER TABLE...
S-Sure!
AND WE TALKED FOR A WHILE.
SHE'D ALWAYS BEEN LOVELY...
BUT HER BEAUTY HAD DEEPENED OVER THE YEARS.
I WAS IN HEAVEN. I WANTED TO KNOW EVERYTHING ABOUT HER.
WHAT WERE YOU DOING IN TOKYO?

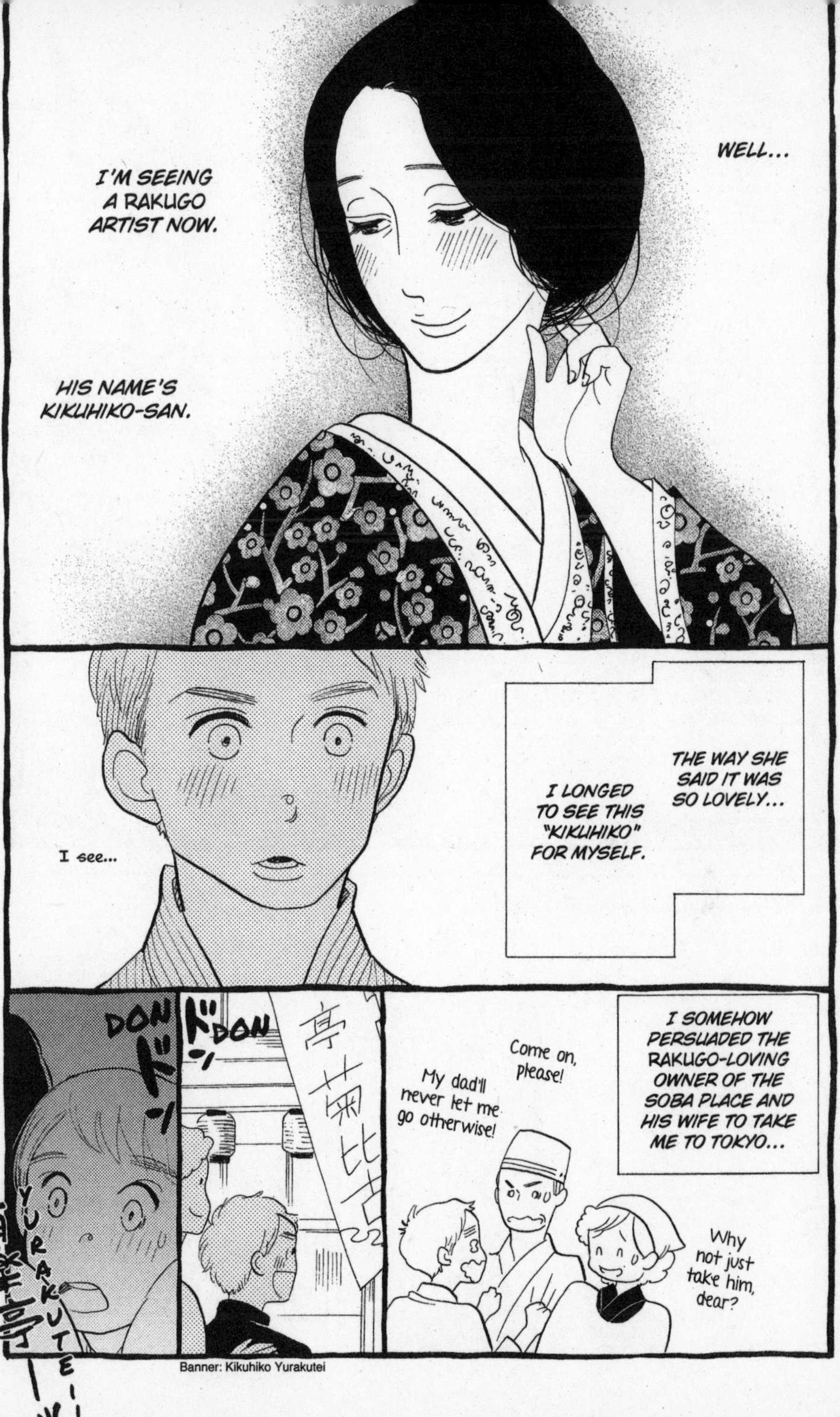
WELL...
I'M SEEING A RAKUGO ARTIST NOW.
HIS NAME'S KIKUHIKO-SAN.
THE WAY SHE SAID IT WAS SO LOVELY...
I LONGED TO SEE THIS "KIKUHIKO" FOR MYSELF.
I see...
I SOMEHOW PERSUADED THE RAKUGO-LOVING OWNER OF THE SOBA PLACE AND HIS WIFE TO TAKE ME TO TOKYO...
Come on, please!
My dad'll never let me go otherwise!
Why not just take him, dear?
ドン DON
亭菊比古
ドーン DON
有楽亭ーッ!
YURAKUTEI!

Banner: Kikuhiko Yurakutei

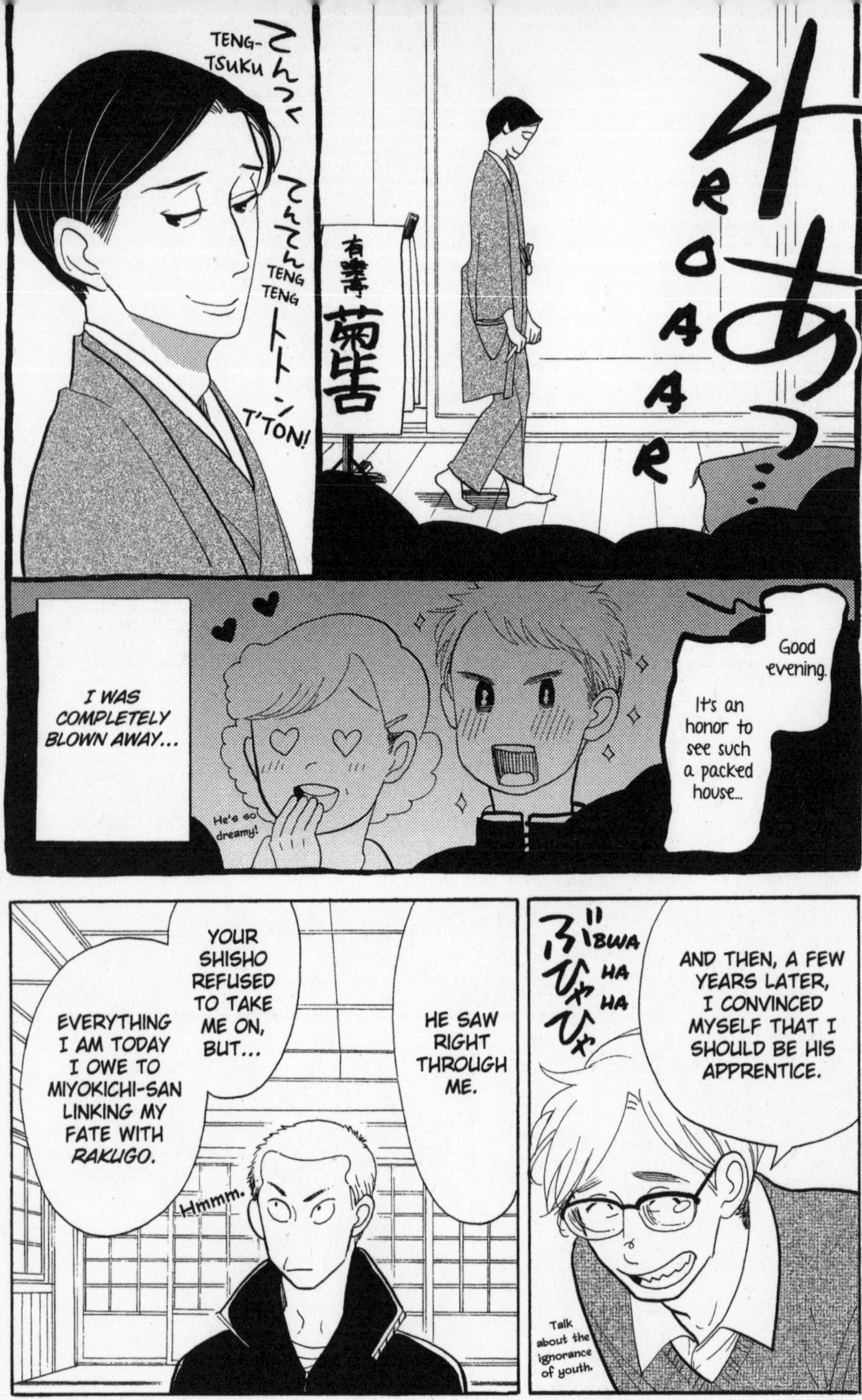
ROAAR
TENG-TSUKU
TENG TENG
T'TON!
Good evening.
It's an honor to see such a packed house...
He's so dreamy!
I WAS COMPLETELY BLOWN AWAY...
BWA HA HA
AND THEN, A FEW YEARS LATER, I CONVINCED MYSELF THAT I SHOULD BE HIS APPRENTICE.
Talk about the ignorance of youth.
HE SAW RIGHT THROUGH ME.
YOUR SHISHO REFUSED TO TAKE ME ON, BUT...
EVERYTHING I AM TODAY I OWE TO MIYOKICHI-SAN LINKING MY FATE WITH *RAKUGO*.
Hmmm.

Sign: Kikuhiko Yurakutei

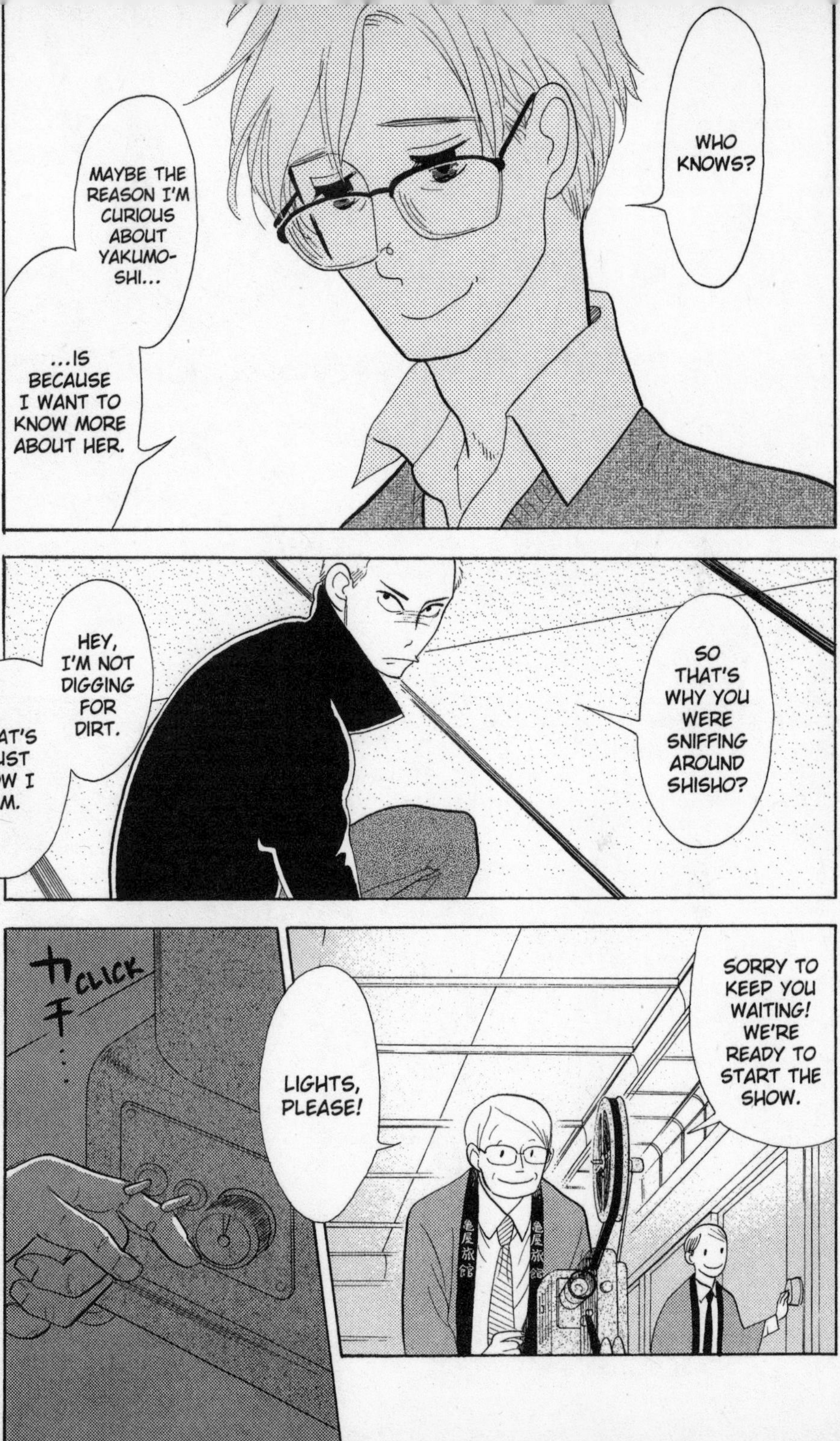
WHO KNOWS?
MAYBE THE REASON I'M CURIOUS ABOUT YAKUMO-SHI...
...IS BECAUSE I WANT TO KNOW MORE ABOUT HER.
SO THAT'S WHY YOU WERE SNIFFING AROUND SHISHO?
HEY, I'M NOT DIGGING FOR DIRT.
THAT'S JUST HOW I AM.
SORRY TO KEEP YOU WAITING! WE'RE READY TO START THE SHOW.
LIGHTS, PLEASE!
カチ CLICK...

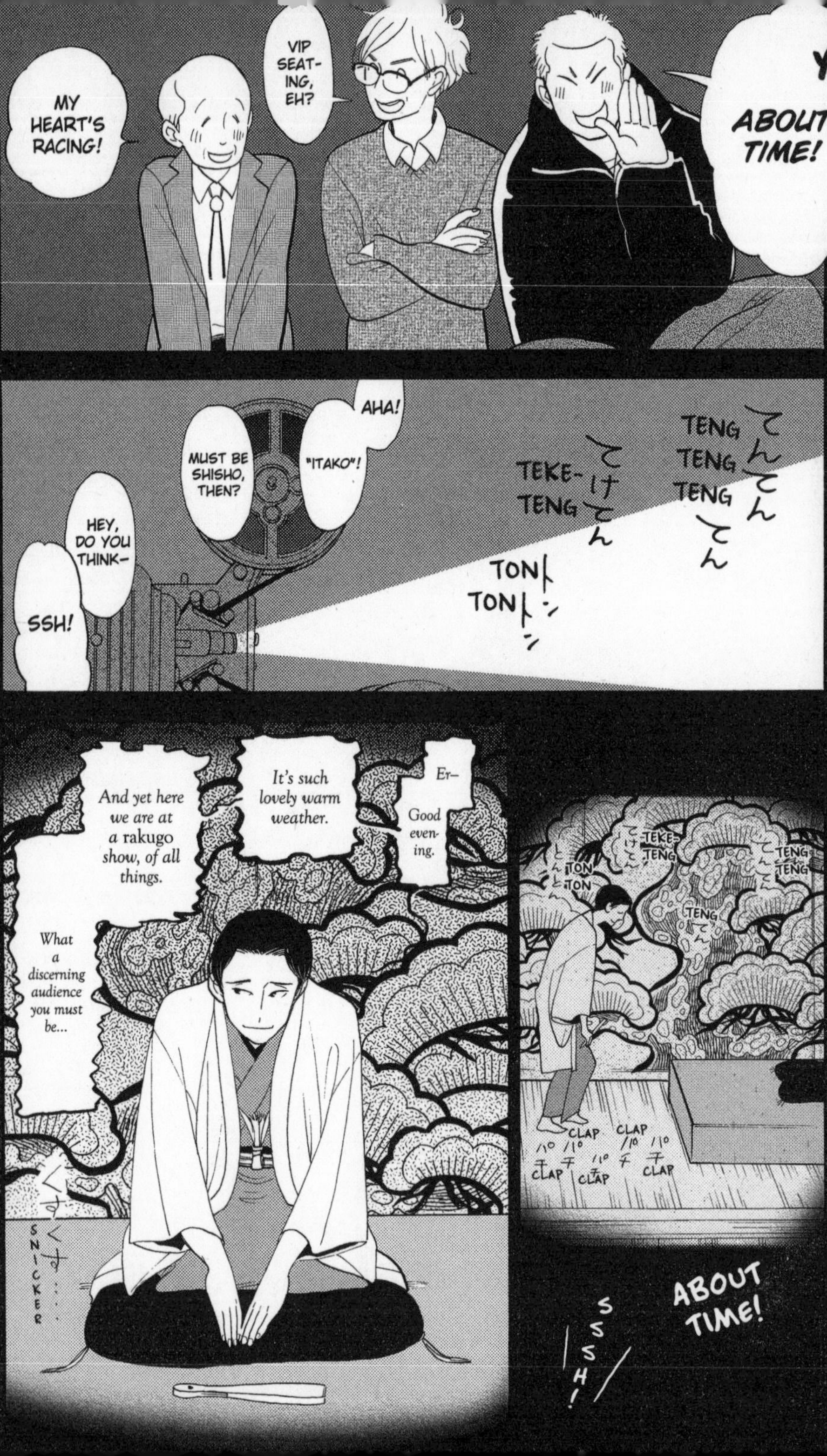
YO!
ABOUT TIME!
VIP SEATING, EH?
MY HEART'S RACING!
TENG TENG TENG
TEKE-TENG
TON TON
AHA!
"ITAKO"!
MUST BE SHISHO, THEN?
HEY, DO YOU THINK—
SSH!
TEKE-TENG
TENG TENG
TENG
TON TON
CLAP CLAP CLAP CLAP CLAP CLAP
ABOUT TIME!
SSSH!
Er— Good evening.
It's such lovely warm weather.
And yet here we are at a rakugo show, of all things.
What a discerning audience you must be...
SNICKER

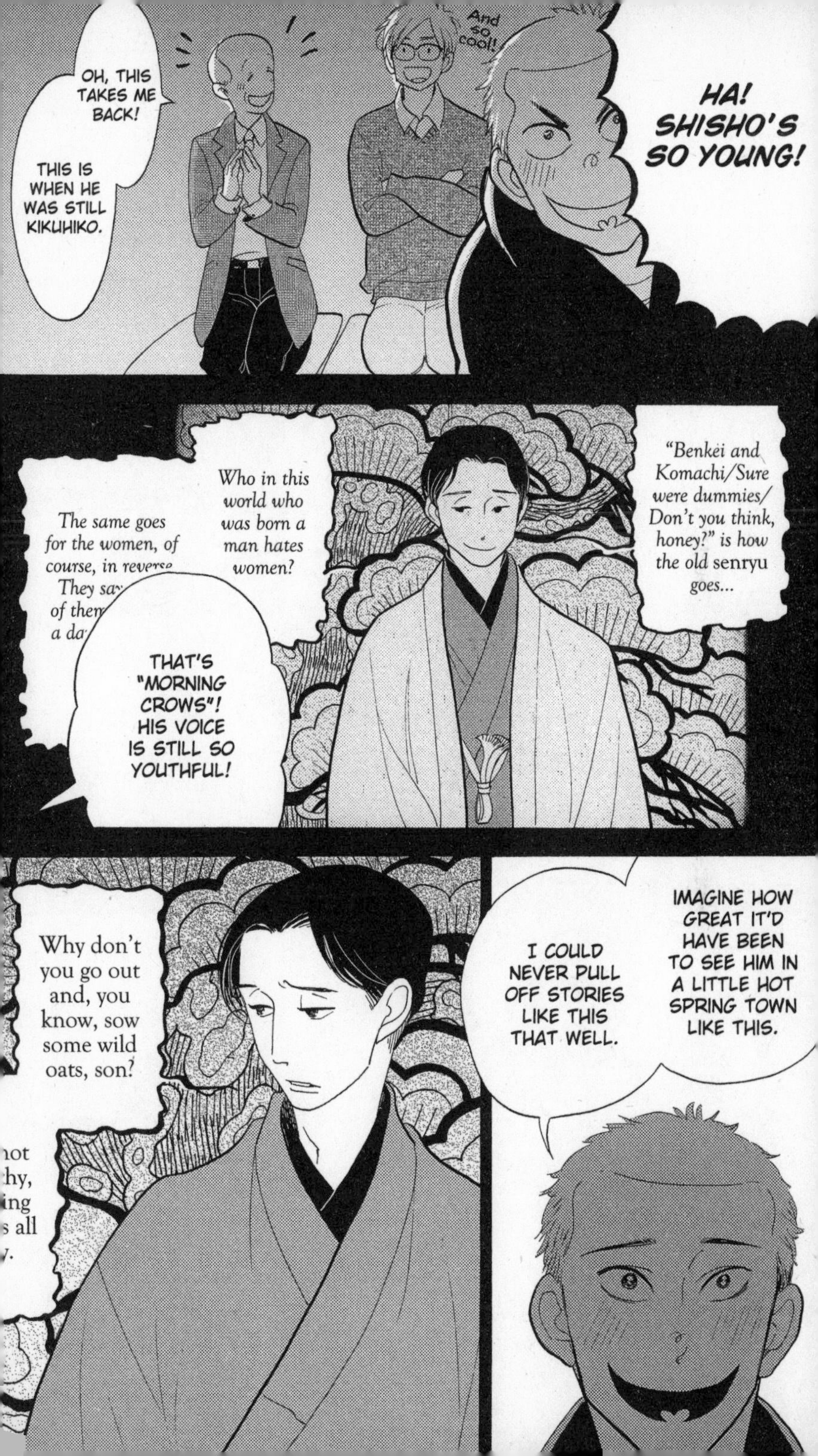
HA! SHISHO'S SO YOUNG!
And so cool!
OH, THIS TAKES ME BACK!
THIS IS WHEN HE WAS STILL KIKUHIKO.
"Benkei and Komachi/Sure were dummies/Don't you think, honey?" is how the old senryu goes...
Who in this world who was born a man hates women?
The same goes for the women, of course, in reverse.
THAT'S "MORNING CROWS"! HIS VOICE IS STILL SO YOUTHFUL!
IMAGINE HOW GREAT IT'D HAVE BEEN TO SEE HIM IN A LITTLE HOT SPRING TOWN LIKE THIS.
I COULD NEVER PULL OFF STORIES LIKE THIS THAT WELL.
Why don't you go out and, you know, sow some wild oats, son?

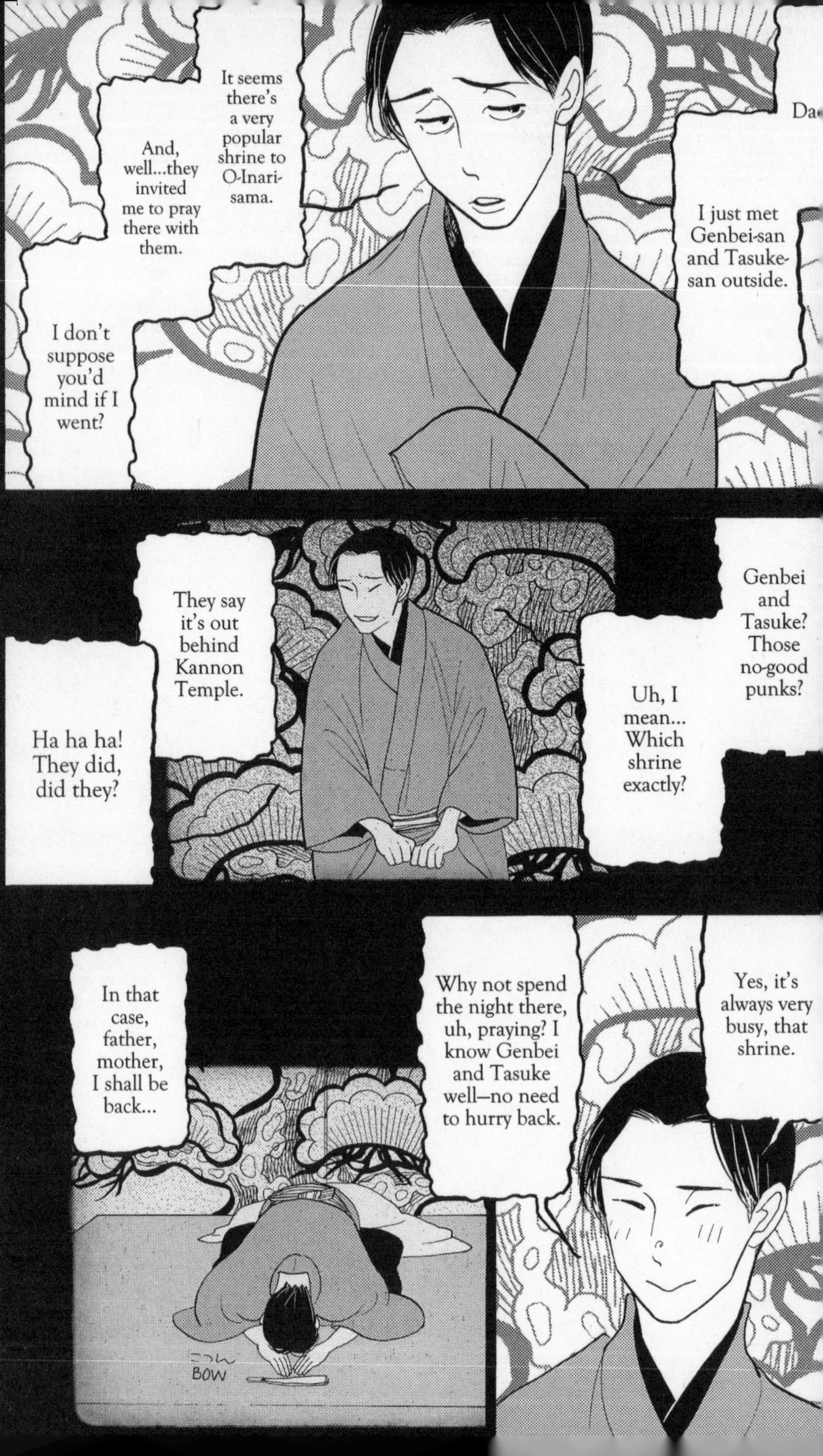
I just met Genbei-san and Tasuke-san outside.
It seems there's a very popular shrine to O-Inari-sama.
And, well...they invited me to pray there with them.
I don't suppose you'd mind if I went?
Genbei and Tasuke? Those no-good punks?
Uh, I mean... Which shrine exactly?
They say it's out behind Kannon Temple.
Ha ha ha! They did, did they?
Yes, it's always very busy, that shrine.
Why not spend the night there, uh, praying? I know Genbei and Tasuke well—no need to hurry back.
In that case, father, mother, I shall be back...
BOW

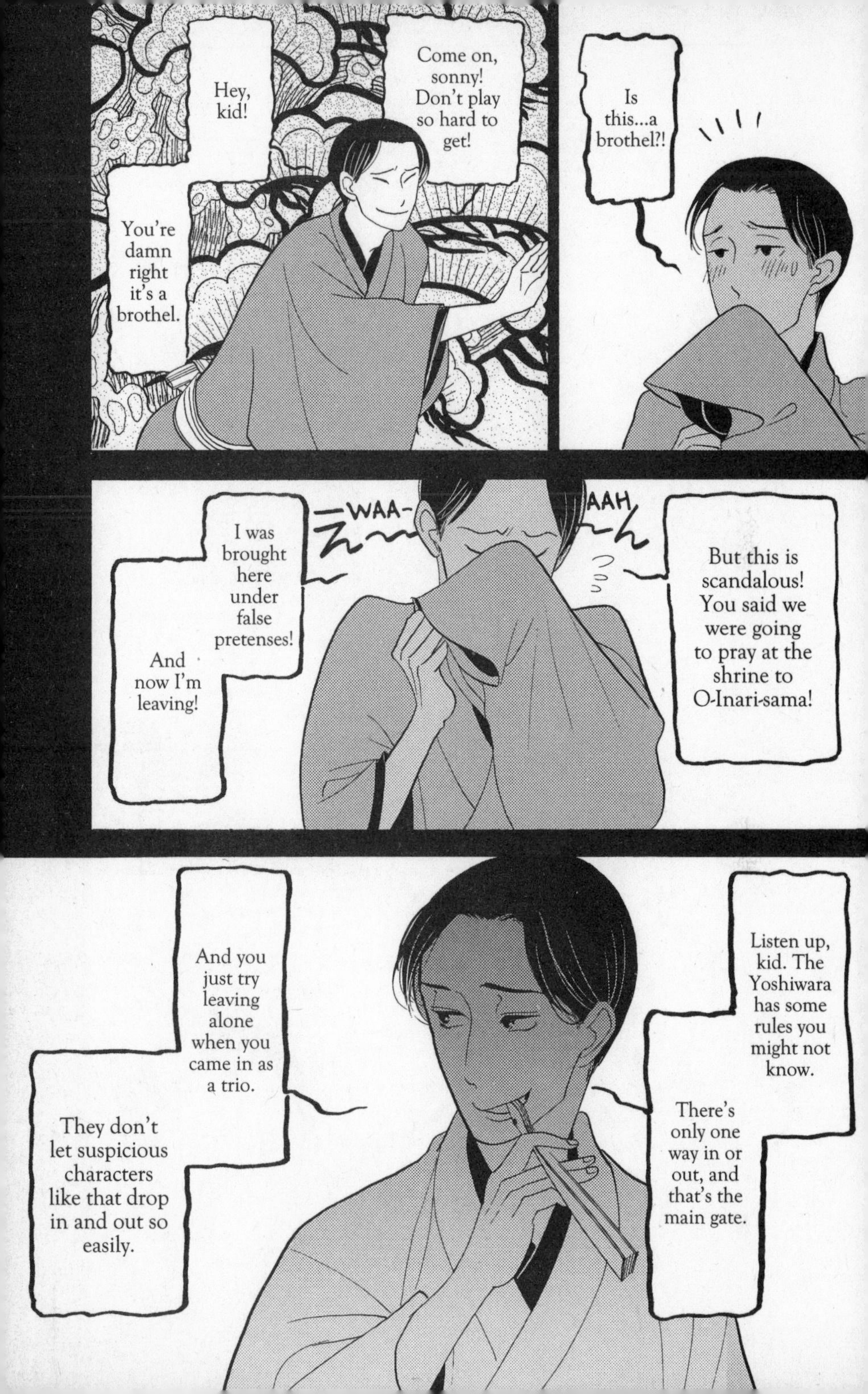
Is this...a brothel?!
Come on, sonny! Don't play so hard to get!
Hey, kid!
You're damn right it's a brothel.
But this is scandalous! You said we were going to pray at the shrine to O-Inari-sama!
WAA-AAH
I was brought here under false pretenses!
And now I'm leaving!
Listen up, kid. The Yoshiwara has some rules you might not know.
There's only one way in or out, and that's the main gate.
And you just try leaving alone when you came in as a trio.
They don't let suspicious characters like that drop in and out so easily.

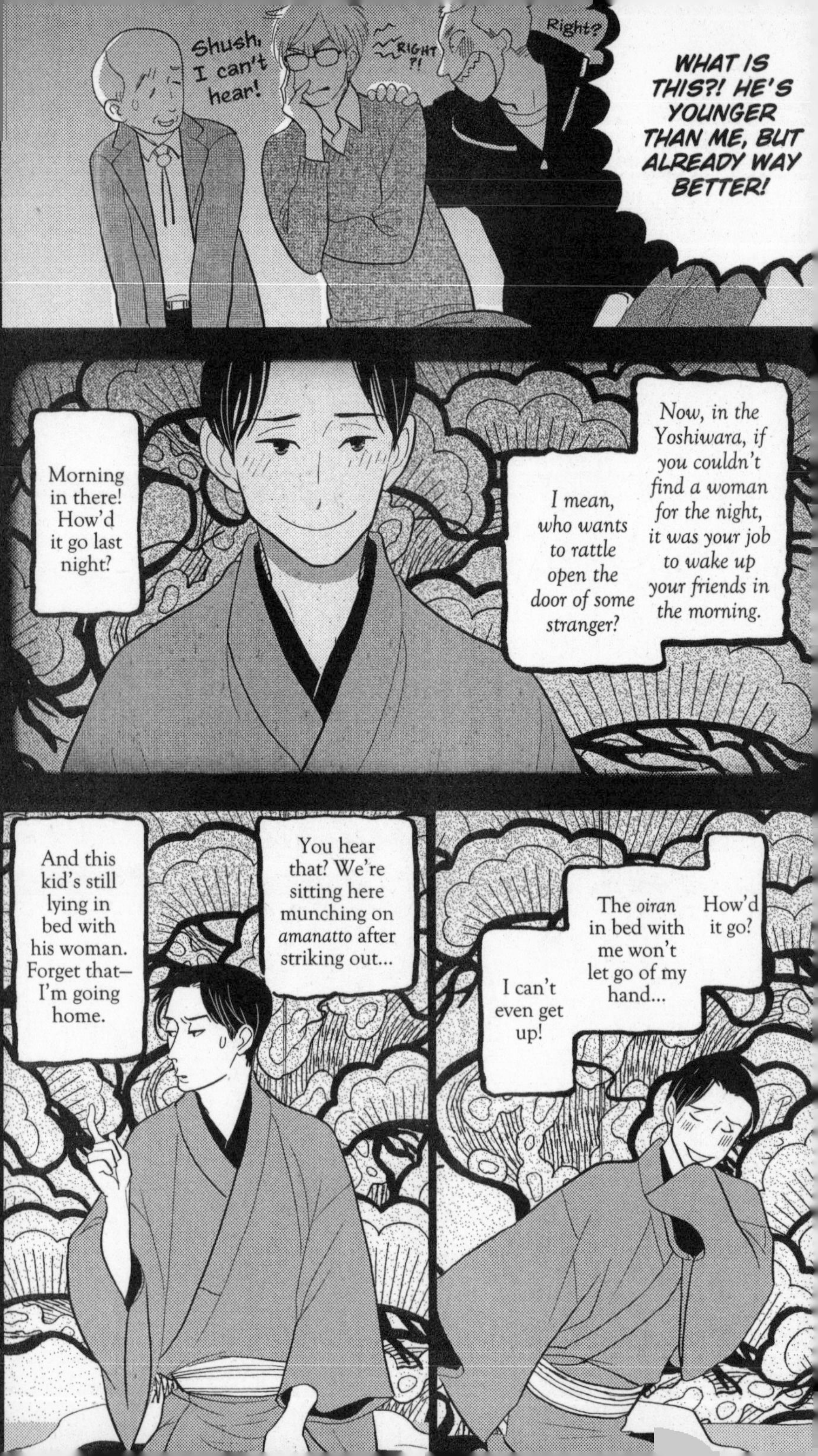
WHAT IS THIS?! HE'S YOUNGER THAN ME, BUT ALREADY WAY BETTER!
Right?
RIGHT ?!
Shush, I can't hear!
Now, in the Yoshiwara, if you couldn't find a woman for the night, it was your job to wake up your friends in the morning.
I mean, who wants to rattle open the door of some stranger?
Morning in there! How'd it go last night?
How'd it go?
The *oiran* in bed with me won't let go of my hand...
I can't even get up!
You hear that? We're sitting here munching on *amanatto* after striking out...
And this kid's still lying in bed with his woman. Forget that–I'm going home.

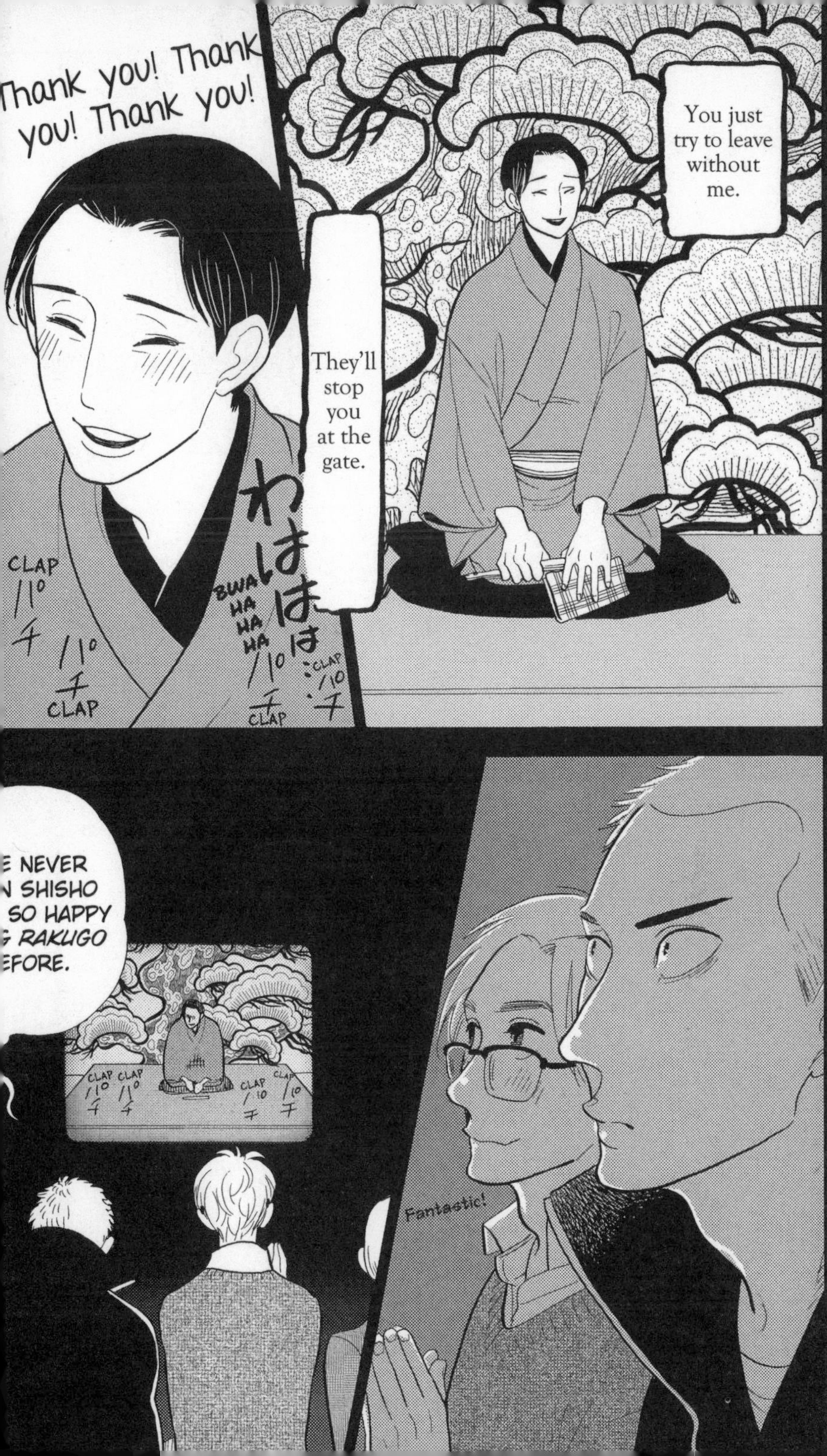

You just try to leave without me.
They'll stop you at the gate.
Thank you! Thank you! Thank you!
わははは
BWA HA HA HA
CLAP パチ
CLAP パチ
CLAP パチ
CLAP パチ
Fantastic!
E NEVER
N SHISHO
SO HAPPY
G RAKUGO
EFORE.
CLAP パチ
CLAP パチ
CLAP パチ
CLAP パチ

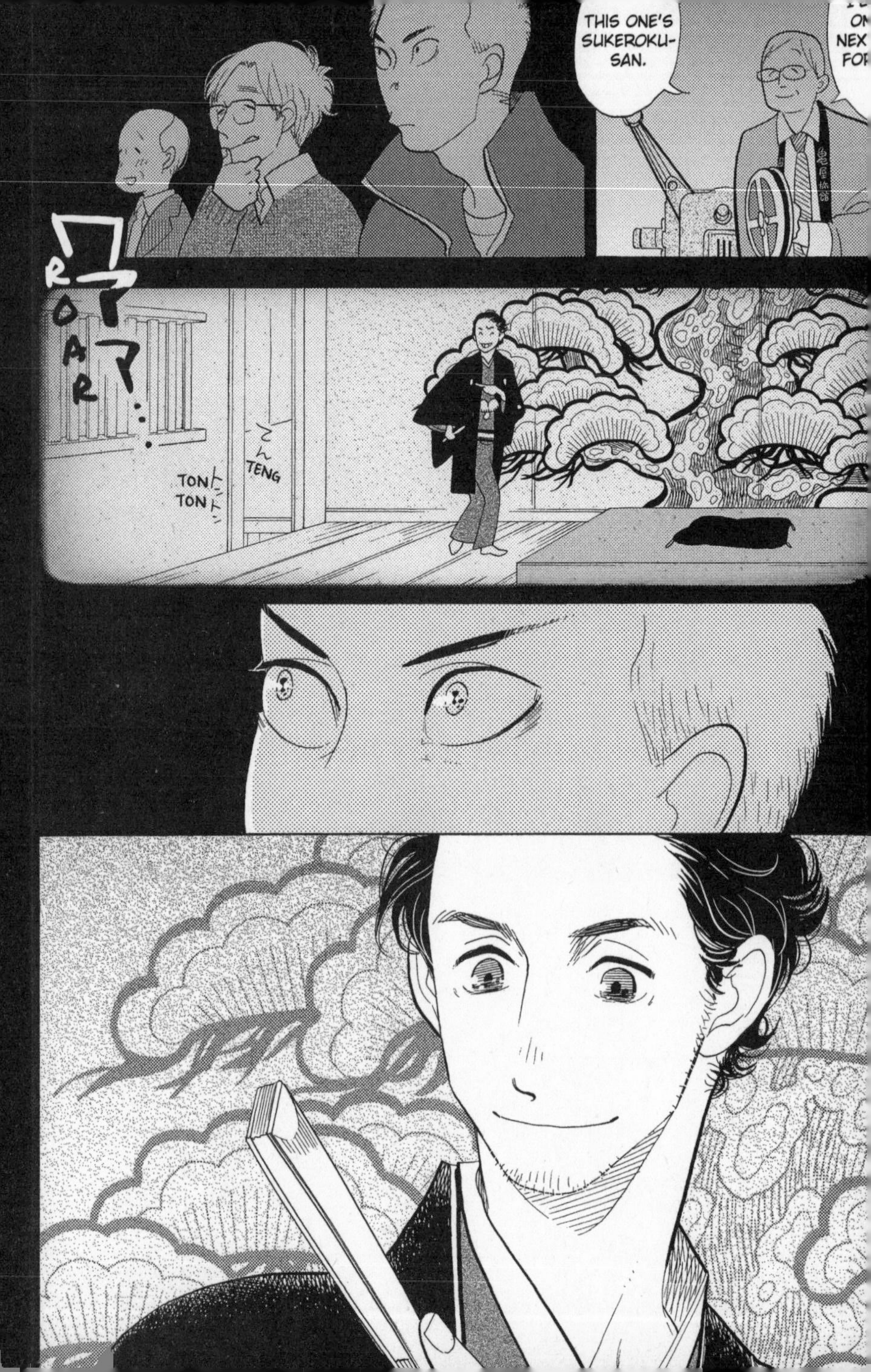
THIS ONE'S SUKEROKU-SAN.
ROAR
TENG
TON TON

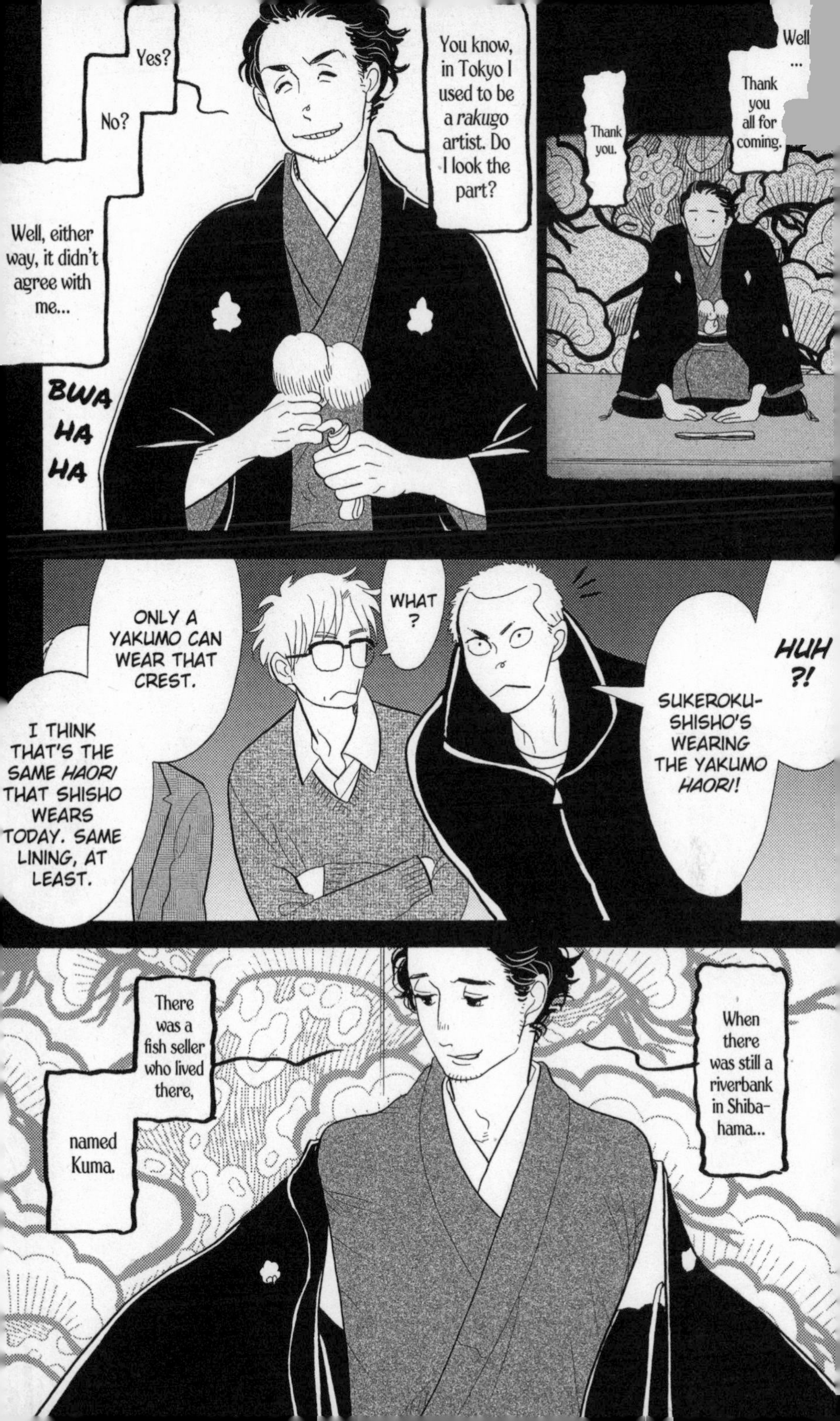
Well...
Thank you all for coming.
Thank you.
You know, in Tokyo I used to be a *rakugo* artist. Do I look the part?
Yes?
No?
Well, either way, it didn't agree with me...
BWA HA HA
HUH ?!
SUKEROKU-SHISHO'S WEARING THE YAKUMO *HAORI*!
WHAT ?
ONLY A YAKUMO CAN WEAR THAT CREST.
I THINK THAT'S THE SAME *HAORI* THAT SHISHO WEARS TODAY. SAME LINING, AT LEAST.
When there was still a riverbank in Shiba-hama...
There was a fish seller who lived there,
named Kuma.

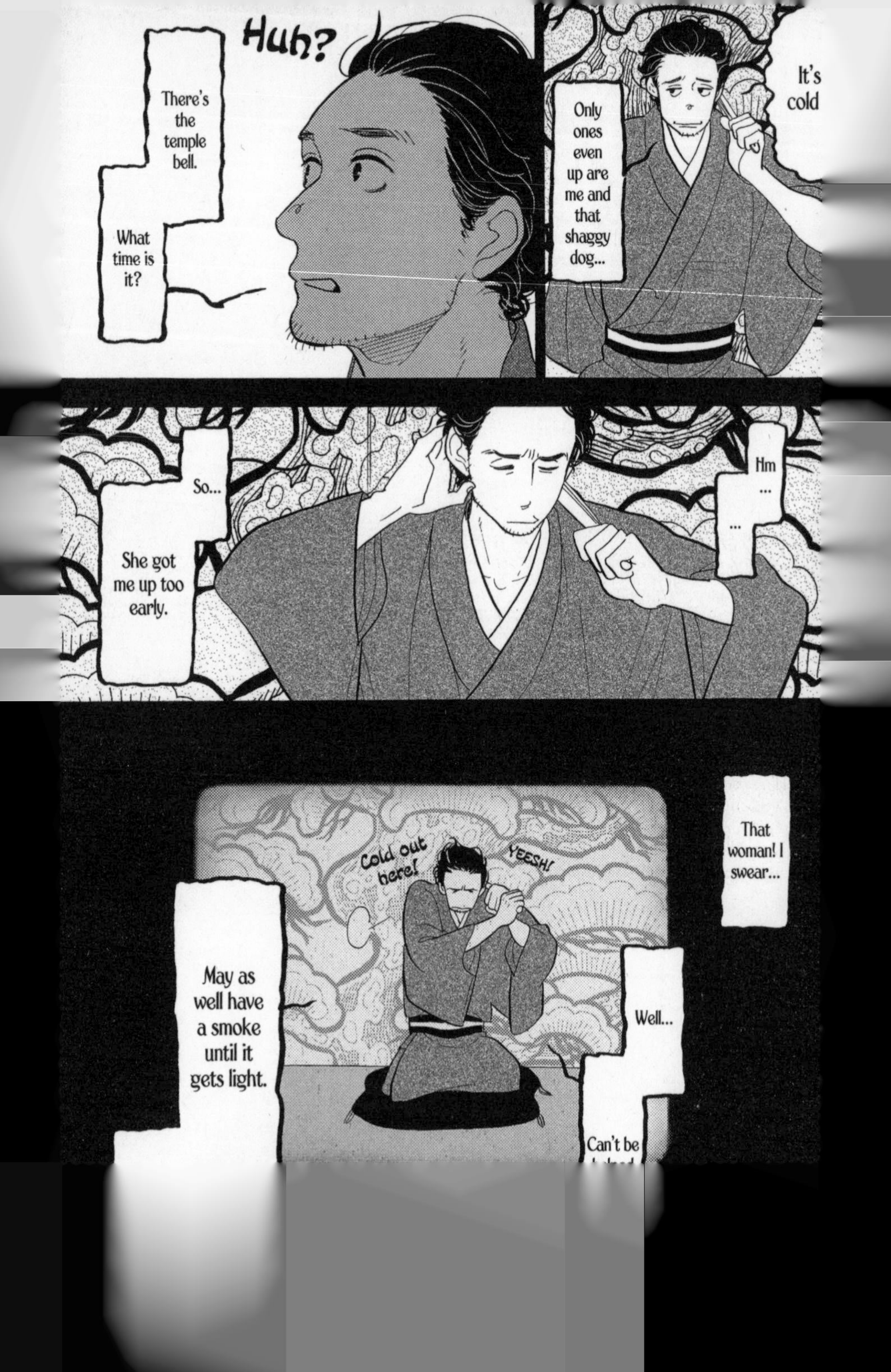
It's cold
Only ones even up are me and that shaggy dog...
Huh?
There's the temple bell.
What time is it?
Hm... ...
So...
She got me up too early.
That woman! I swear...
Well...
Can't be
YEESH!
Cold out here!
May as well have a smoke until it gets light.

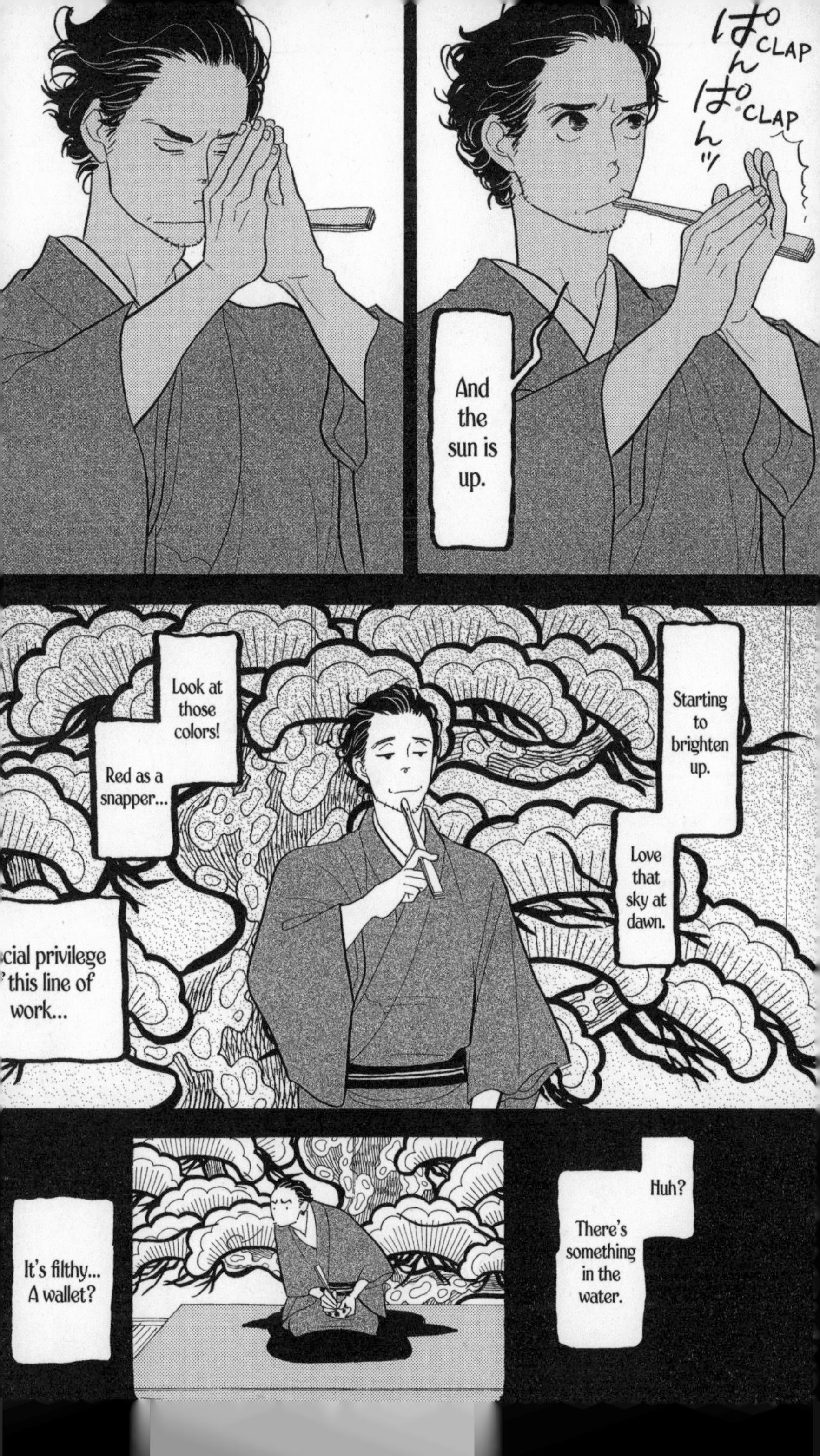
ぱん ぱんッ
CLAP CLAP
And the sun is up.
Starting to brighten up.
Love that sky at dawn.
Look at those colors!
Red as a snapper...
cial privilege
f this line of
work...
Huh?
There's something in the water.
It's filthy... A wallet?

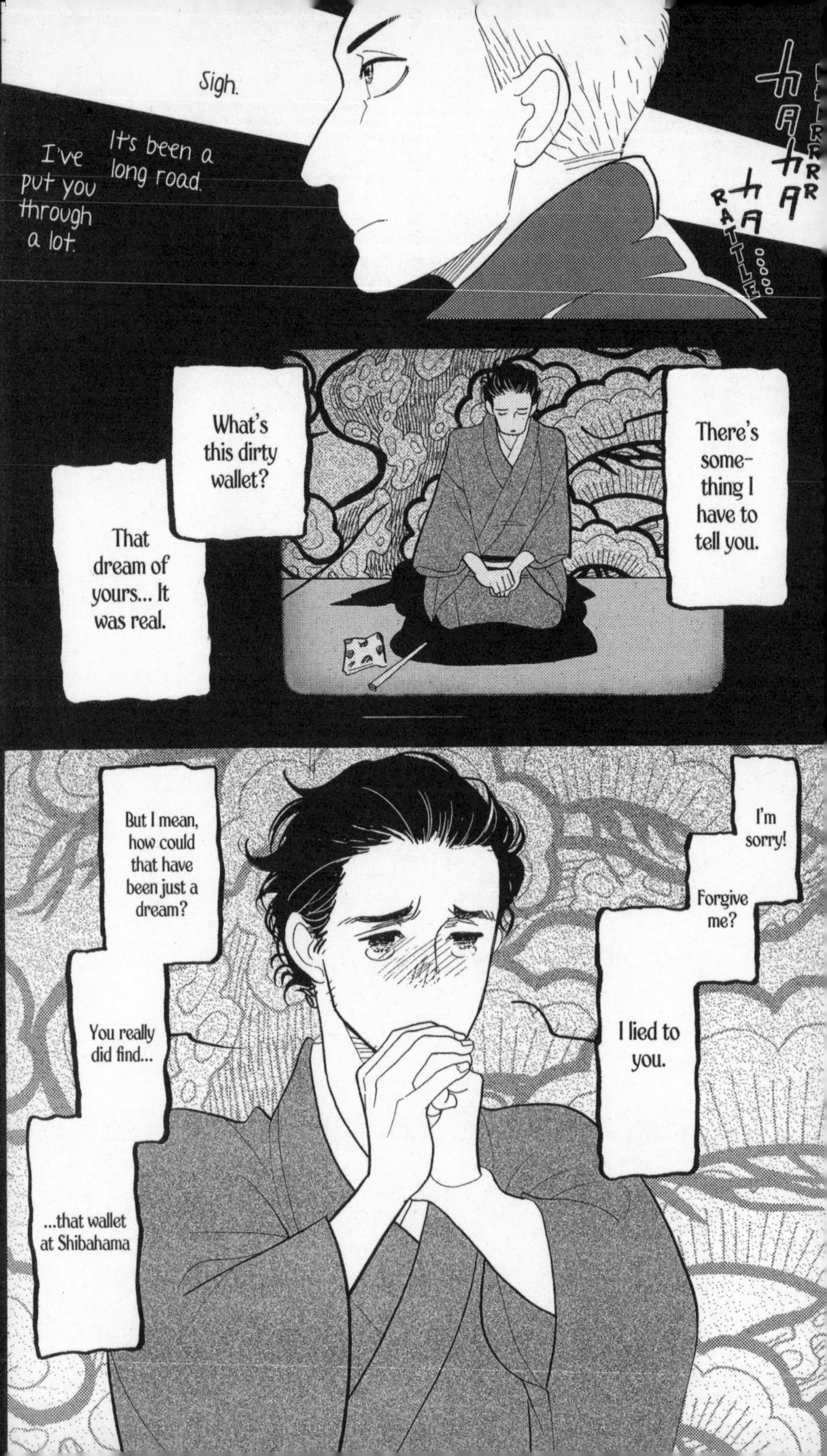
RATTLE...
Sigh.
It's been a long road.
I've put you through a lot.
There's something I have to tell you.
What's this dirty wallet?
That dream of yours... It was real.
I'm sorry!
Forgive me?
I lied to you.
But I mean, how could that have been just a dream?
You really did find...
...that wallet at Shibahama

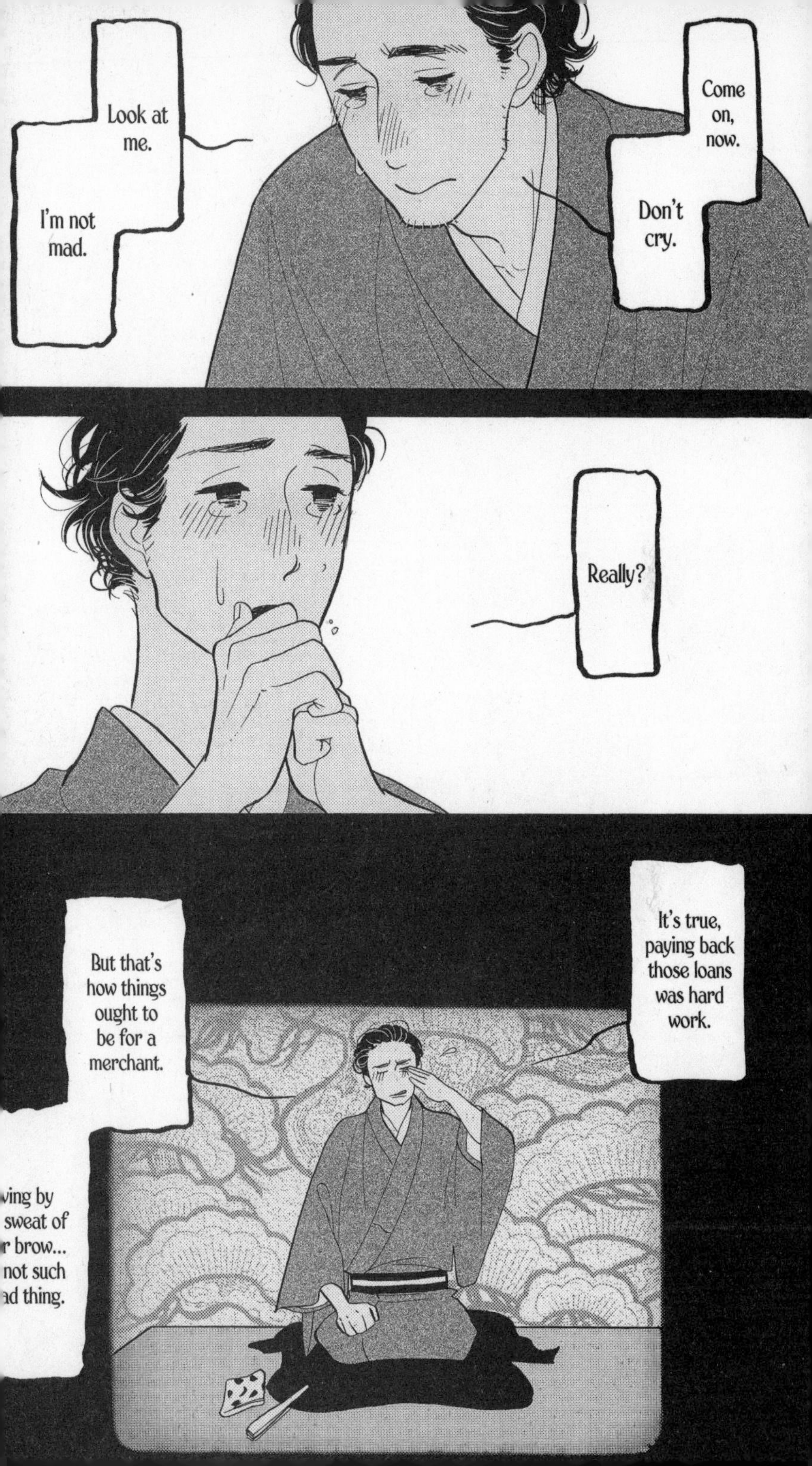
Come on, now.
Don't cry.
Look at me.
I'm not mad.
Really?
It's true, paying back those loans was hard work.
But that's how things ought to be for a merchant.
ving by sweat of r brow... not such ad thing.

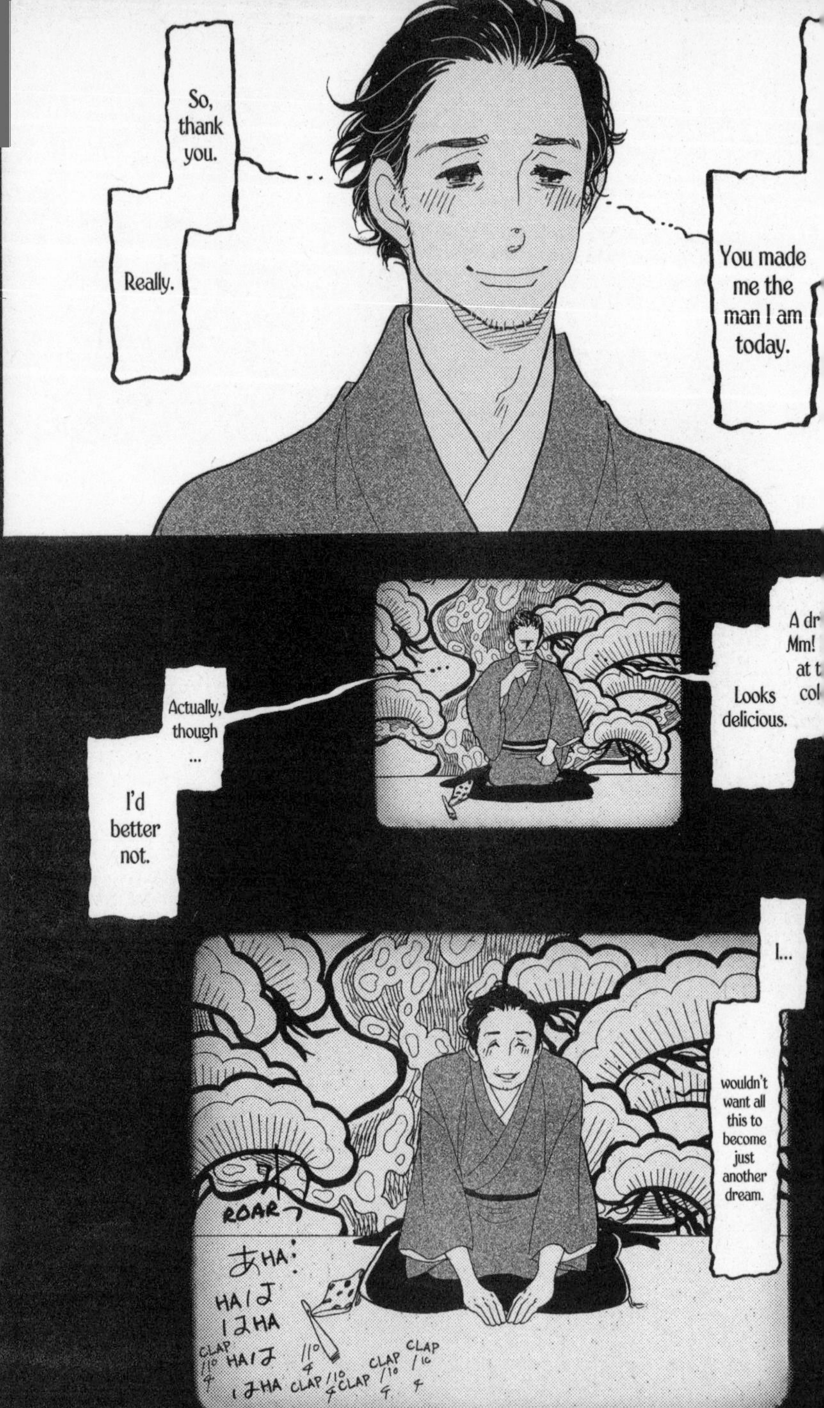
You made me the man I am today.
So, thank you.
Really.
Mm!
Looks delicious.
Actually, though ...
I'd better not.
I...
wouldn't want all this to become just another dream.
ROAR
HA HA HA HA HA HA
CLAP CLAP CLAP CLAP CLAP

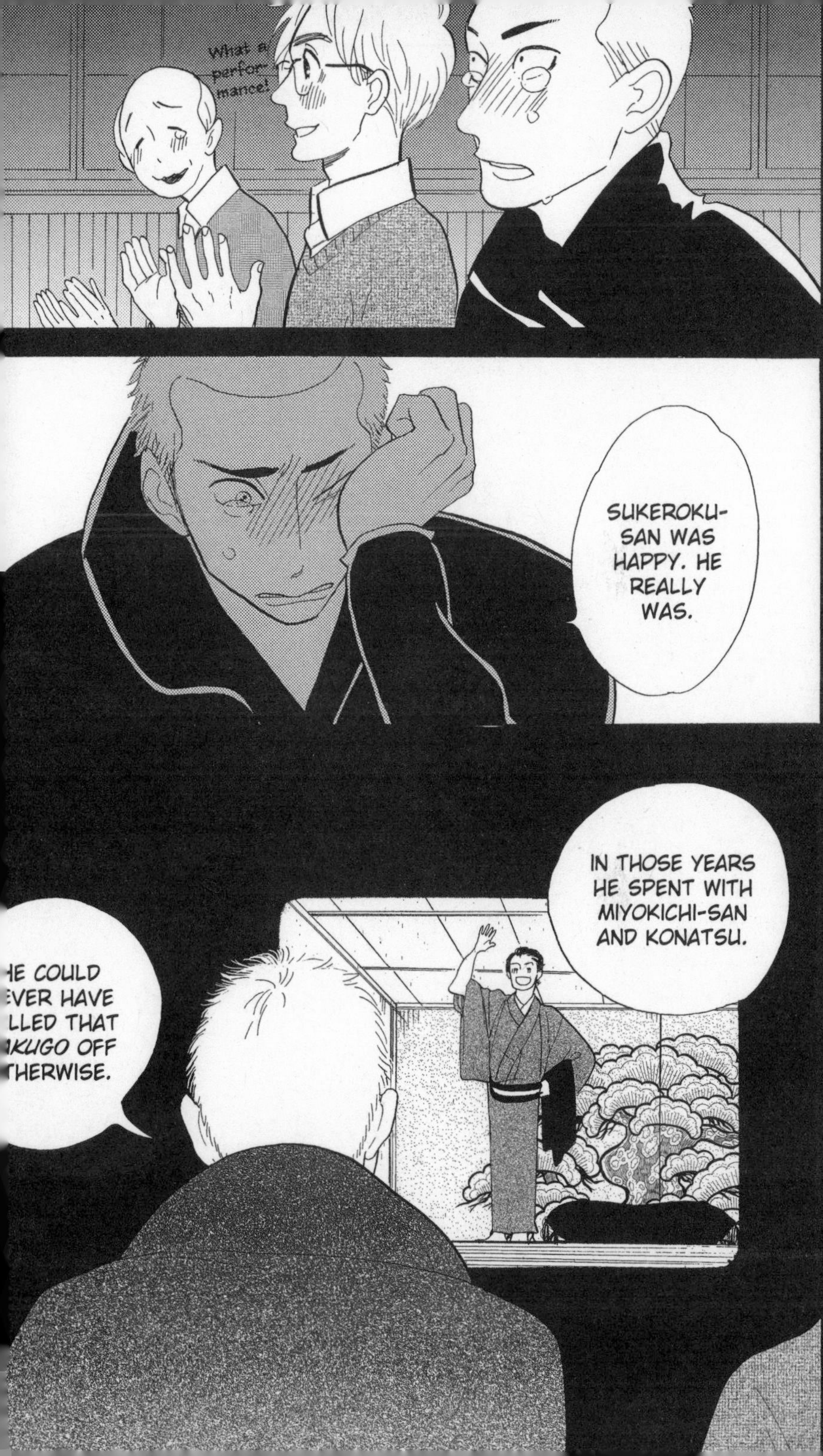
What a perfor-mance!
SUKEROKU-SAN WAS HAPPY. HE REALLY WAS.
IN THOSE YEARS HE SPENT WITH MIYOKICHI-SAN AND KONATSU.
HE COULD EVER HAVE LLED THAT KUGO OFF THERWISE.

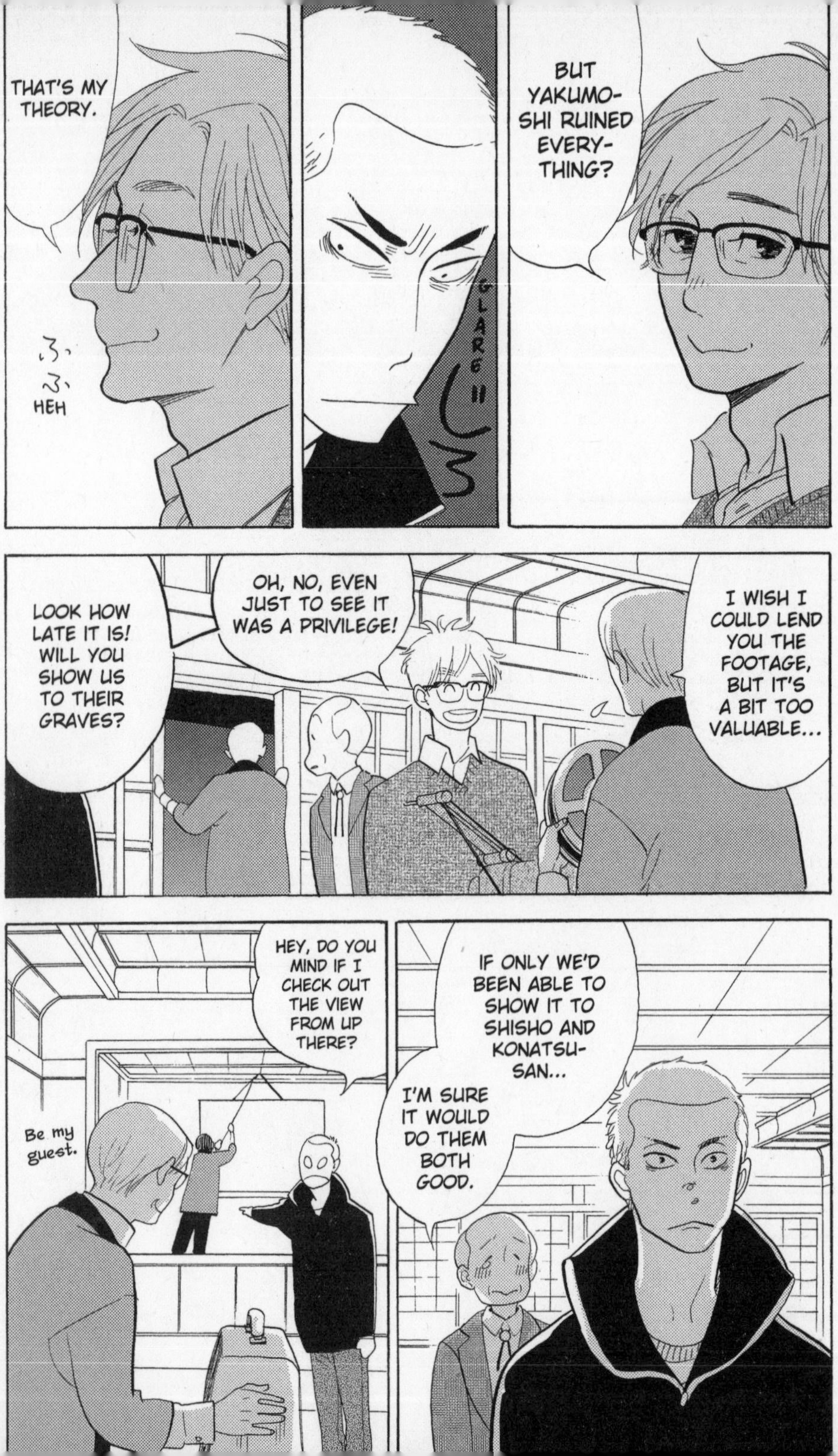
BUT YAKUMO-SHI RUINED EVERY-THING?
GLARE
じろ
THAT'S MY THEORY.
ふふ
HEH
I WISH I COULD LEND YOU THE FOOTAGE, BUT IT'S A BIT TOO VALUABLE...
OH, NO, EVEN JUST TO SEE IT WAS A PRIVILEGE!
LOOK HOW LATE IT IS! WILL YOU SHOW US TO THEIR GRAVES?
IF ONLY WE'D BEEN ABLE TO SHOW IT TO SHISHO AND KONATSU-SAN...
I'M SURE IT WOULD DO THEM BOTH GOOD.
HEY, DO YOU MIND IF I CHECK OUT THE VIEW FROM UP THERE?
Be my guest.

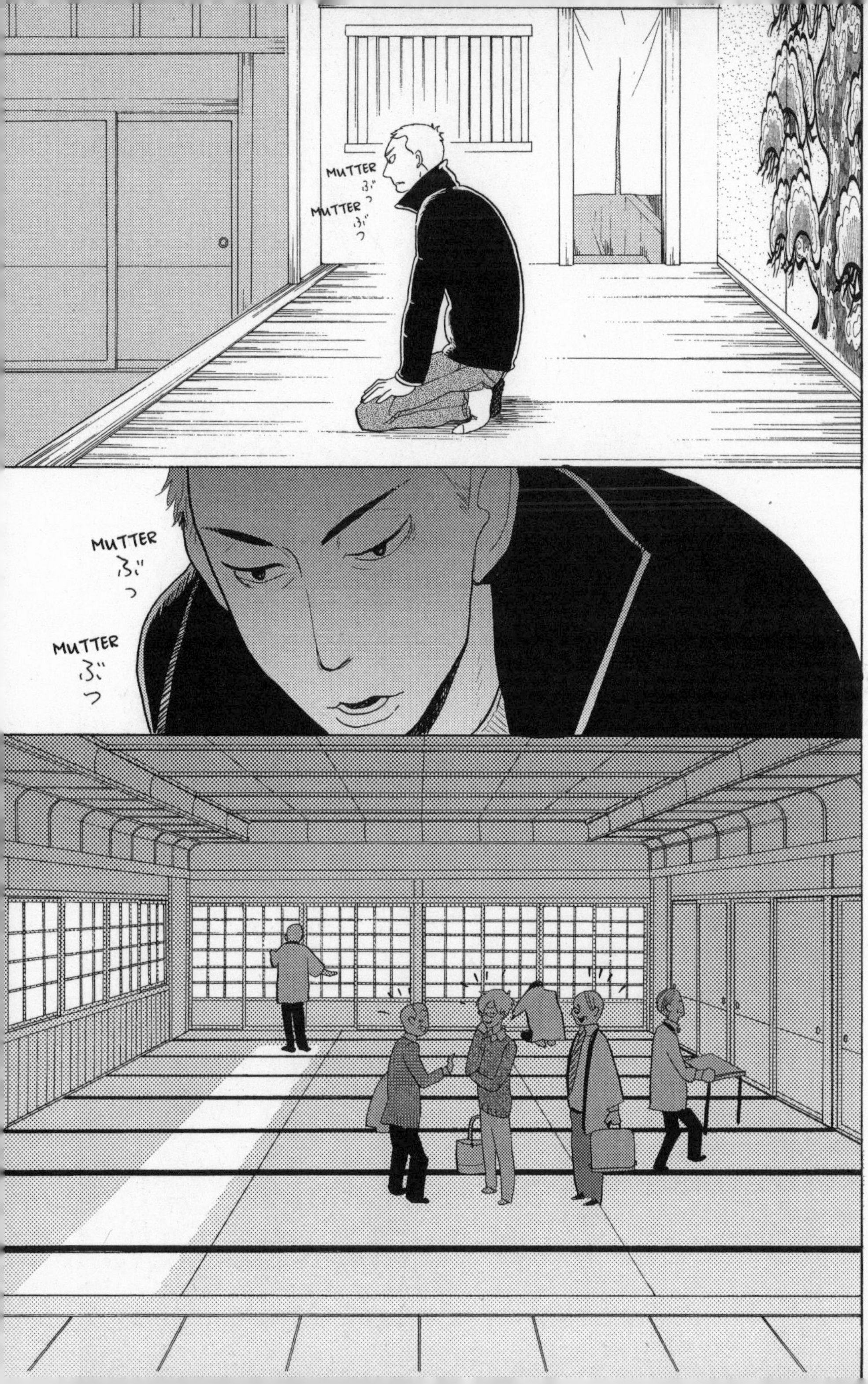
MUTTER
ぶつ
MUTTER
ぶつ
MUTTER
ぶつ
MUTTER
ぶつ

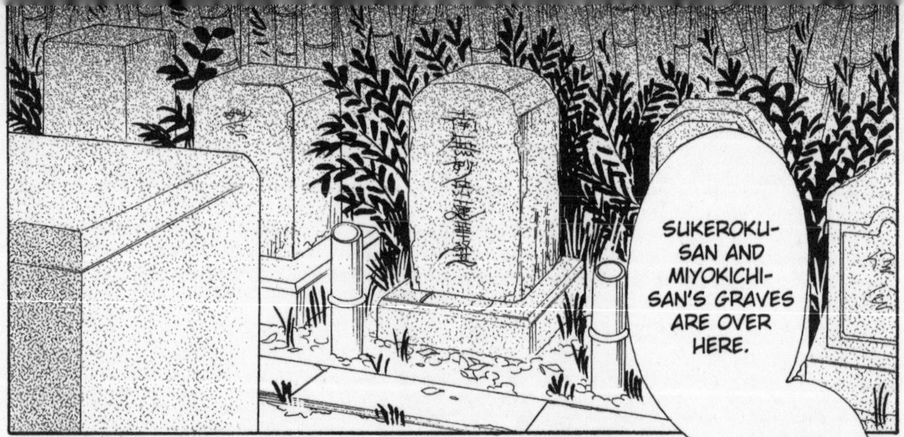
SUKEROKU-SAN AND MIYOKICHI-SAN'S GRAVES ARE OVER HERE.
Gravestone: *Namu Myoho Renge Kyo*

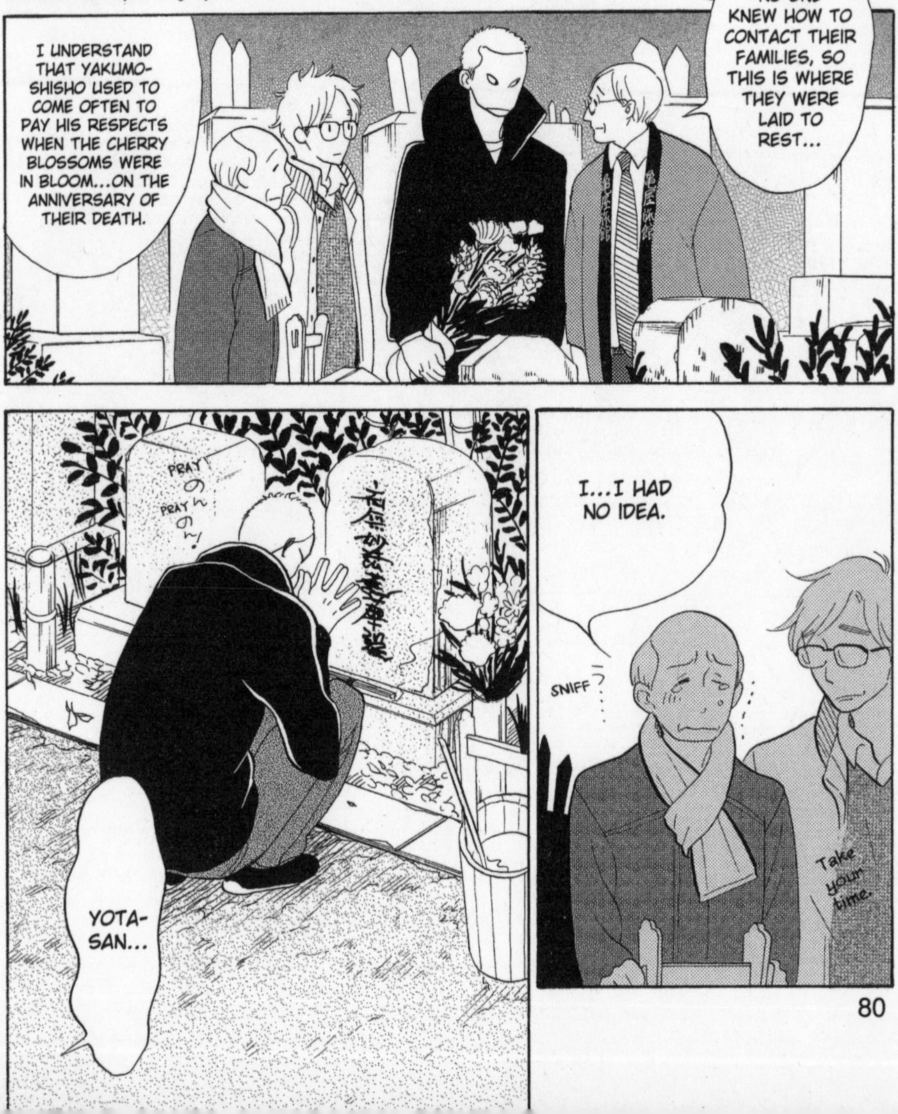
NO ONE KNEW HOW TO CONTACT THEIR FAMILIES, SO THIS IS WHERE THEY WERE LAID TO REST...
I UNDERSTAND THAT YAKUMO-SHISHO USED TO COME OFTEN TO PAY HIS RESPECTS WHEN THE CHERRY BLOSSOMS WERE IN BLOOM...ON THE ANNIVERSARY OF THEIR DEATH.
I...I HAD NO IDEA.
SNIFF
Take your time.
PRAY
PRAY
YOTA-SAN...

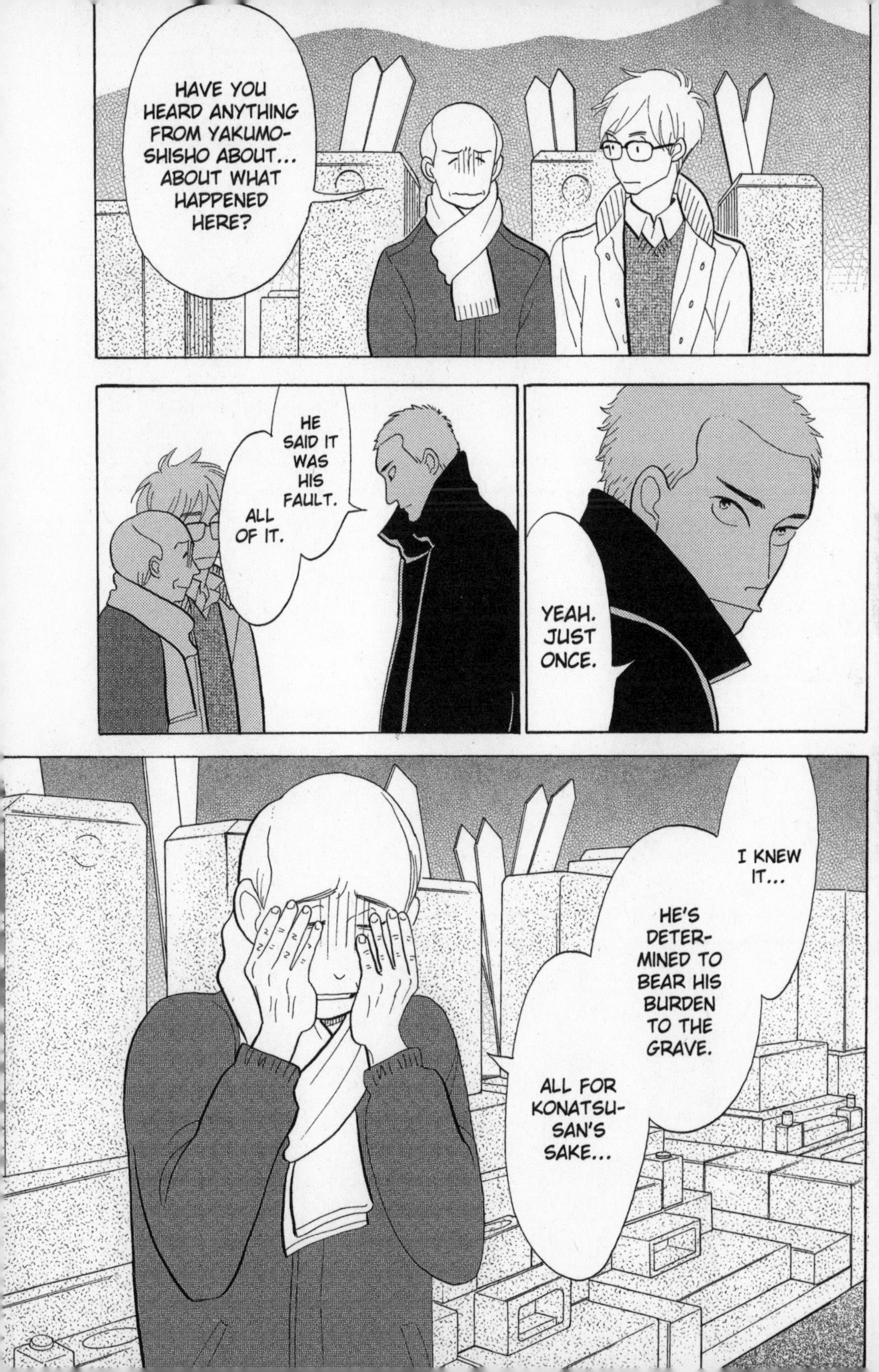
HAVE YOU HEARD ANYTHING FROM YAKUMO-SHISHO ABOUT... ABOUT WHAT HAPPENED HERE?
YEAH. JUST ONCE.
HE SAID IT WAS HIS FAULT.
ALL OF IT.
I KNEW IT...
HE'S DETER-MINED TO BEAR HIS BURDEN TO THE GRAVE.
ALL FOR KONATSU-SAN'S SAKE...

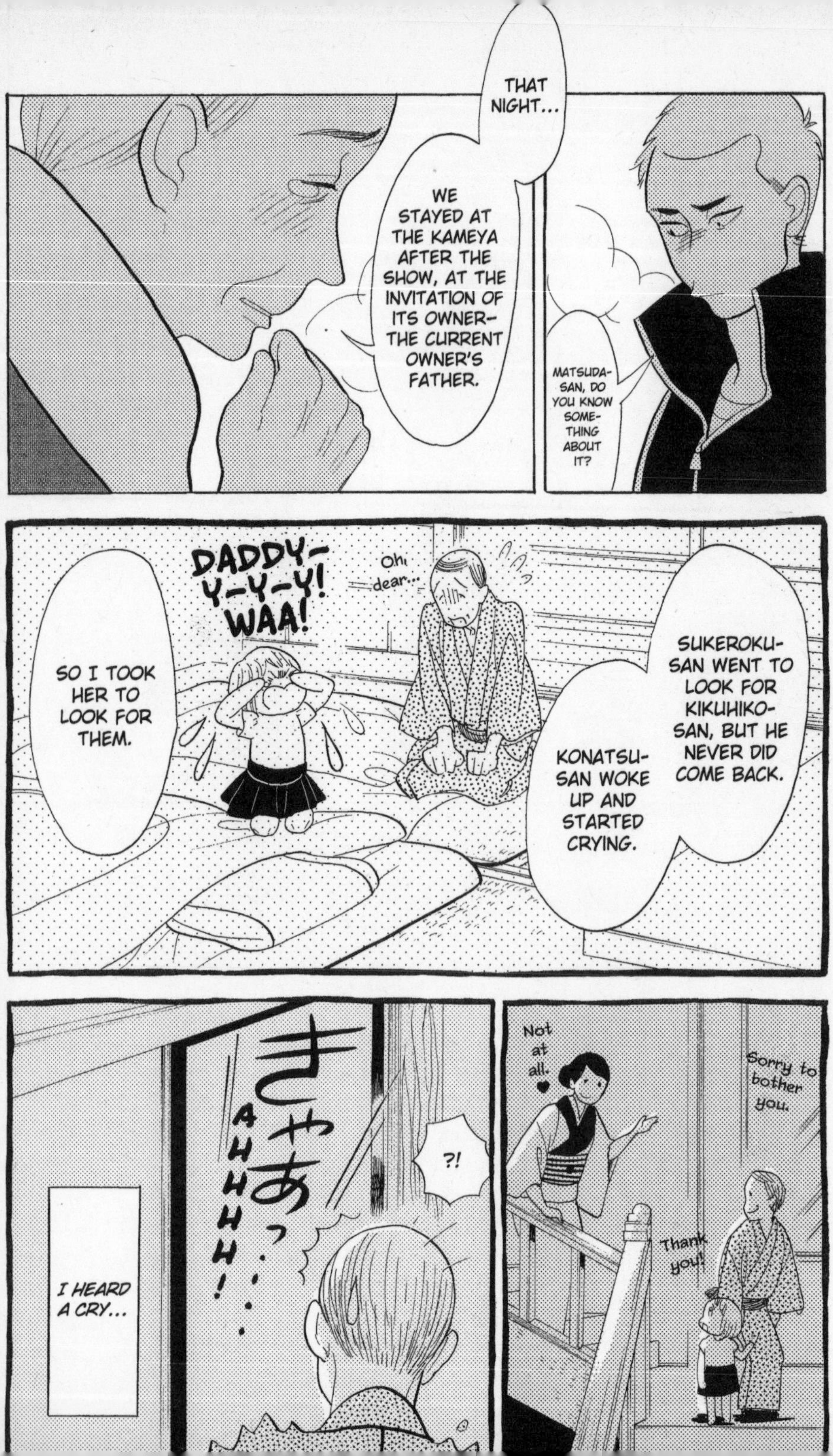
MATSUDA-SAN, DO YOU KNOW SOMETHING ABOUT IT?
THAT NIGHT...
WE STAYED AT THE KAMEYA AFTER THE SHOW, AT THE INVITATION OF ITS OWNER–THE CURRENT OWNER'S FATHER.
SUKEROKU-SAN WENT TO LOOK FOR KIKUHIKO-SAN, BUT HE NEVER DID COME BACK.
KONATSU-SAN WOKE UP AND STARTED CRYING.
Oh, dear...
DADDY-Y-Y-Y! WAA!
SO I TOOK HER TO LOOK FOR THEM.
Sorry to bother you.
Not at all.
Thank you!
?!
きゃあっ……
AHHHHH!
I HEARD A CRY...

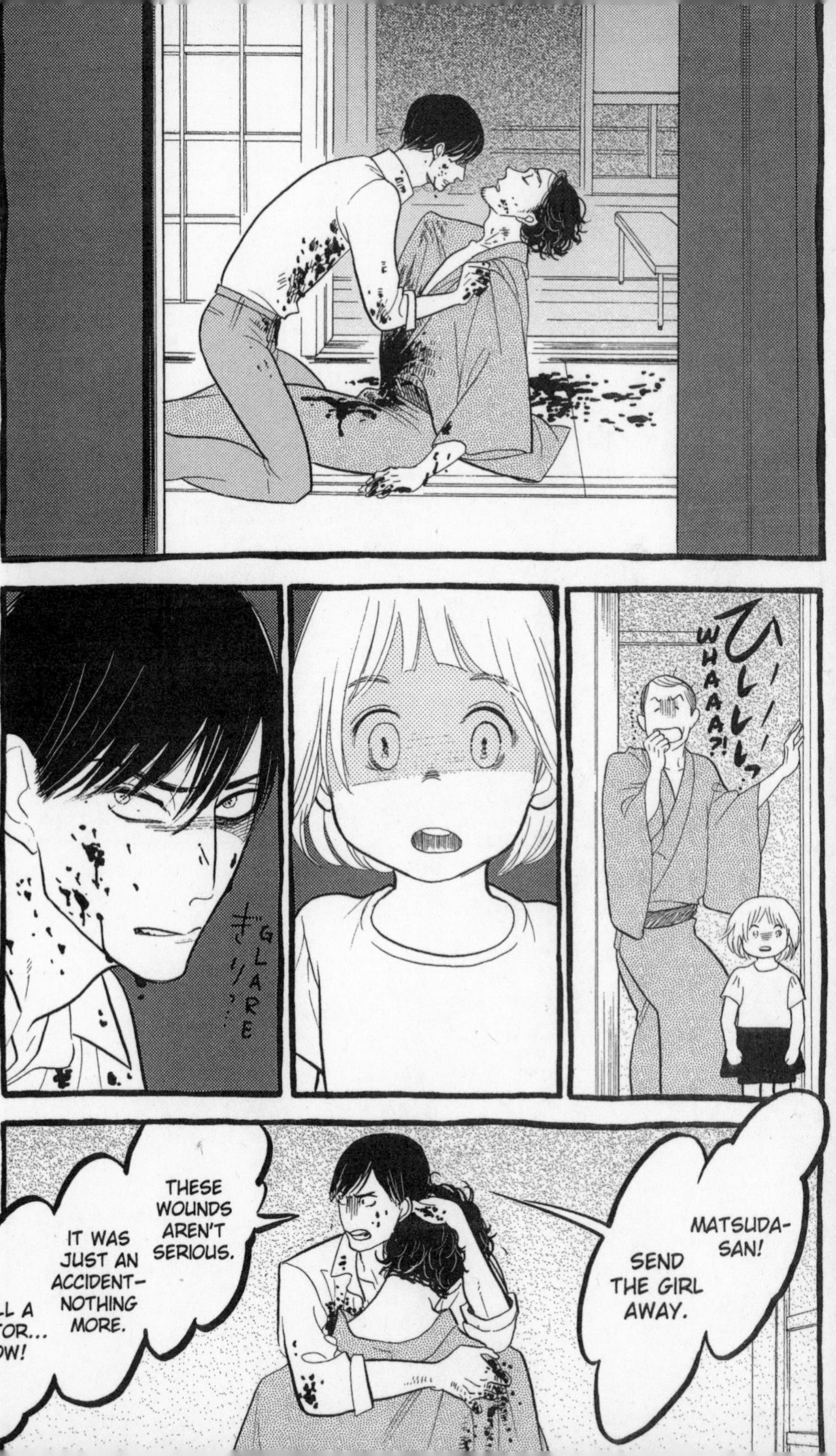
WHAAAA?!
GLARE
MATSUDA-SAN!
SEND THE GIRL AWAY.
THESE WOUNDS AREN'T SERIOUS.
IT WAS JUST AN ACCIDENT—NOTHING MORE.
CALL A DOCTOR... NOW!

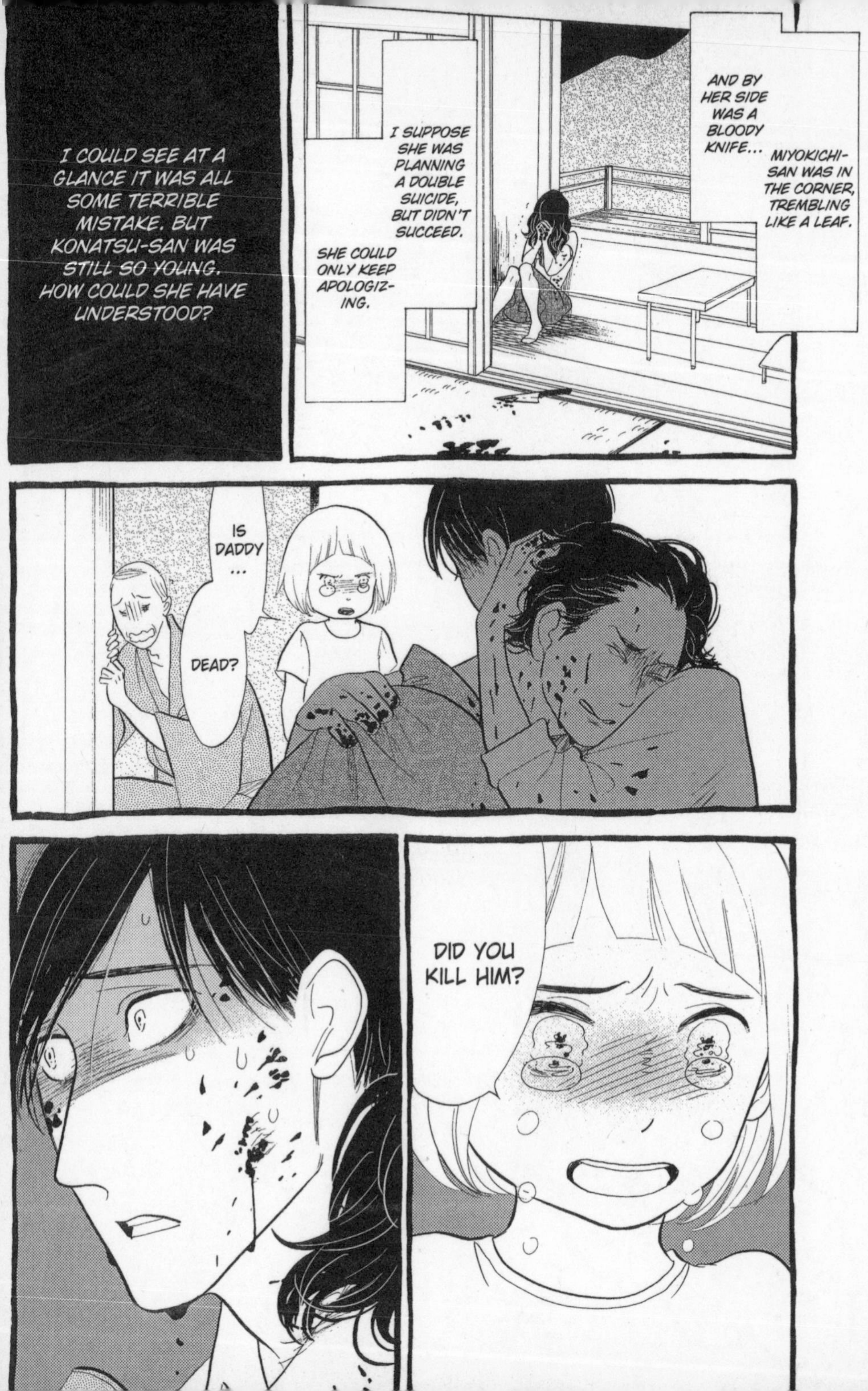
AND BY HER SIDE WAS A BLOODY KNIFE...
MIYOKICHI-SAN WAS IN THE CORNER, TREMBLING LIKE A LEAF.
I SUPPOSE SHE WAS PLANNING A DOUBLE SUICIDE, BUT DIDN'T SUCCEED.
SHE COULD ONLY KEEP APOLOGIZING.
I COULD SEE AT A GLANCE IT WAS ALL SOME TERRIBLE MISTAKE. BUT KONATSU-SAN WAS STILL SO YOUNG. HOW COULD SHE HAVE UNDERSTOOD?
IS DADDY ...
DEAD?
DID YOU KILL HIM?

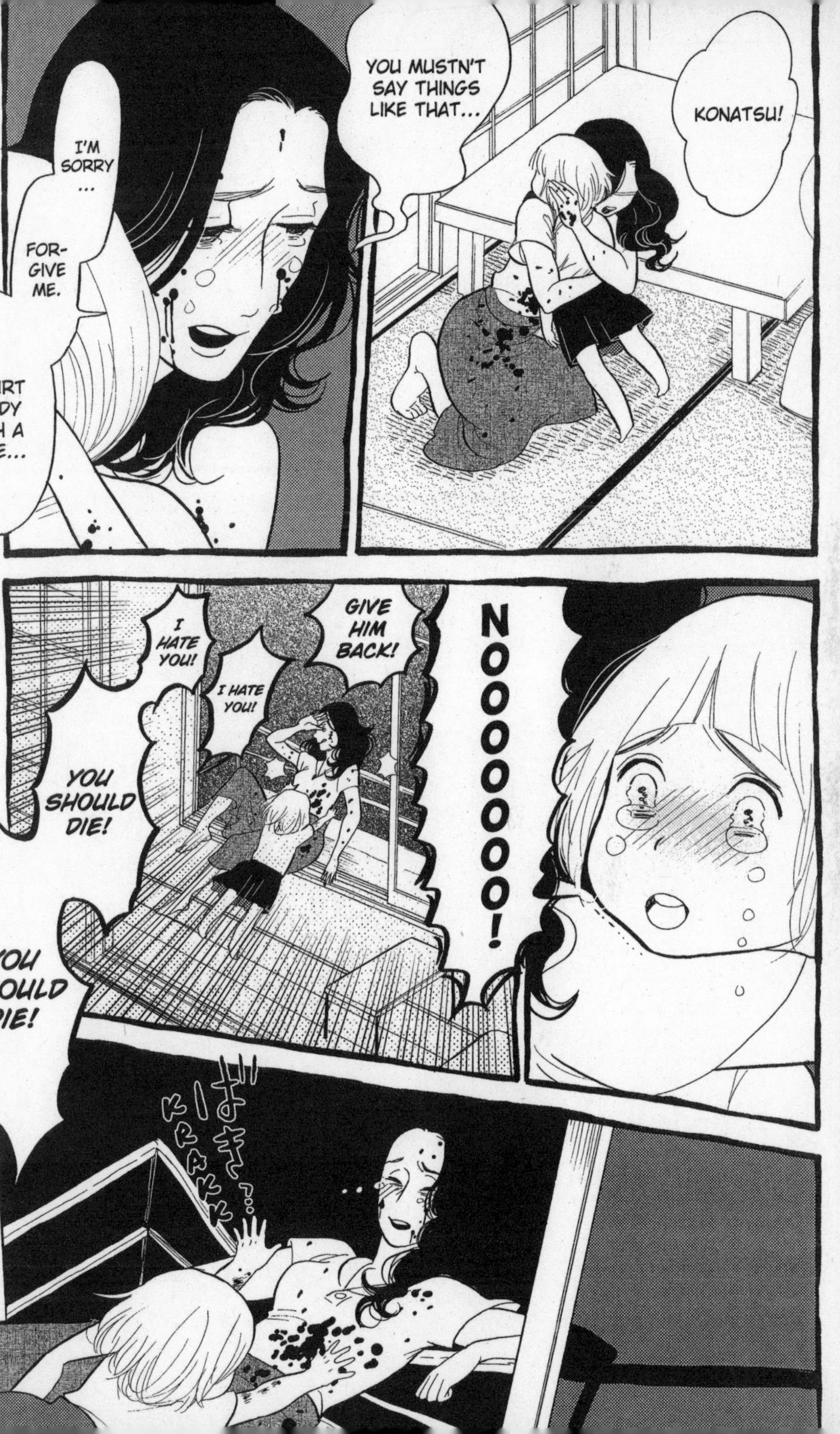
KONATSU!
YOU MUSTN'T SAY THINGS LIKE THAT...
I'M SORRY ...
FOR-GIVE ME.
I HURT DADDY WITH A KNIFE...
NOOOOOOOO!
GIVE HIM BACK!
I HATE YOU!
I HATE YOU!
YOU SHOULD DIE!
YOU SHOULD DIE!
ばきっ
KRAKK

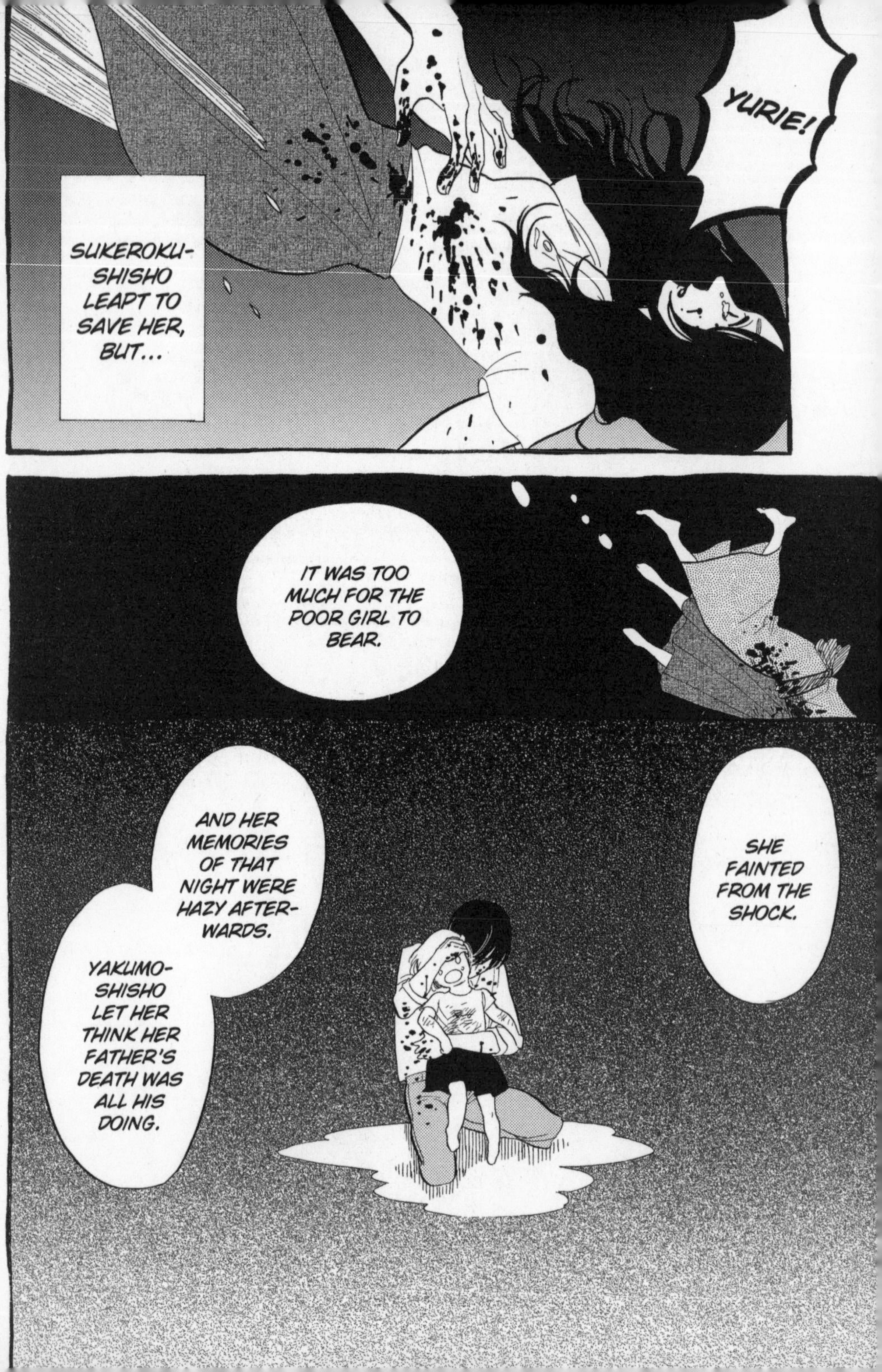
YURIE!
SUKEROKU-SHISHO LEAPT TO SAVE HER, BUT...
IT WAS TOO MUCH FOR THE POOR GIRL TO BEAR.
SHE FAINTED FROM THE SHOCK.
AND HER MEMORIES OF THAT NIGHT WERE HAZY AFTER-WARDS.
YAKUMO-SHISHO LET HER THINK HER FATHER'S DEATH WAS ALL HIS DOING.

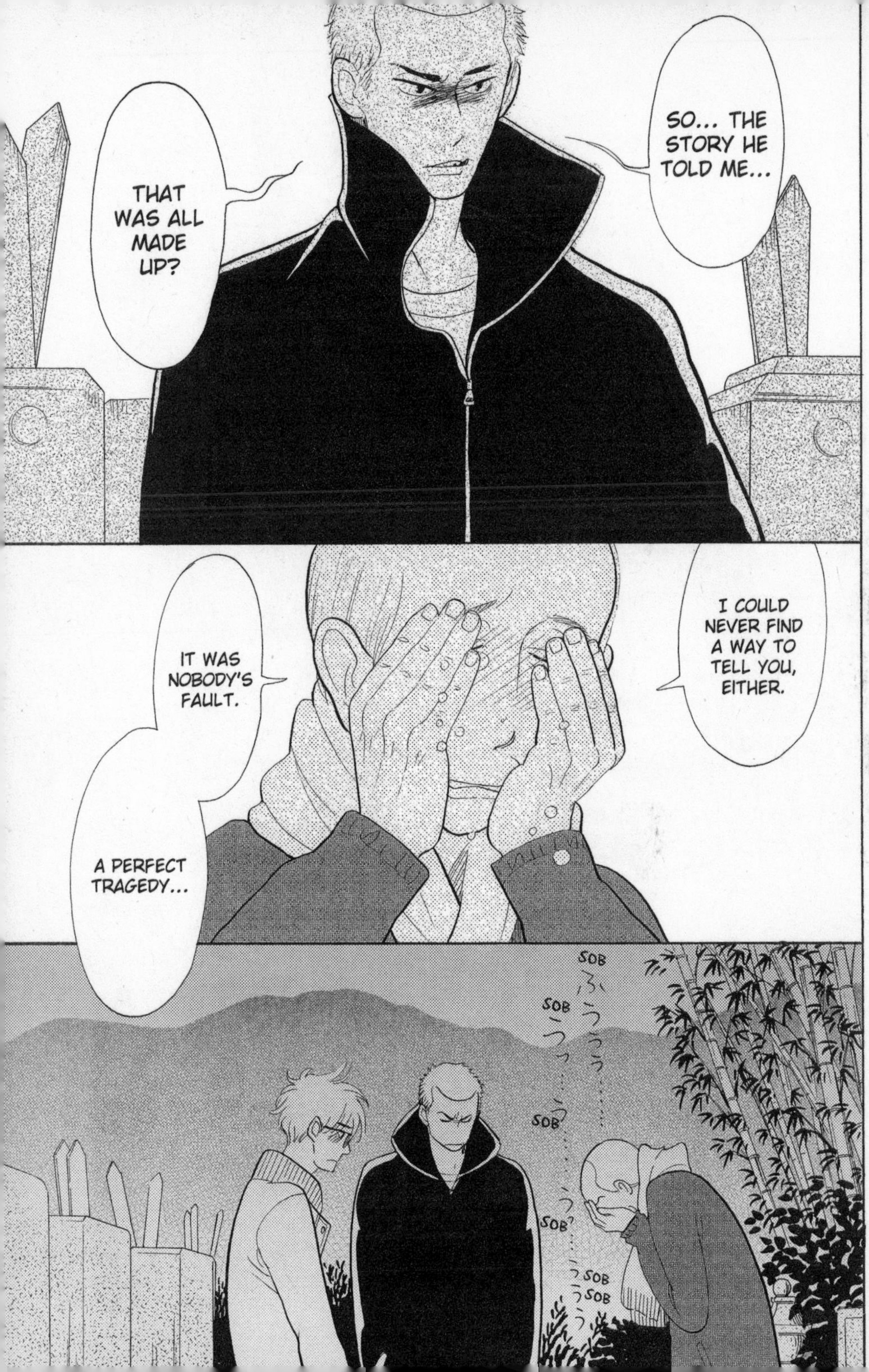
SO... THE STORY HE TOLD ME...
THAT WAS ALL MADE UP?
I COULD NEVER FIND A WAY TO TELL YOU, EITHER.
IT WAS NOBODY'S FAULT.
A PERFECT TRAGEDY...
SOB
SOB
SOB
SOB
SOB
SOB

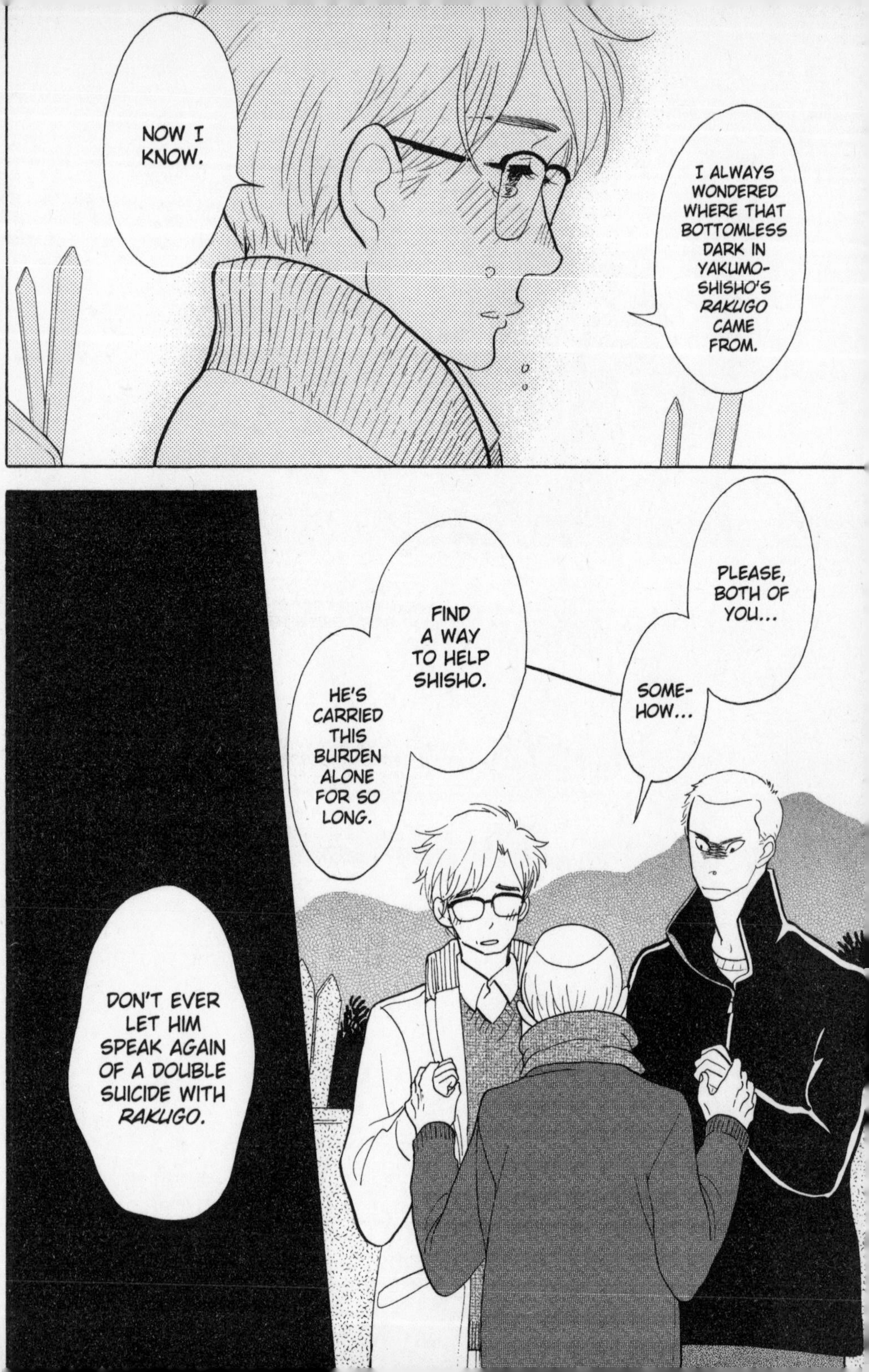
I ALWAYS WONDERED WHERE THAT BOTTOMLESS DARK IN YAKUMO-SHISHO'S *RAKUGO* CAME FROM.
NOW I KNOW.
PLEASE, BOTH OF YOU...
SOME-HOW...
FIND A WAY TO HELP SHISHO.
HE'S CARRIED THIS BURDEN ALONE FOR SO LONG.
DON'T EVER LET HIM SPEAK AGAIN OF A DOUBLE SUICIDE WITH *RAKUGO*.

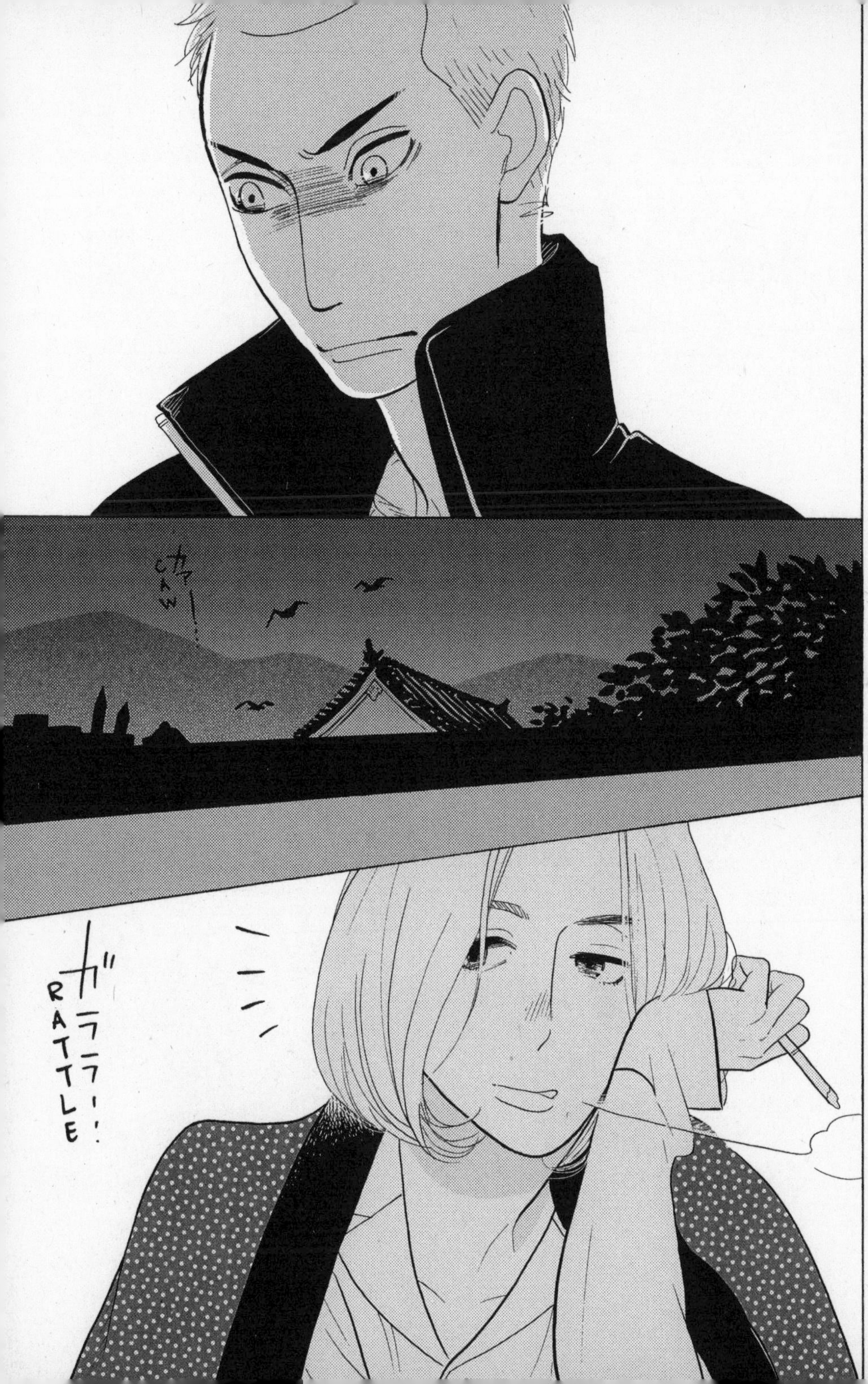
CAW
RATTLE

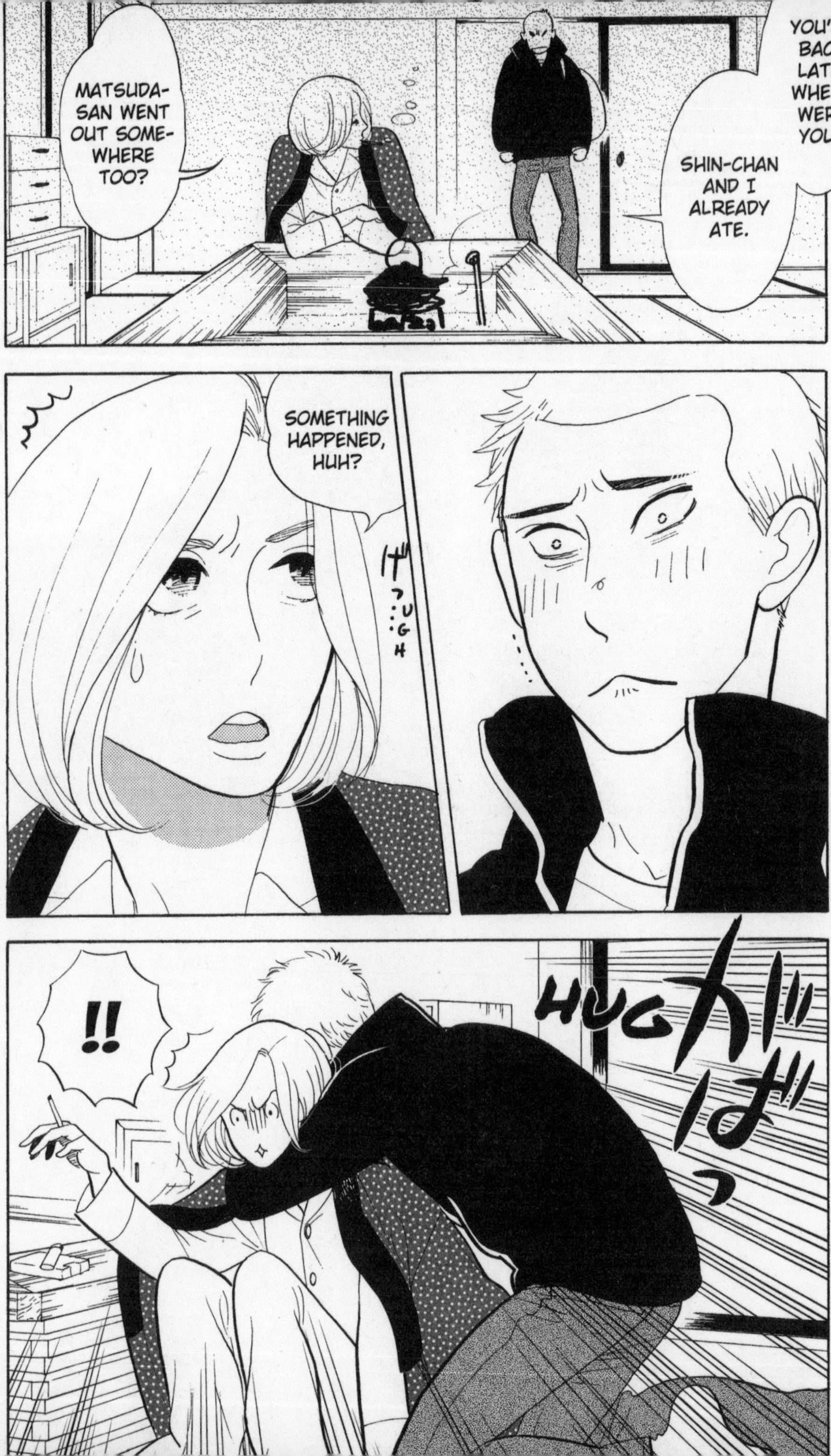
YOU'RE BACK LATE. WHERE WERE YOU?
SHIN-CHAN AND I ALREADY ATE.
MATSUDA-SAN WENT OUT SOMEWHERE TOO?
SOMETHING HAPPENED, HUH?
UGH
HUG
!!

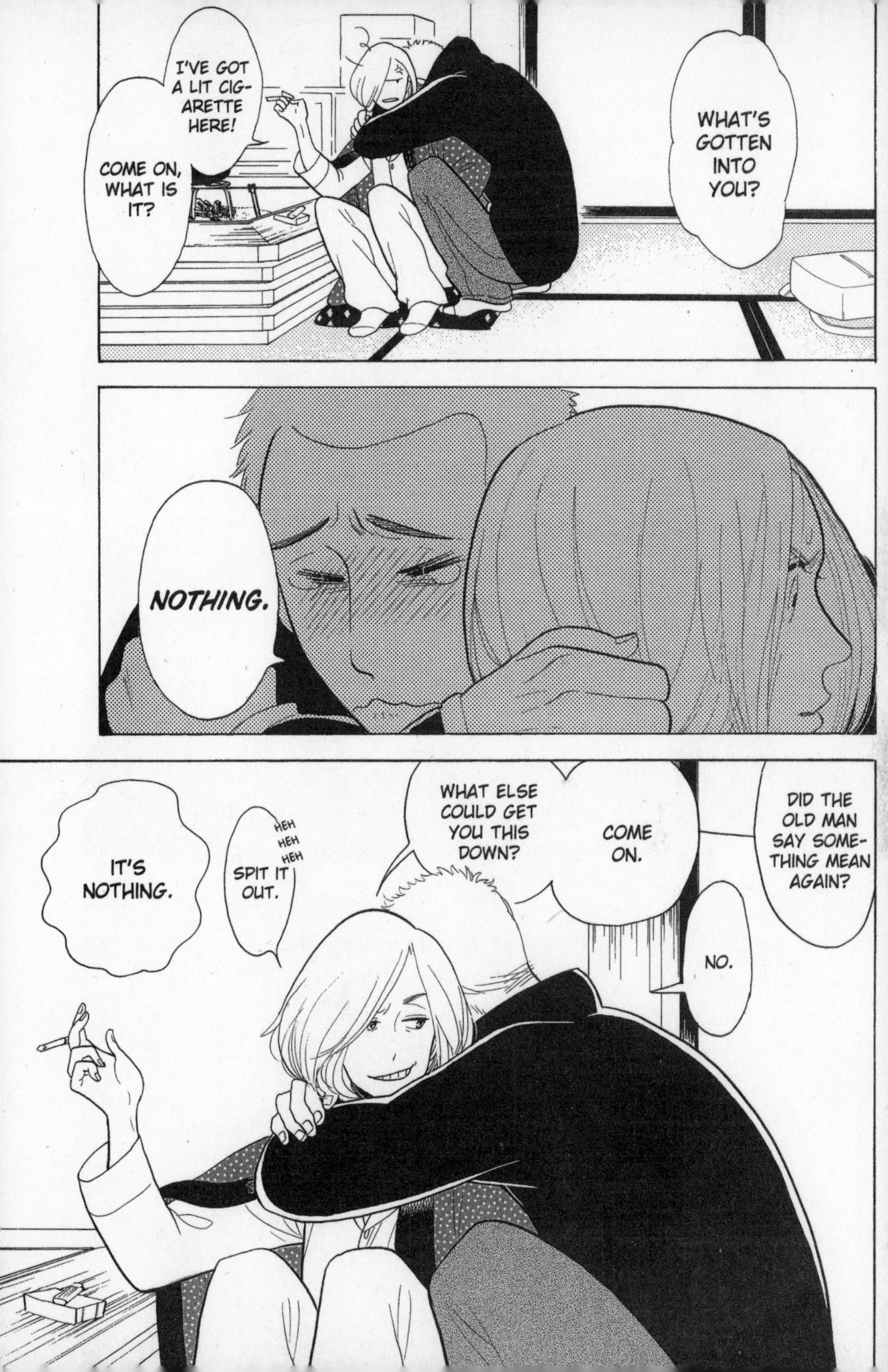
WHAT'S GOTTEN INTO YOU?
I'VE GOT A LIT CIG-ARETTE HERE!
COME ON, WHAT IS IT?
NOTHING.
DID THE OLD MAN SAY SOME-THING MEAN AGAIN?
NO.
COME ON.
WHAT ELSE COULD GET YOU THIS DOWN?
HEH HEH HEH
SPIT IT OUT.
IT'S NOTHING.

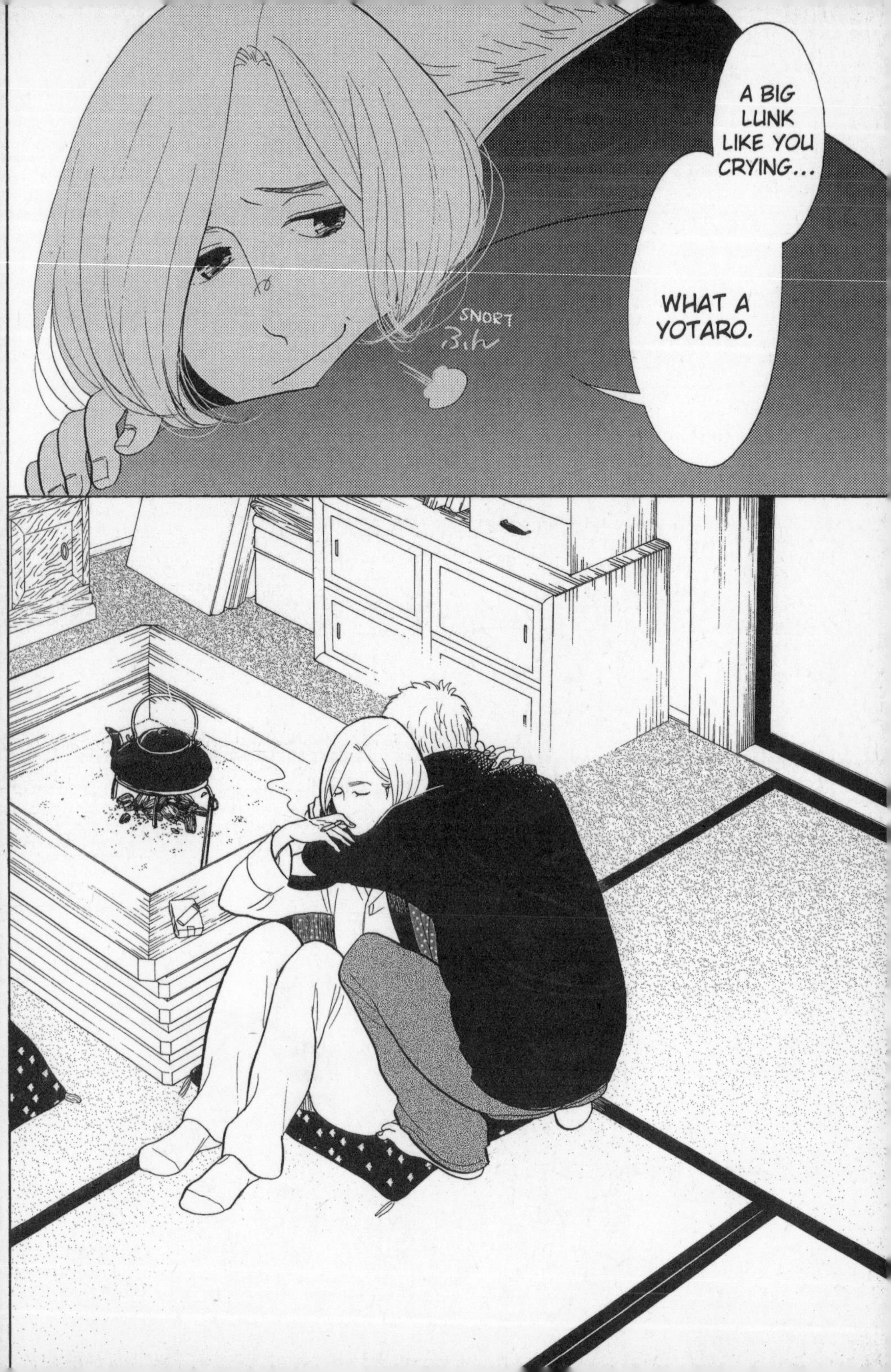
A BIG LUNK LIKE YOU CRYING...
WHAT A YOTARO.
SNORT

DESCENDING STORIES

SHOWA GENROKU RAKUGO SHINJU

HARUKO KUMOTA

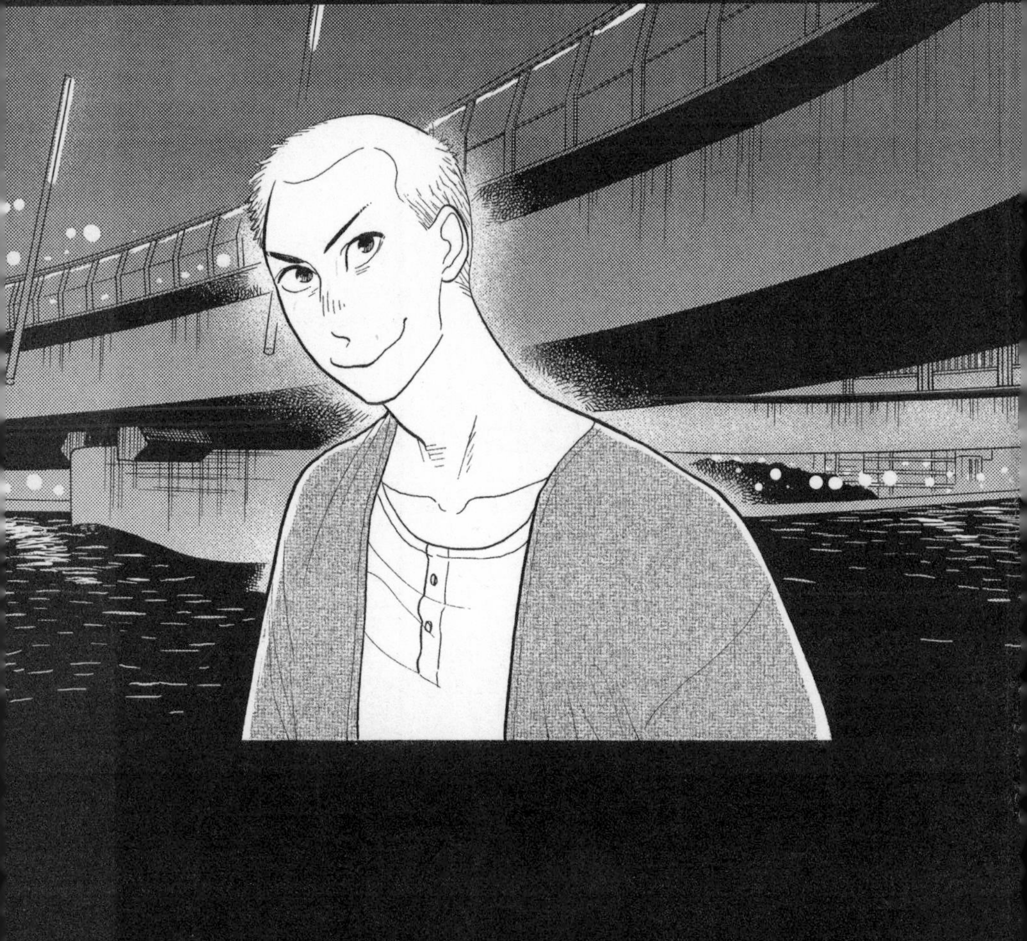

DESCENDING STORIES

SHOWA GENROKU RAKUGO SHINJU

SUKEROKU AGAIN: 11

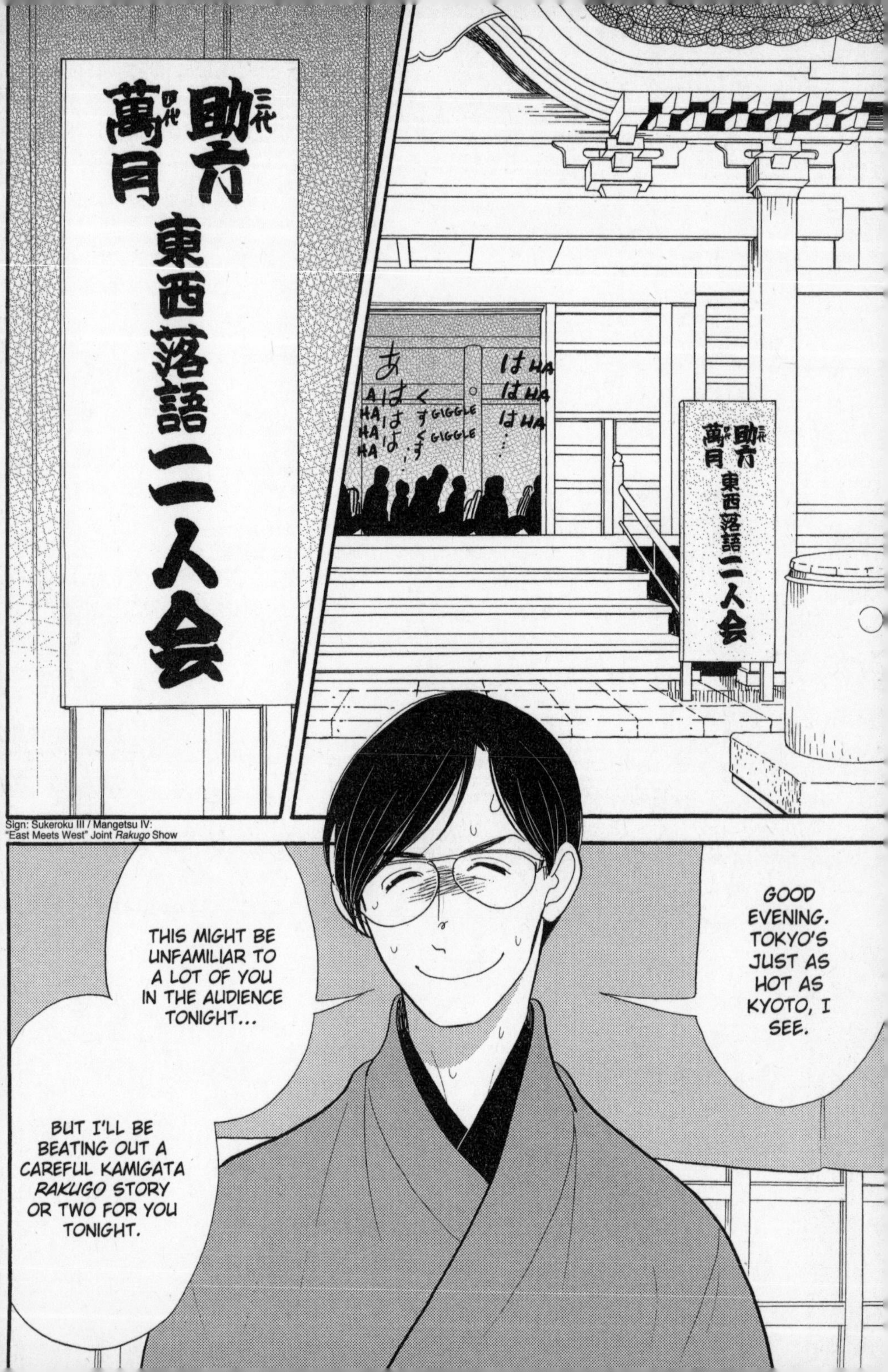
はHA はHA はHA
あははは A HA HA HA
くすくす GIGGLE GIGGLE
三代 助六 四代 萬月 東西落語二人会
三代 助六 四代 萬月 東西落語二人会
Sign: Sukeroku III / Mangetsu IV: "East Meets West" Joint *Rakugo* Show
GOOD EVENING. TOKYO'S JUST AS HOT AS KYOTO, I SEE.
THIS MIGHT BE UNFAMILIAR TO A LOT OF YOU IN THE AUDIENCE TONIGHT...
BUT I'LL BE BEATING OUT A CAREFUL KAMIGATA *RAKUGO* STORY OR TWO FOR YOU TONIGHT.

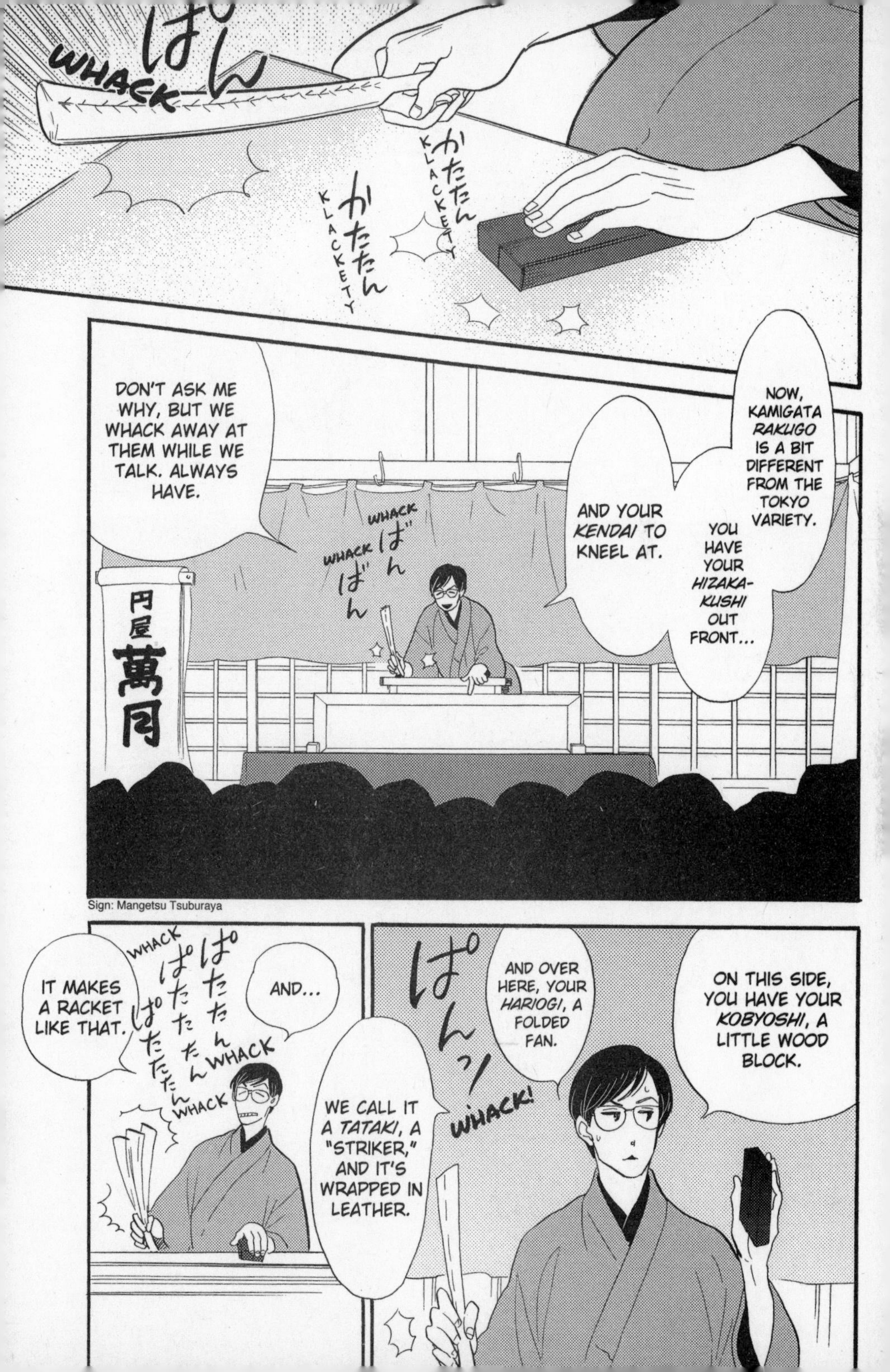
ぱん
WHACK
かたたん
KLACKETY
かたたん
KLACKETY
NOW, KAMIGATA *RAKUGO* IS A BIT DIFFERENT FROM THE TOKYO VARIETY.
YOU HAVE YOUR *HIZAKAKUSHI* OUT FRONT...
AND YOUR *KENDAI* TO KNEEL AT.
WHACK ばん
WHACK ばん
DON'T ASK ME WHY, BUT WE WHACK AWAY AT THEM WHILE WE TALK. ALWAYS HAVE.
円屋 萬月
ON THIS SIDE, YOU HAVE YOUR *KOBYOSHI*, A LITTLE WOOD BLOCK.
AND OVER HERE, YOUR *HARIOGI*, A FOLDED FAN.
ぱんッ!
WHACK!
WE CALL IT A *TATAKI*, A "STRIKER," AND IT'S WRAPPED IN LEATHER.
AND...
ぱたたん
WHACK
ぱたたん
WHACK
ぱたたん
WHACK
IT MAKES A RACKET LIKE THAT.
Sign: Mangetsu Tsuburaya

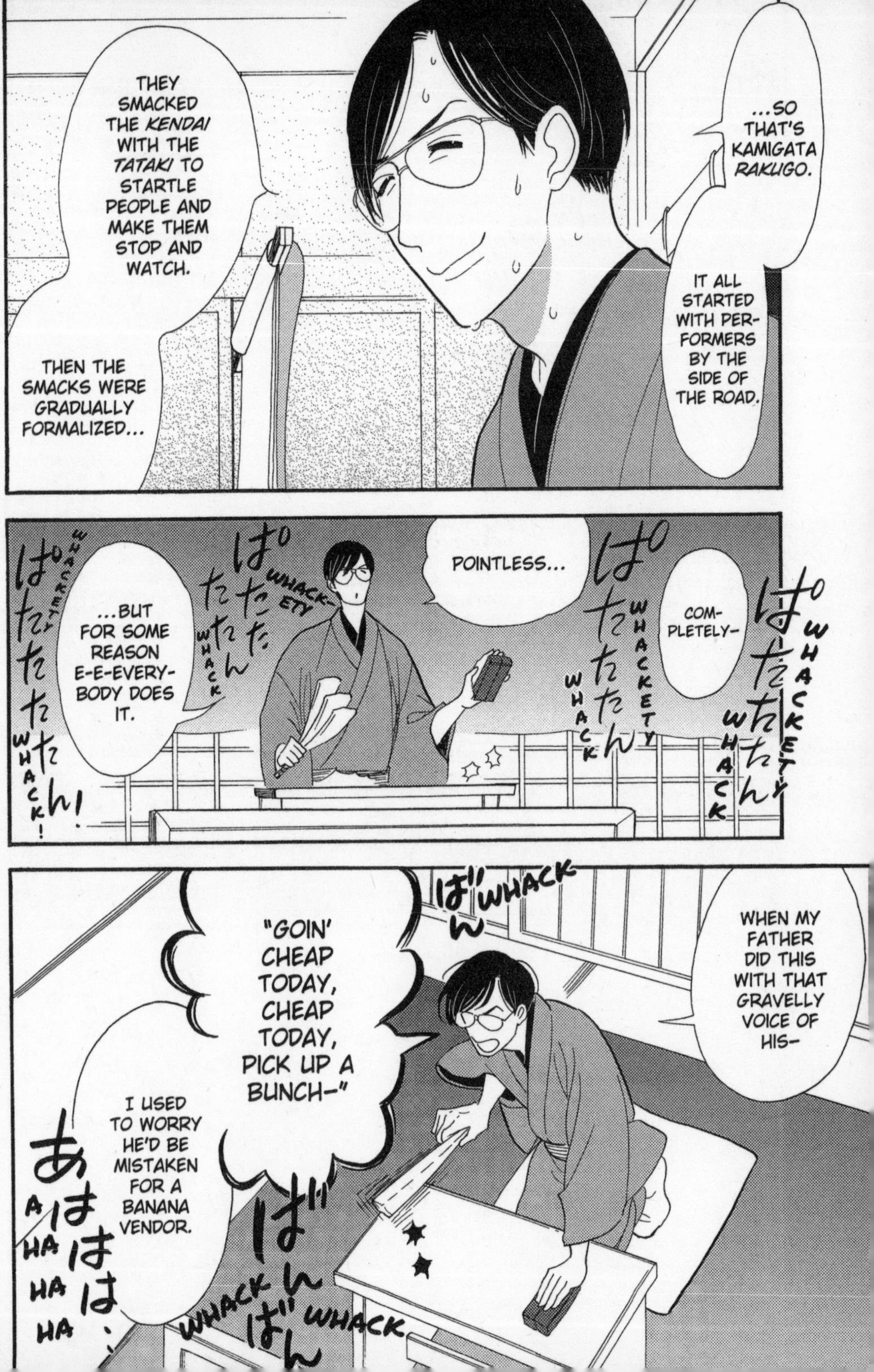
...SO THAT'S KAMIGATA *RAKUGO.*
IT ALL STARTED WITH PER-FORMERS BY THE SIDE OF THE ROAD.
THEY SMACKED THE *KENDAI* WITH THE *TATAKI* TO STARTLE PEOPLE AND MAKE THEM STOP AND WATCH.
THEN THE SMACKS WERE GRADUALLY FORMALIZED...
ぱたたん
WHACKETY WHACK
COM-PLETELY-
ぱたたん
WHACKETY WHACK
POINTLESS...
ぱたたたん
WHACKETY WHACK
...BUT FOR SOME REASON E-E-EVERY-BODY DOES IT.
ぱたたたたん!
WHACKETY WHACK!
WHEN MY FATHER DID THIS WITH THAT GRAVELLY VOICE OF HIS-
ばん
WHACK
"GOIN' CHEAP TODAY, CHEAP TODAY, PICK UP A BUNCH-"
ばんばん
WHACK WHACK
I USED TO WORRY HE'D BE MISTAKEN FOR A BANANA VENDOR.
あははは
A HA HA HA

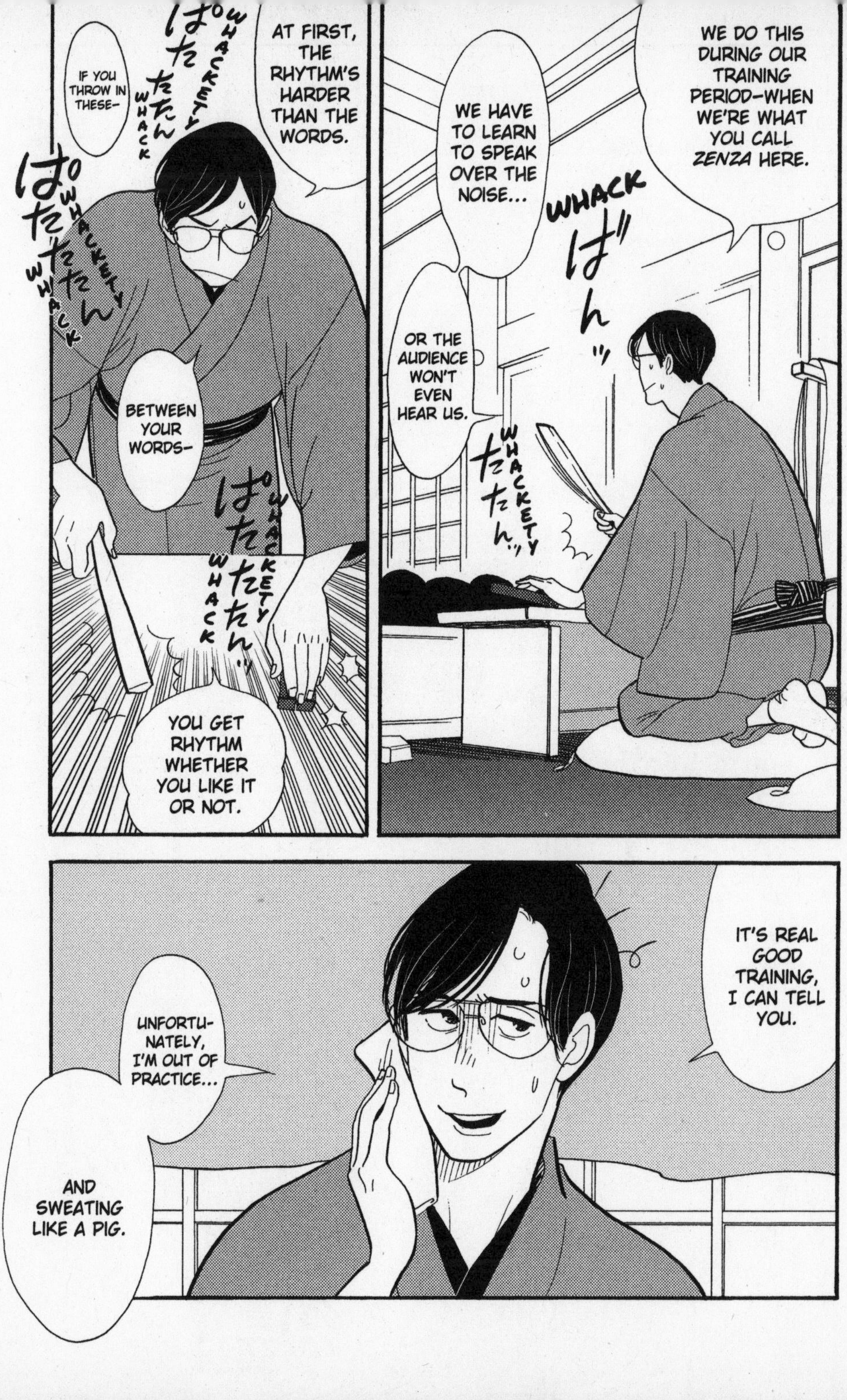
WE DO THIS DURING OUR TRAINING PERIOD—WHEN WE'RE WHAT YOU CALL ZENZA HERE.
WE HAVE TO LEARN TO SPEAK OVER THE NOISE...
WHACK
ばん
OR THE AUDIENCE WON'T EVEN HEAR US.
WHACKETY
たたん
AT FIRST, THE RHYTHM'S HARDER THAN THE WORDS.
WHACKETY WHACK
ぱたたたん
IF YOU THROW IN THESE—
WHACKETY WHACK
ぱたたたん
BETWEEN YOUR WORDS—
WHACKETY WHACK
ぱたたたん
YOU GET RHYTHM WHETHER YOU LIKE IT OR NOT.
IT'S REAL GOOD TRAINING, I CAN TELL YOU.
UNFORTU-NATELY, I'M OUT OF PRACTICE...
AND SWEATING LIKE A PIG.

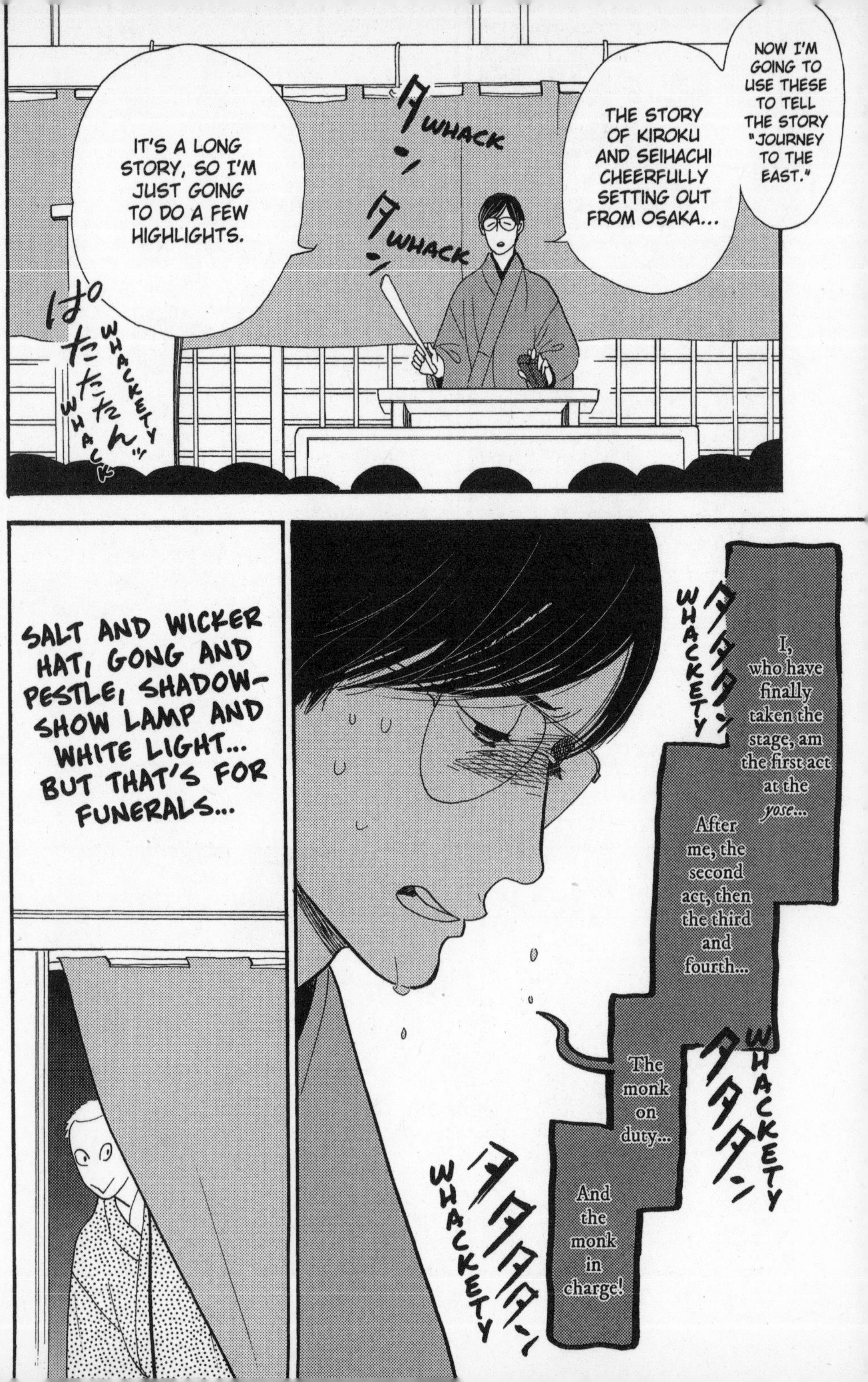
NOW I'M GOING TO USE THESE TO TELL THE STORY "JOURNEY TO THE EAST."
THE STORY OF KIROKU AND SEIHACHI CHEERFULLY SETTING OUT FROM OSAKA...
タ WHACK
タ WHACK
IT'S A LONG STORY, SO I'M JUST GOING TO DO A FEW HIGHLIGHTS.
ぱたたたん WHACKETY WHACK
タタタン WHACKETY
I, who have finally taken the stage, am the first act at the *yose*...
After me, the second act, then the third and fourth...
The monk on duty...
And the monk in charge!
タタタン WHACKETY
タタタタ WHACKETY
SALT AND WICKER HAT, GONG AND PESTLE, SHADOW-SHOW LAMP AND WHITE LIGHT... BUT THAT'S FOR FUNERALS...

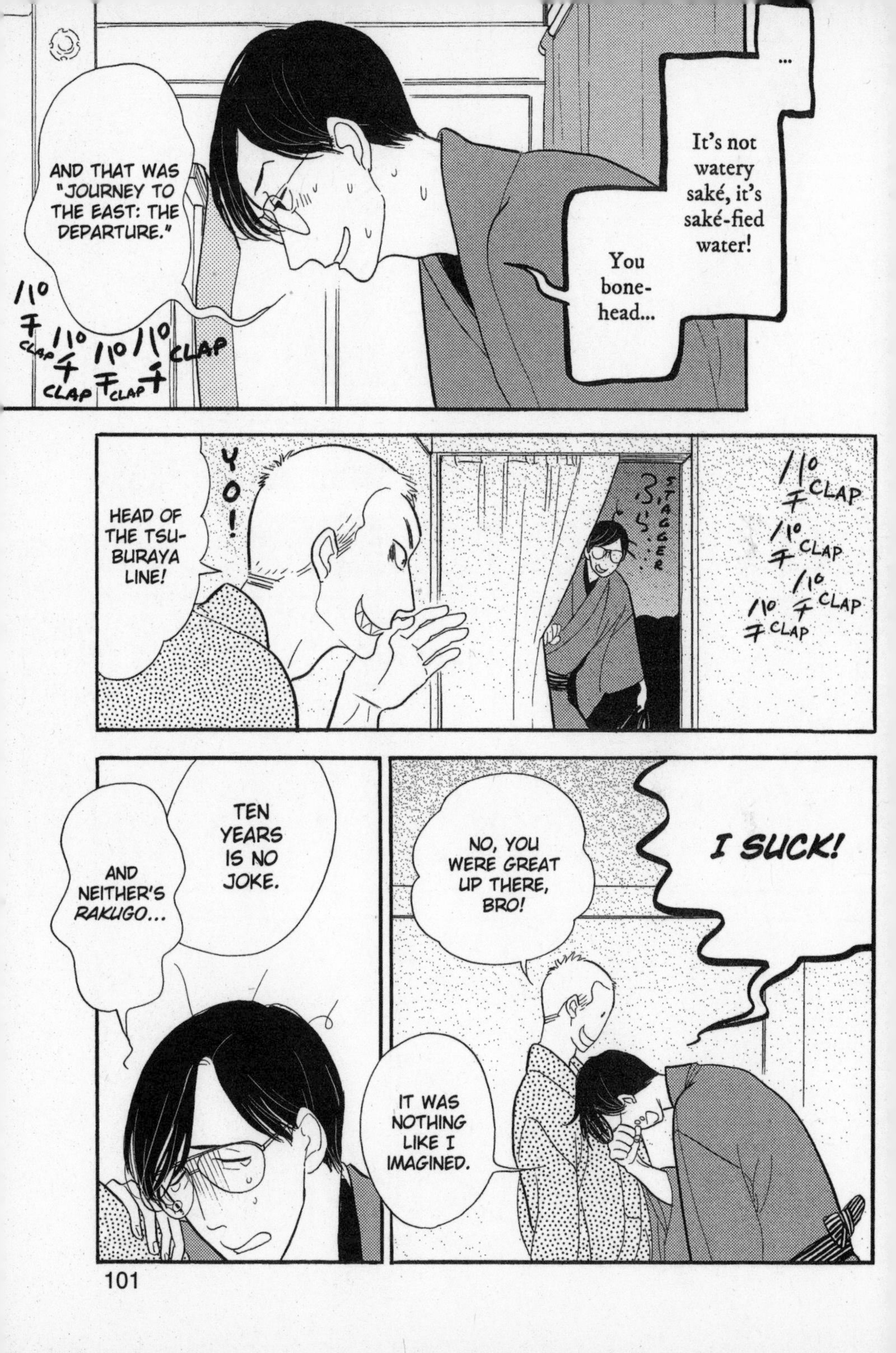
...
It's not watery saké, it's saké-fied water!
You bone-head...
AND THAT WAS "JOURNEY TO THE EAST: THE DEPARTURE."
CLAP CLAP CLAP CLAP
CLAP CLAP CLAP CLAP
STAGGER
YO!
HEAD OF THE TSU-BURAYA LINE!
I SUCK!
NO, YOU WERE GREAT UP THERE, BRO!
TEN YEARS IS NO JOKE.
AND NEITHER'S *RAKUGO*...
IT WAS NOTHING LIKE I IMAGINED.

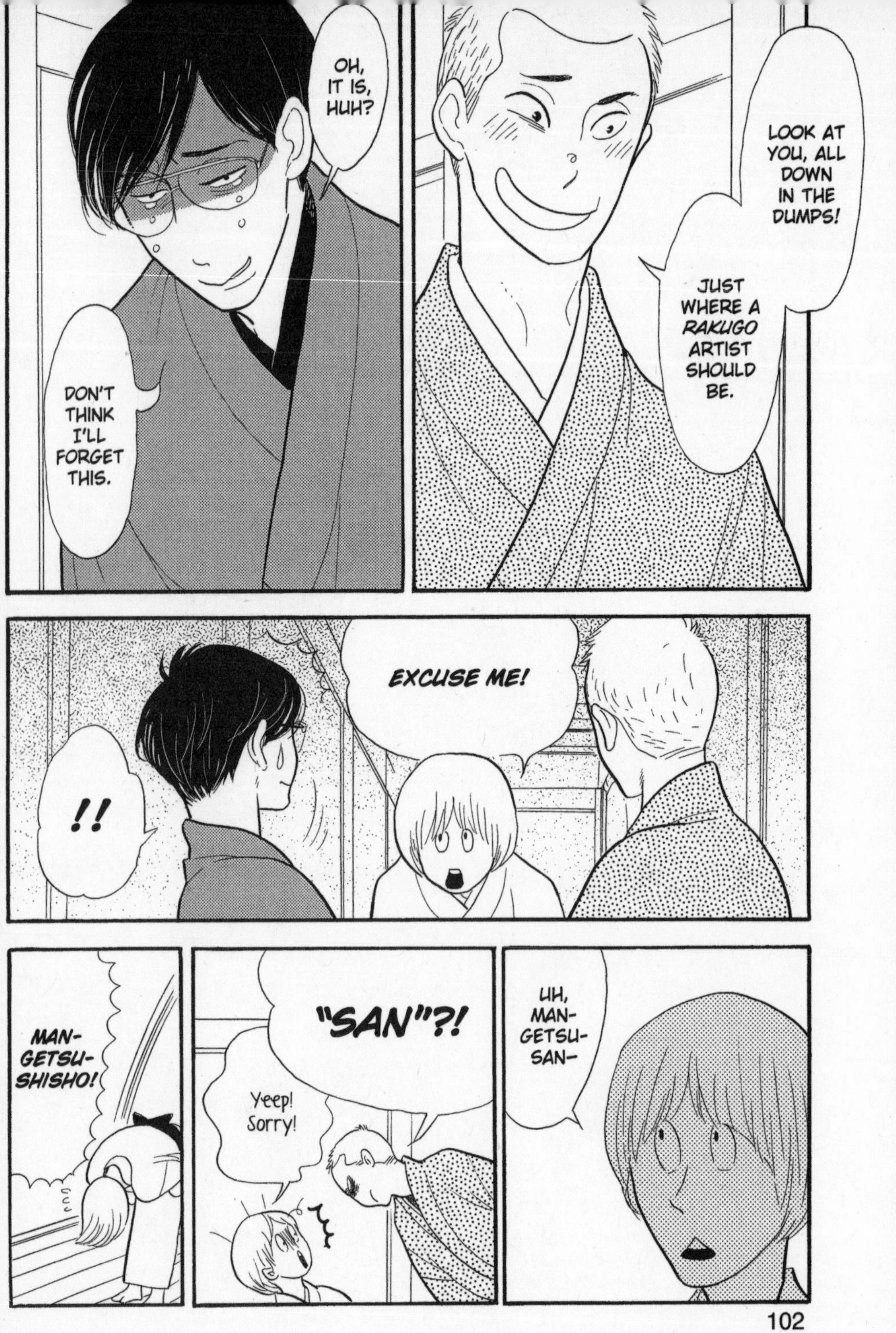
LOOK AT YOU, ALL DOWN IN THE DUMPS!
JUST WHERE A *RAKUGO* ARTIST SHOULD BE.
OH, IT IS, HUH?
DON'T THINK I'LL FORGET THIS.
EXCUSE ME!
!!
UH, MANGETSU-SAN-
"SAN"?!
Yeep! Sorry!
MANGETSU-SHISHO!

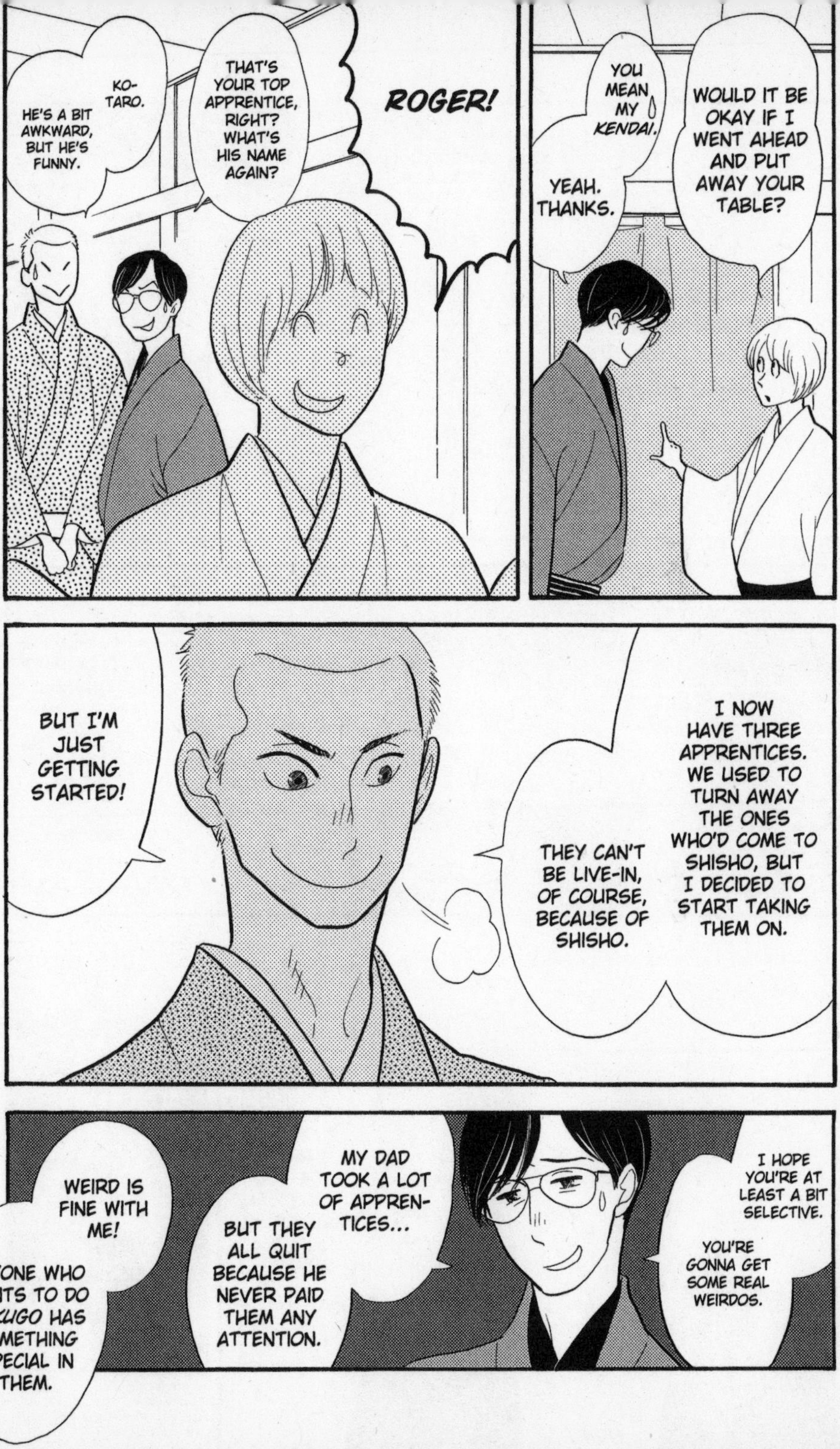
WOULD IT BE OKAY IF I WENT AHEAD AND PUT AWAY YOUR TABLE?
YOU MEAN MY *KENDAI*.
YEAH. THANKS.
ROGER!
THAT'S YOUR TOP APPRENTICE, RIGHT? WHAT'S HIS NAME AGAIN?
KO-TARO.
HE'S A BIT AWKWARD, BUT HE'S FUNNY.
I NOW HAVE THREE APPRENTICES. WE USED TO TURN AWAY THE ONES WHO'D COME TO SHISHO, BUT I DECIDED TO START TAKING THEM ON.
THEY CAN'T BE LIVE-IN, OF COURSE, BECAUSE OF SHISHO.
BUT I'M JUST GETTING STARTED!
I HOPE YOU'RE AT LEAST A BIT SELECTIVE.
YOU'RE GONNA GET SOME REAL WEIRDOS.
MY DAD TOOK A LOT OF APPREN-TICES...
BUT THEY ALL QUIT BECAUSE HE NEVER PAID THEM ANY ATTENTION.
WEIRD IS FINE WITH ME!
ANYONE WHO WANTS TO DO *RAKUGO* HAS SOMETHING SPECIAL IN THEM.

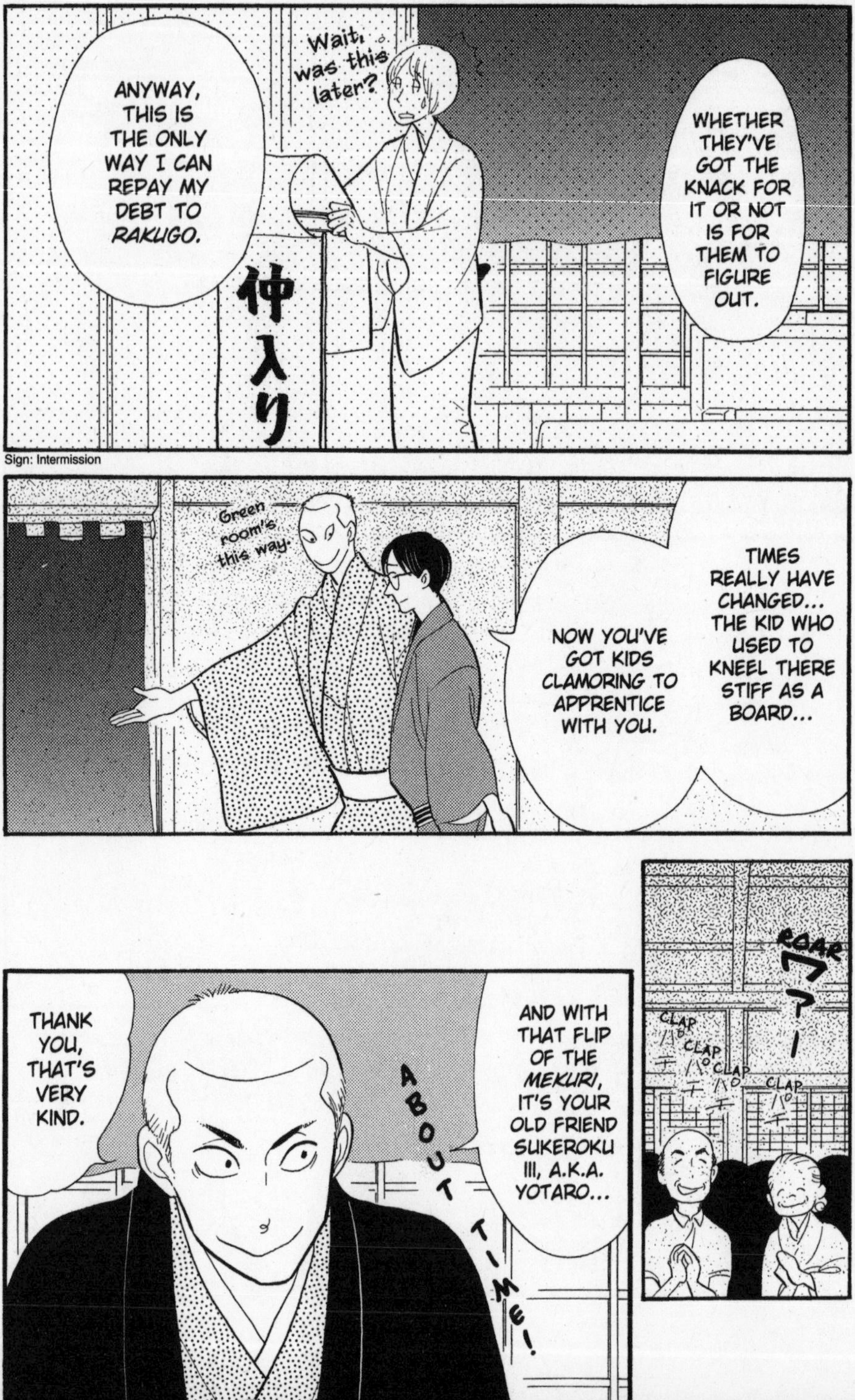
WHETHER THEY'VE GOT THE KNACK FOR IT OR NOT IS FOR THEM TO FIGURE OUT.
Wait, was this later?
ANYWAY, THIS IS THE ONLY WAY I CAN REPAY MY DEBT TO *RAKUGO*.
仲入り
TIMES REALLY HAVE CHANGED... THE KID WHO USED TO KNEEL THERE STIFF AS A BOARD...
NOW YOU'VE GOT KIDS CLAMORING TO APPRENTICE WITH YOU.
Green room's this way.
ROAR
ワァー
CLAP
パチ
CLAP
パチ
CLAP
パチ
CLAP
パチ
AND WITH THAT FLIP OF THE *MEKURI*, IT'S YOUR OLD FRIEND SUKEROKU III, A.K.A. YOTARO...
ABOUT TIME!
THANK YOU, THAT'S VERY KIND.
Sign: Intermission

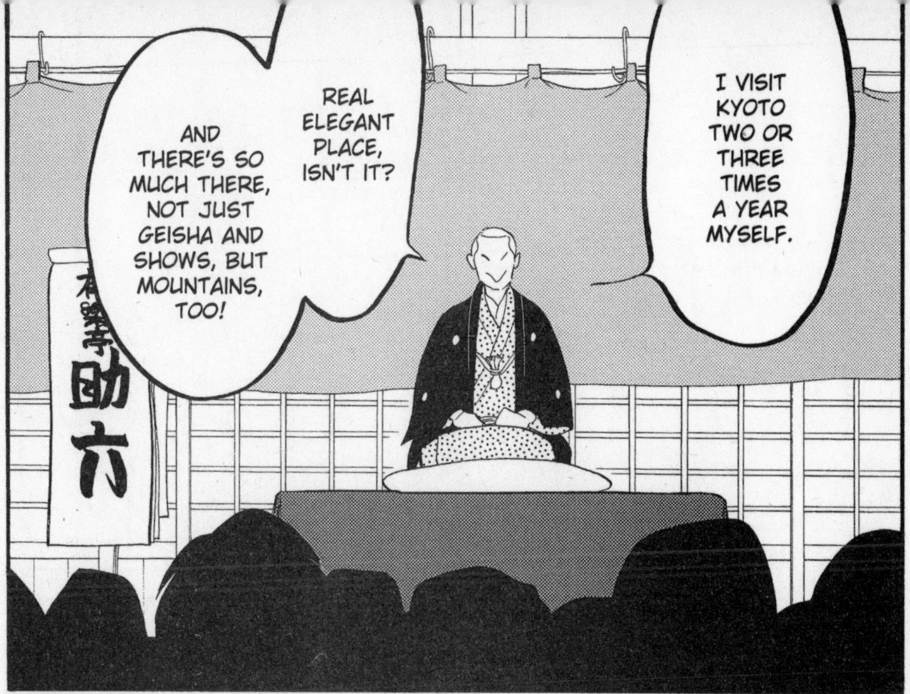
I VISIT KYOTO TWO OR THREE TIMES A YEAR MYSELF.
REAL ELEGANT PLACE, ISN'T IT?
AND THERE'S SO MUCH THERE, NOT JUST GEISHA AND SHOWS, BUT MOUNTAINS, TOO!
助六

Sign: Sukeroku Yurakutei

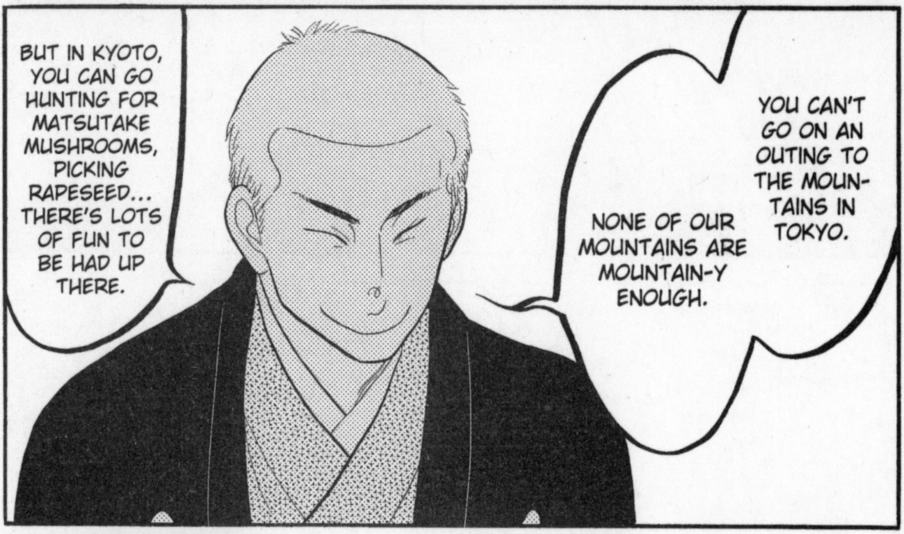
YOU CAN'T GO ON AN OUTING TO THE MOUN-TAINS IN TOKYO.
NONE OF OUR MOUNTAINS ARE MOUNTAIN-Y ENOUGH.
BUT IN KYOTO, YOU CAN GO HUNTING FOR MATSUTAKE MUSHROOMS, PICKING RAPESEED... THERE'S LOTS OF FUN TO BE HAD UP THERE.

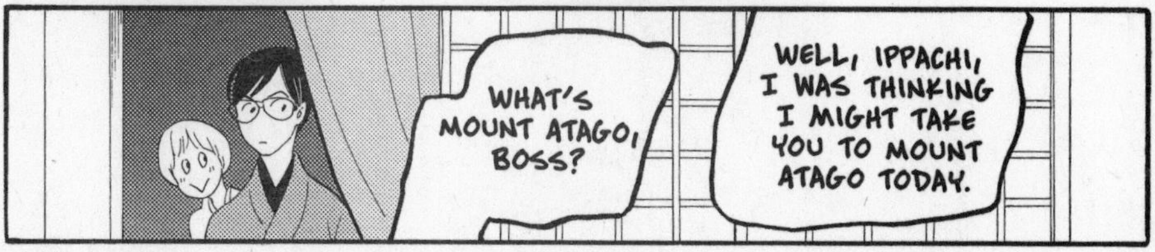
WELL, IPPACHI, I WAS THINKING I MIGHT TAKE YOU TO MOUNT ATAGO TODAY.
WHAT'S MOUNT ATAGO, BOSS?

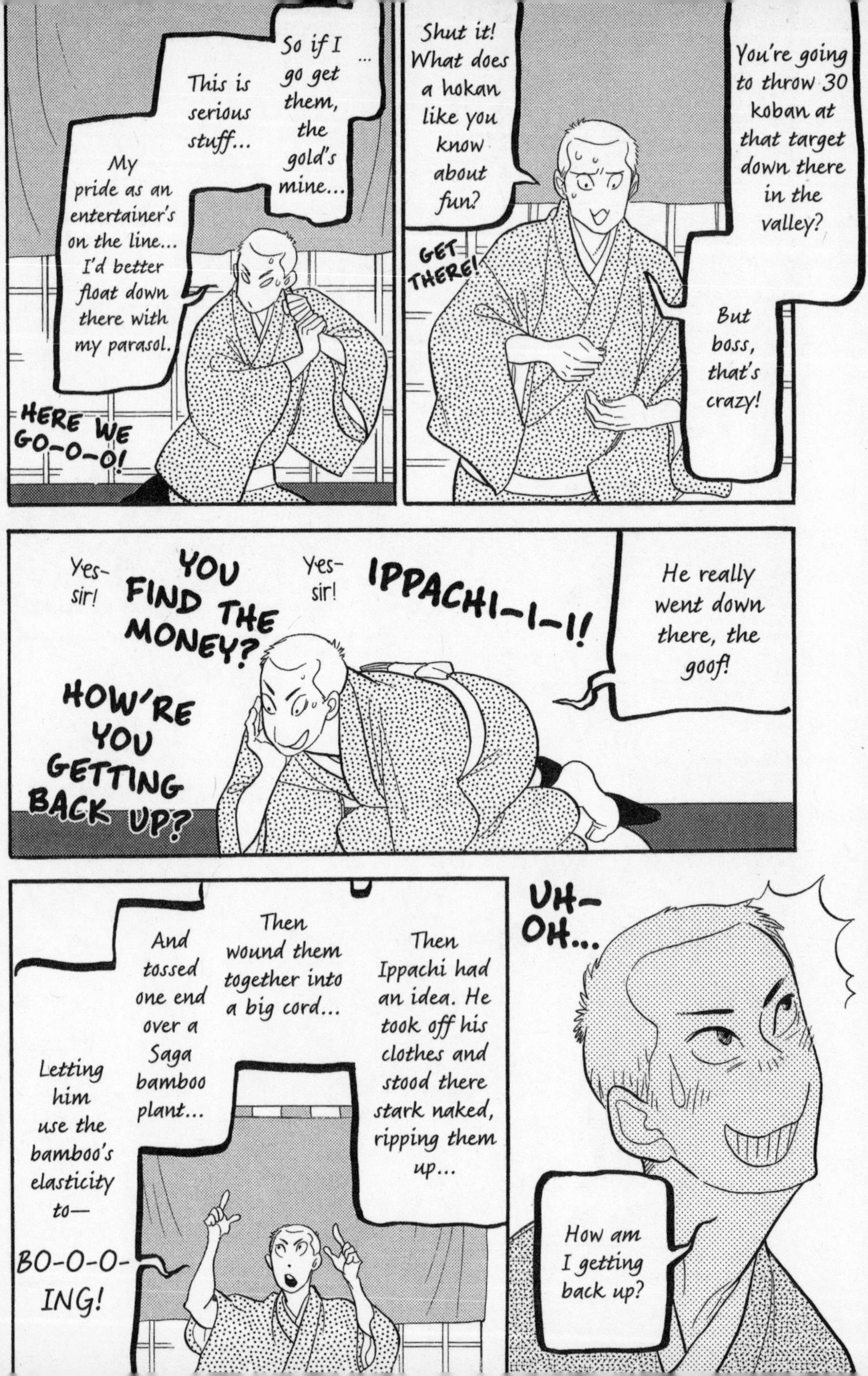

You're going to throw 30 koban at that target down there in the valley?
But boss, that's crazy!
Shut it! What does a hokan like you know about fun?
GET THERE!
So if I go get them, the gold's mine...
...
This is serious stuff...
My pride as an entertainer's on the line... I'd better float down there with my parasol.
HERE WE GO-O-O!
He really went down there, the goof!
IPPACHI-I-I!
Yes-sir!
YOU FIND THE MONEY?
Yes-sir!
HOW'RE YOU GETTING BACK UP?
UH-OH...
How am I getting back up?
Then Ippachi had an idea. He took off his clothes and stood there stark naked, ripping them up...
Then wound them together into a big cord...
And tossed one end over a Saga bamboo plant...
Letting him use the bamboo's elasticity to—
BO-O-O-ING!

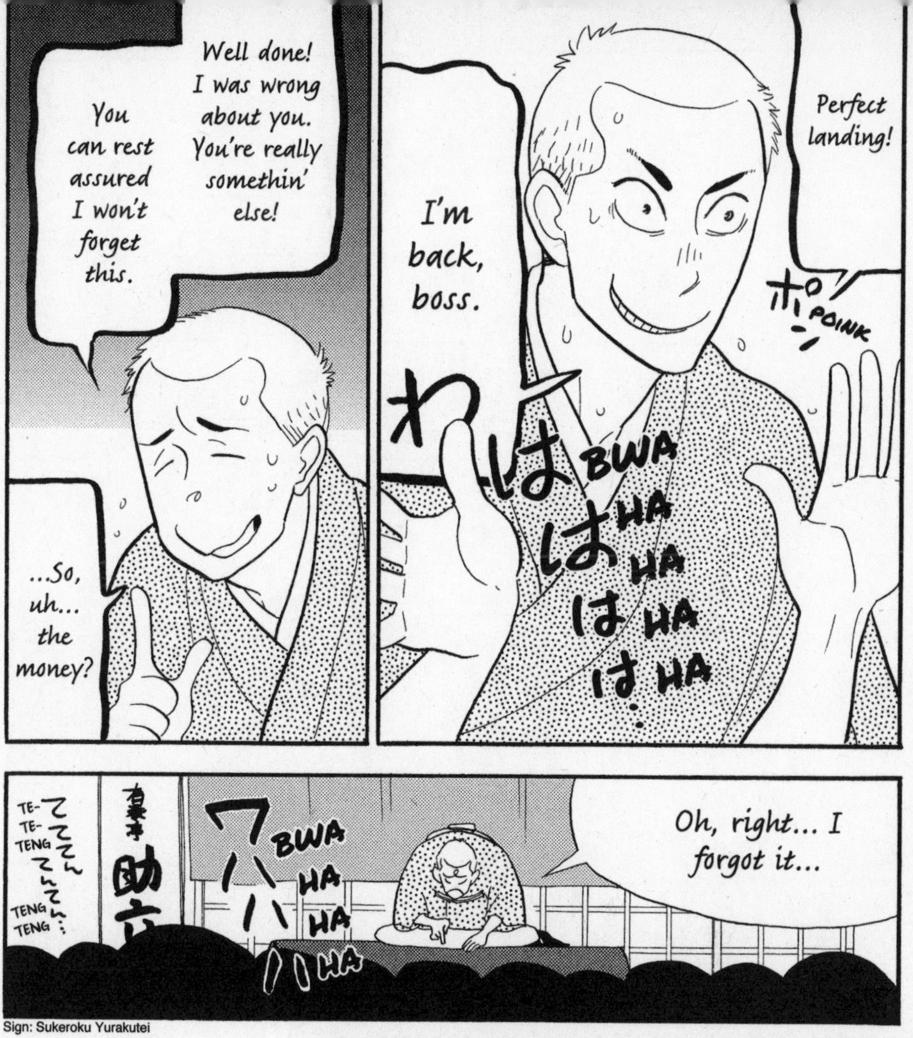
Perfect landing!
I'm back, boss.
POINK
BWA HA HA HA HA
Well done! I was wrong about you. You're really somethin' else!
You can rest assured I won't forget this.
...So, uh... the money?
Oh, right... I forgot it...
BWA HA HA HA
TE-TE-TENG TENG TENG

Sign: Sukeroku Yurakutei

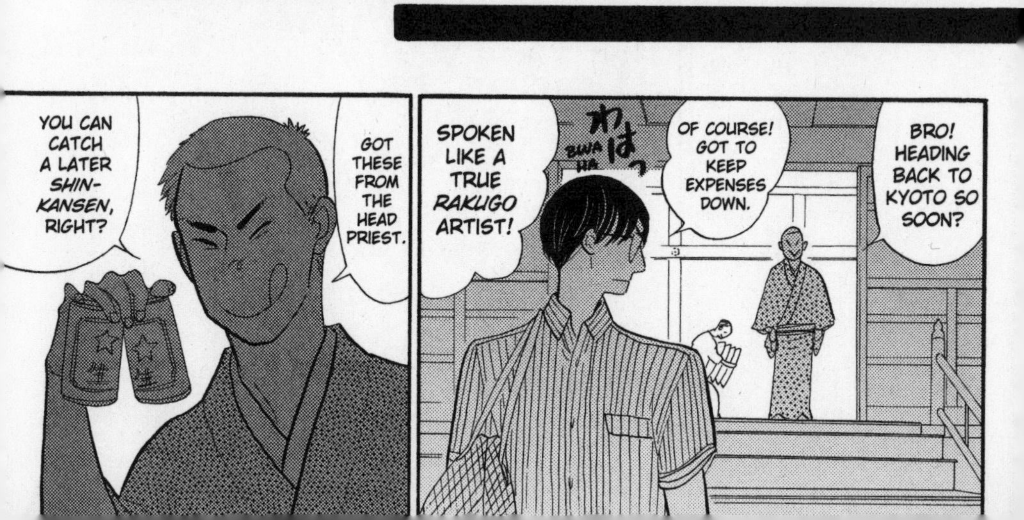
BRO! HEADING BACK TO KYOTO SO SOON?
OF COURSE! GOT TO KEEP EXPENSES DOWN.
BWA HA
SPOKEN LIKE A TRUE *RAKUGO* ARTIST!
GOT THESE FROM THE HEAD PRIEST.
YOU CAN CATCH A LATER *SHIN-KANSEN*, RIGHT?

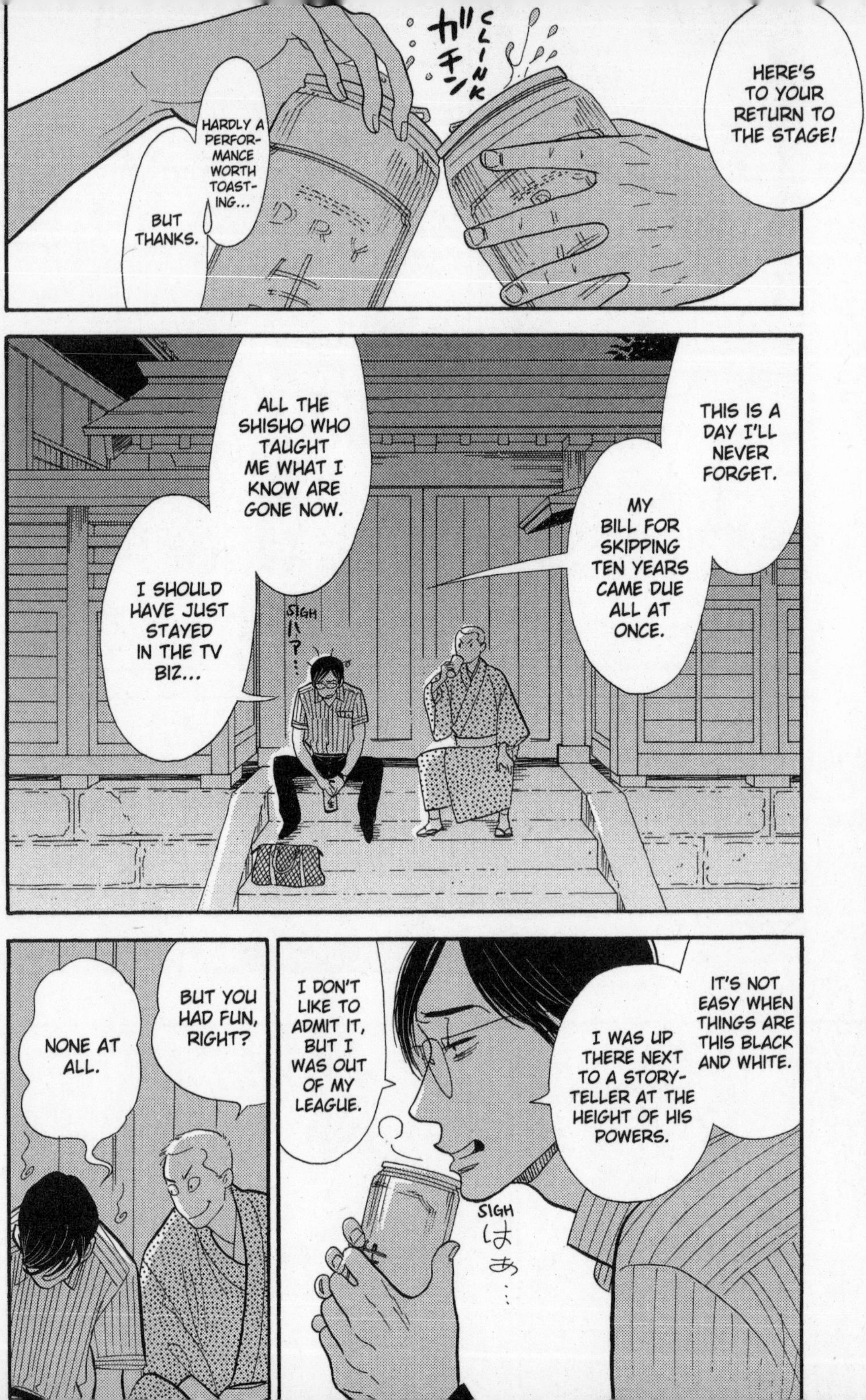
HERE'S TO YOUR RETURN TO THE STAGE!
CLINK
ガチン
HARDLY A PERFORMANCE WORTH TOASTING...
BUT THANKS.
THIS IS A DAY I'LL NEVER FORGET.
MY BILL FOR SKIPPING TEN YEARS CAME DUE ALL AT ONCE.
ALL THE SHISHO WHO TAUGHT ME WHAT I KNOW ARE GONE NOW.
SIGH
ハァ...
I SHOULD HAVE JUST STAYED IN THE TV BIZ...
IT'S NOT EASY WHEN THINGS ARE THIS BLACK AND WHITE.
I WAS UP THERE NEXT TO A STORY-TELLER AT THE HEIGHT OF HIS POWERS.
I DON'T LIKE TO ADMIT IT, BUT I WAS OUT OF MY LEAGUE.
SIGH
はあ...
BUT YOU HAD FUN, RIGHT?
NONE AT ALL.

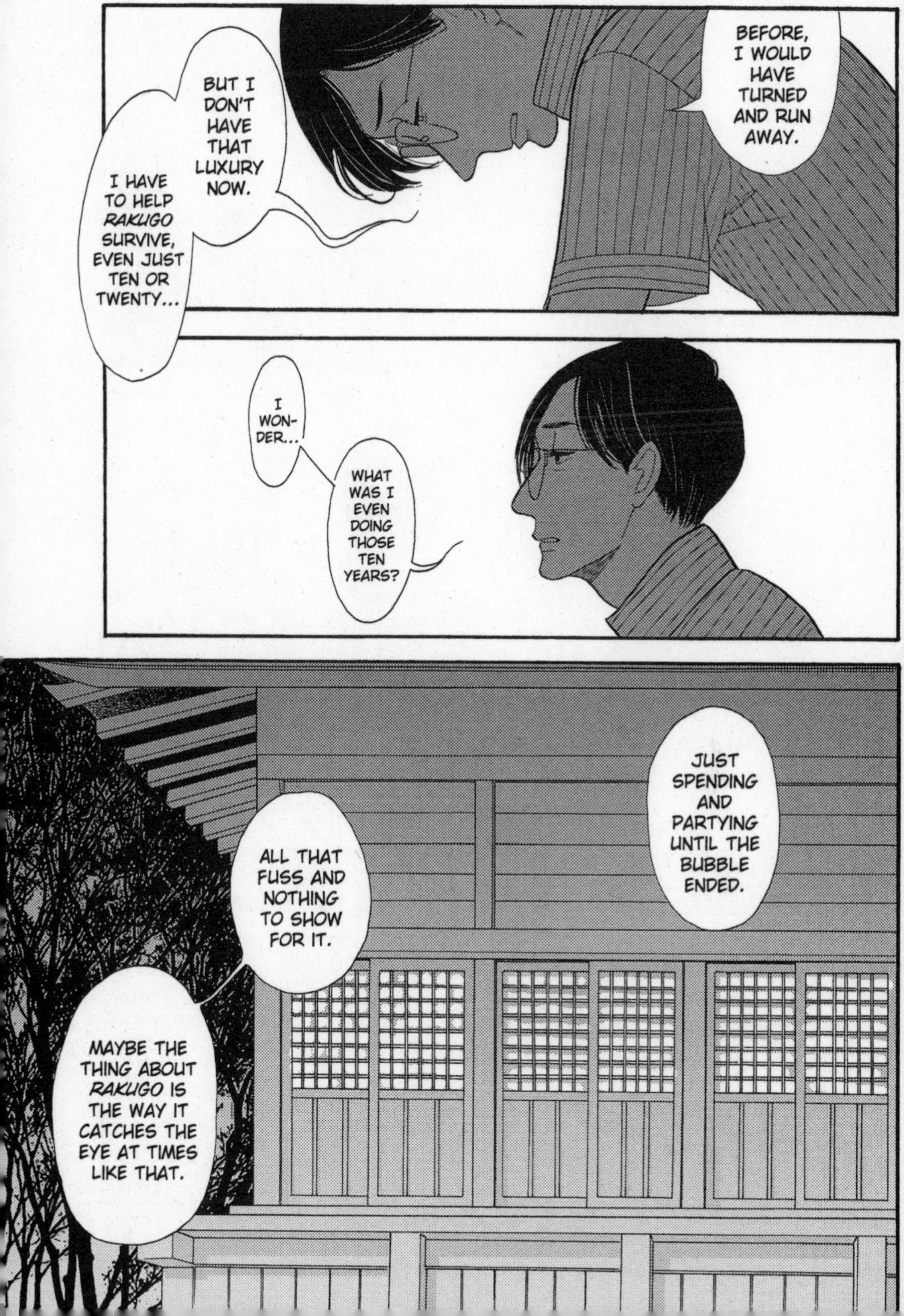
BEFORE, I WOULD HAVE TURNED AND RUN AWAY.
BUT I DON'T HAVE THAT LUXURY NOW.
I HAVE TO HELP *RAKUGO* SURVIVE, EVEN JUST TEN OR TWENTY...
I WONDER...
WHAT WAS I EVEN DOING THOSE TEN YEARS?
JUST SPENDING AND PARTYING UNTIL THE BUBBLE ENDED.
ALL THAT FUSS AND NOTHING TO SHOW FOR IT.
MAYBE THE THING ABOUT *RAKUGO* IS THE WAY IT CATCHES THE EYE AT TIMES LIKE THAT.

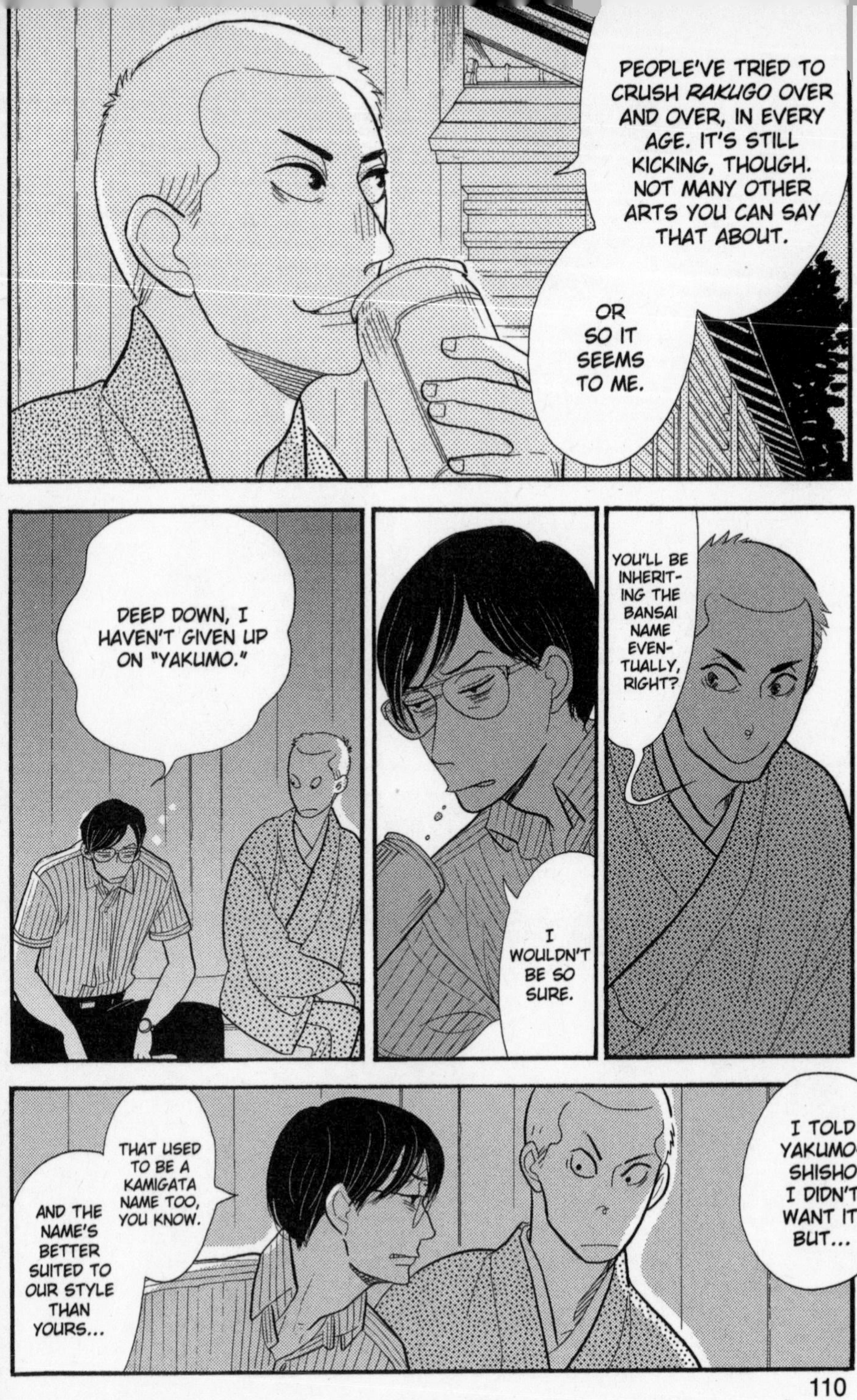
PEOPLE'VE TRIED TO CRUSH *RAKUGO* OVER AND OVER, IN EVERY AGE. IT'S STILL KICKING, THOUGH. NOT MANY OTHER ARTS YOU CAN SAY THAT ABOUT.
OR SO IT SEEMS TO ME.
YOU'LL BE INHERITING THE BANSAI NAME EVENTUALLY, RIGHT?
I WOULDN'T BE SO SURE.
DEEP DOWN, I HAVEN'T GIVEN UP ON "YAKUMO."
I TOLD YAKUMO-SHISHO I DIDN'T WANT IT, BUT...
THAT USED TO BE A KAMIGATA NAME TOO, YOU KNOW.
AND THE NAME'S BETTER SUITED TO OUR STYLE THAN YOURS...

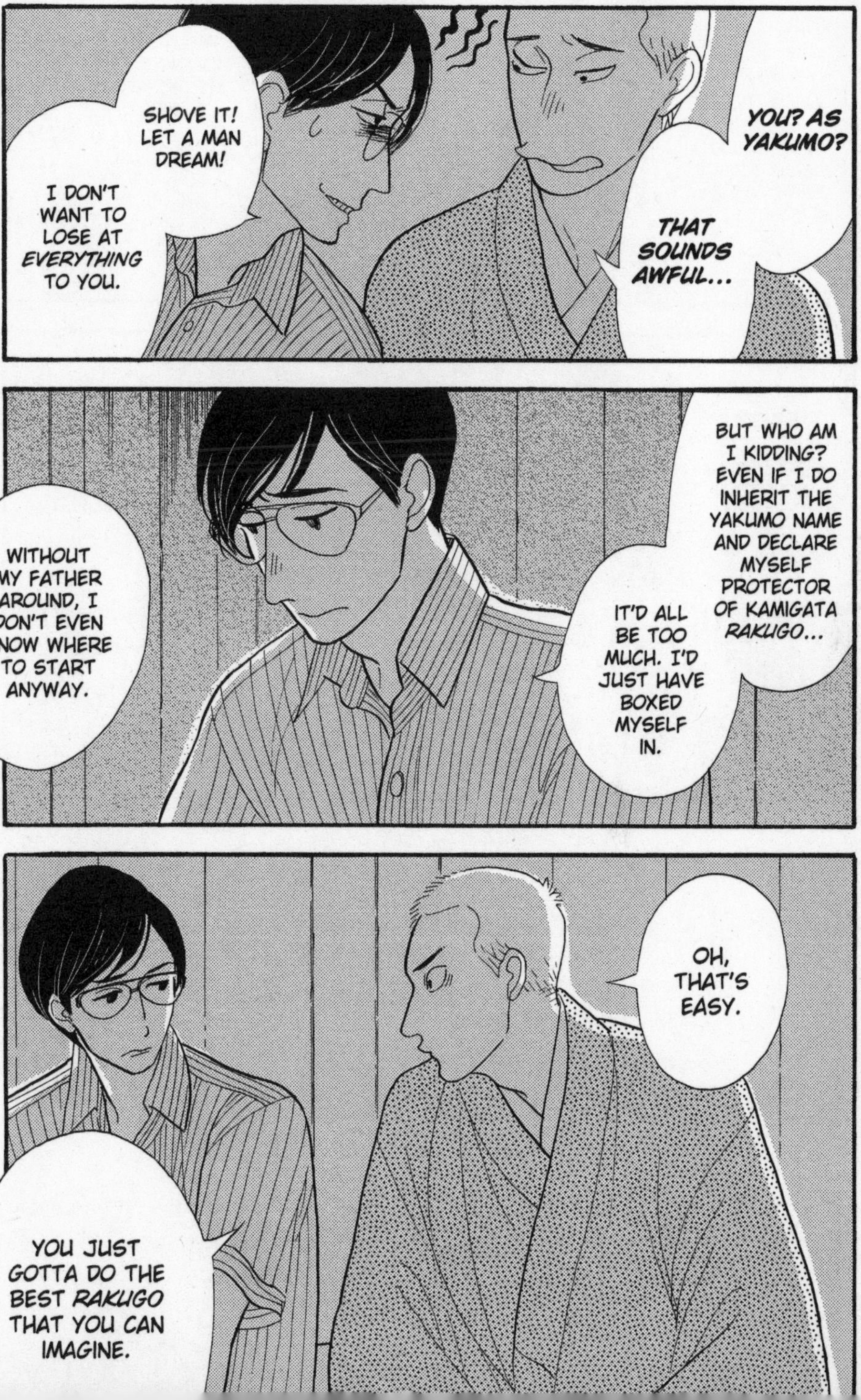
YOU? AS YAKUMO?
THAT SOUNDS AWFUL...
SHOVE IT! LET A MAN DREAM!
I DON'T WANT TO LOSE AT EVERYTHING TO YOU.
BUT WHO AM I KIDDING? EVEN IF I DO INHERIT THE YAKUMO NAME AND DECLARE MYSELF PROTECTOR OF KAMIGATA RAKUGO...
IT'D ALL BE TOO MUCH. I'D JUST HAVE BOXED MYSELF IN.
WITHOUT MY FATHER AROUND, I DON'T EVEN KNOW WHERE TO START ANYWAY.
OH, THAT'S EASY.
YOU JUST GOTTA DO THE BEST RAKUGO THAT YOU CAN IMAGINE.

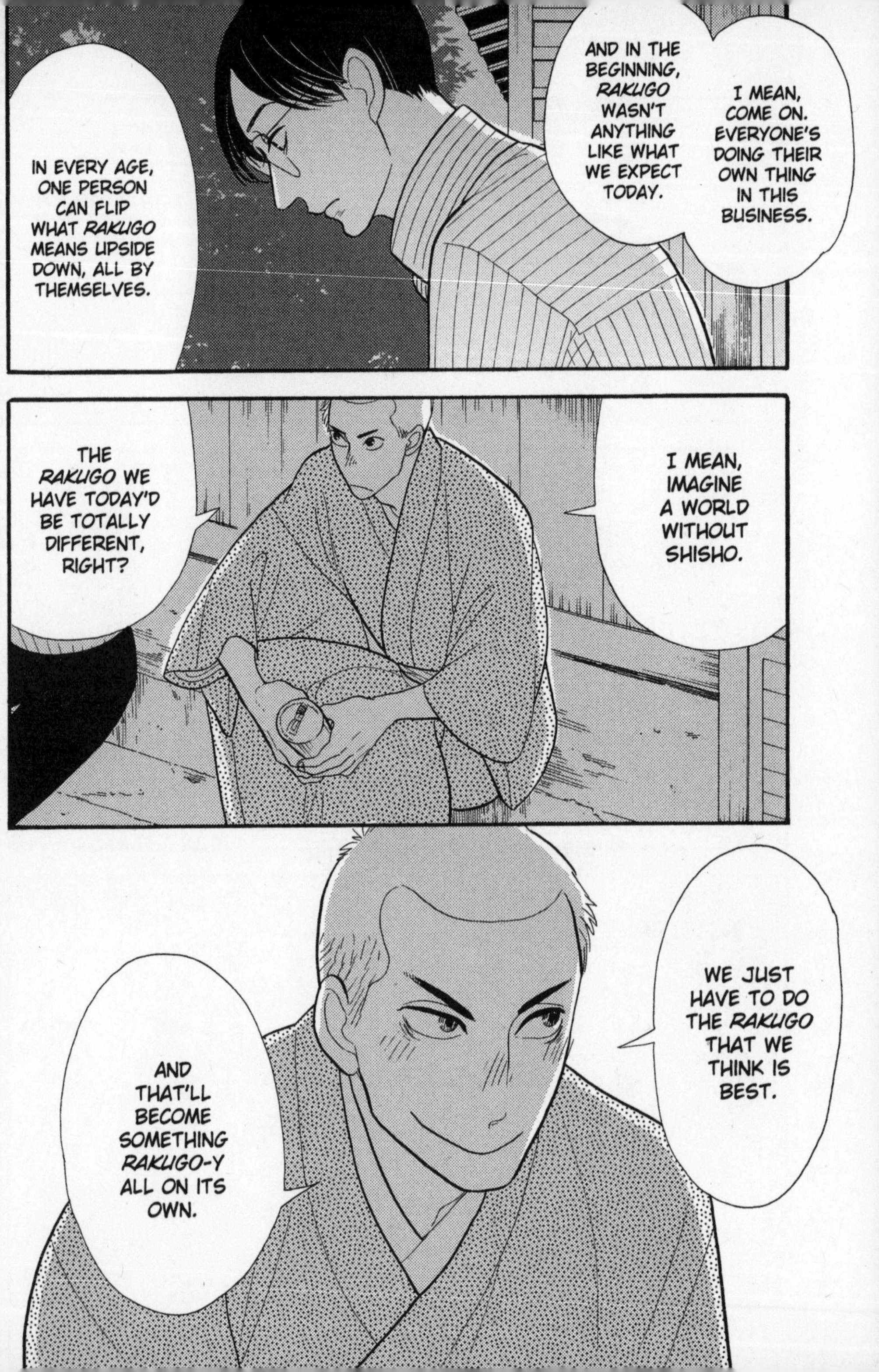
I MEAN, COME ON. EVERYONE'S DOING THEIR OWN THING IN THIS BUSINESS.
AND IN THE BEGINNING, *RAKUGO* WASN'T ANYTHING LIKE WHAT WE EXPECT TODAY.
IN EVERY AGE, ONE PERSON CAN FLIP WHAT *RAKUGO* MEANS UPSIDE DOWN, ALL BY THEMSELVES.
I MEAN, IMAGINE A WORLD WITHOUT SHISHO.
THE *RAKUGO* WE HAVE TODAY'D BE TOTALLY DIFFERENT, RIGHT?
WE JUST HAVE TO DO THE *RAKUGO* THAT WE THINK IS BEST.
AND THAT'LL BECOME SOMETHING *RAKUGO*-Y ALL ON ITS OWN.

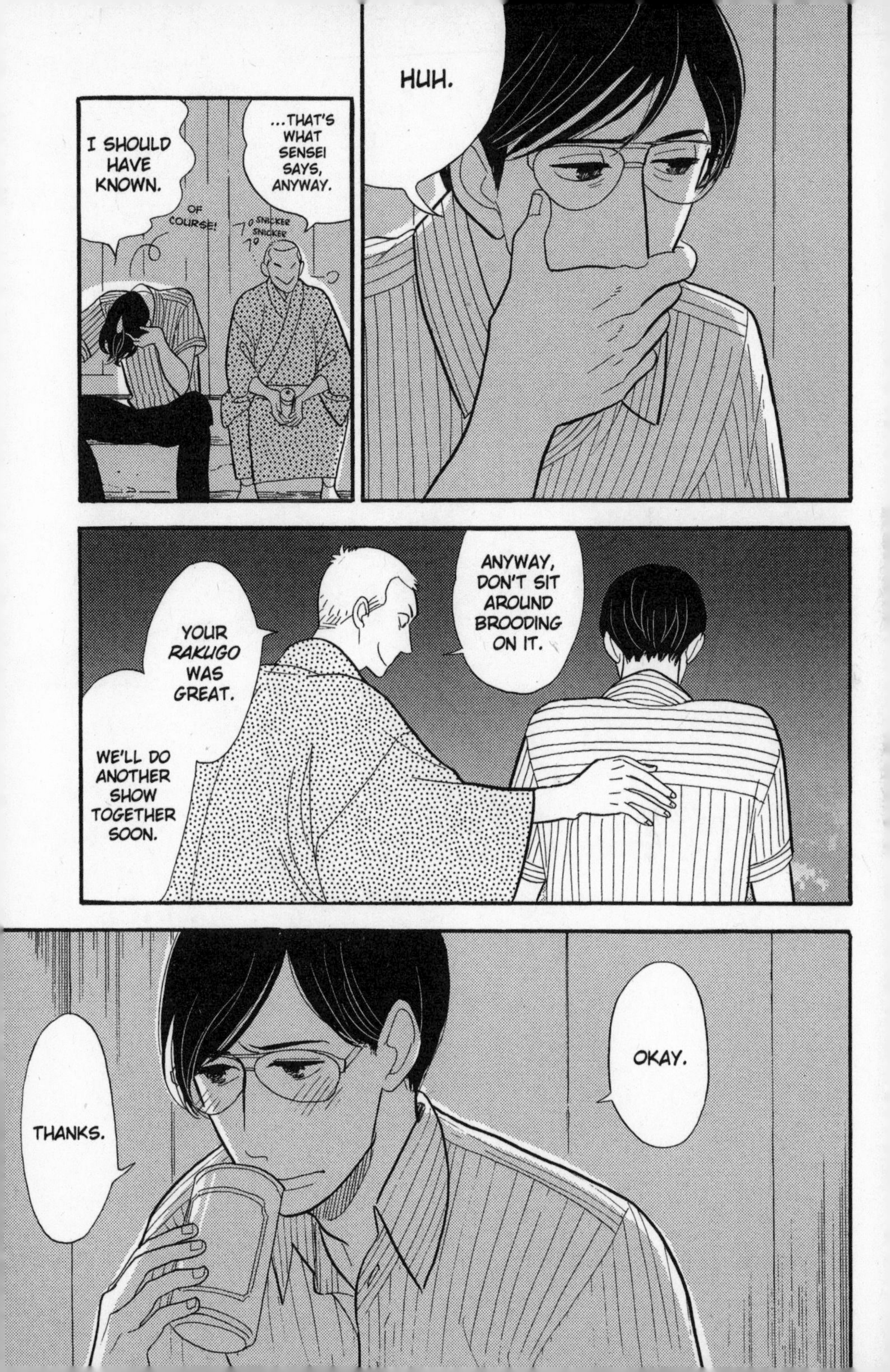
HUH.
...THAT'S WHAT SENSEI SAYS, ANYWAY.
I SHOULD HAVE KNOWN.
SNICKER SNICKER
OF COURSE!
ANYWAY, DON'T SIT AROUND BROODING ON IT.
YOUR *RAKUGO* WAS GREAT.
WE'LL DO ANOTHER SHOW TOGETHER SOON.
OKAY.
THANKS.

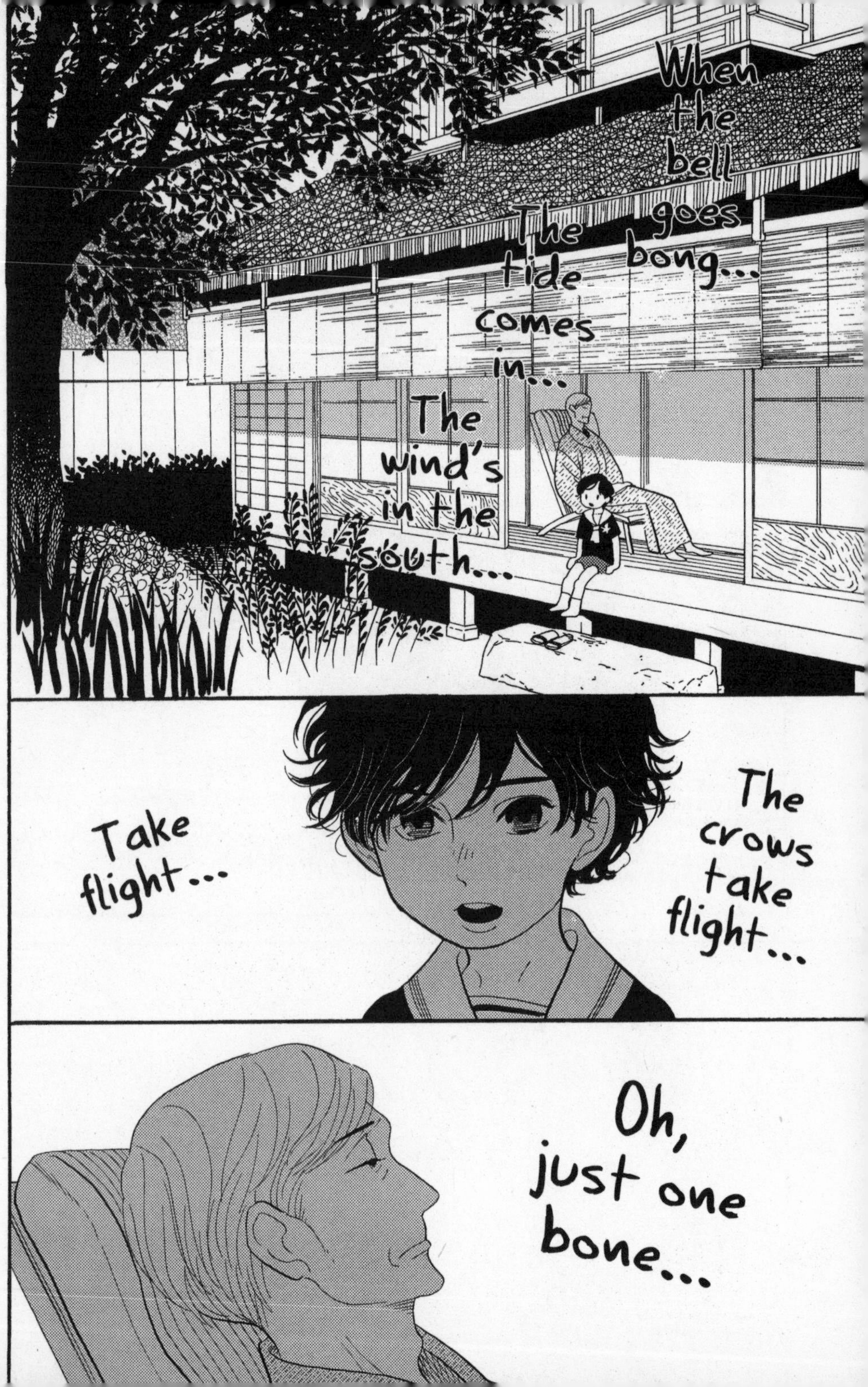
When the bell goes bong...
The tide comes in...
The wind's in the south...
The crows take flight...
Take flight...
Oh, just one bone...

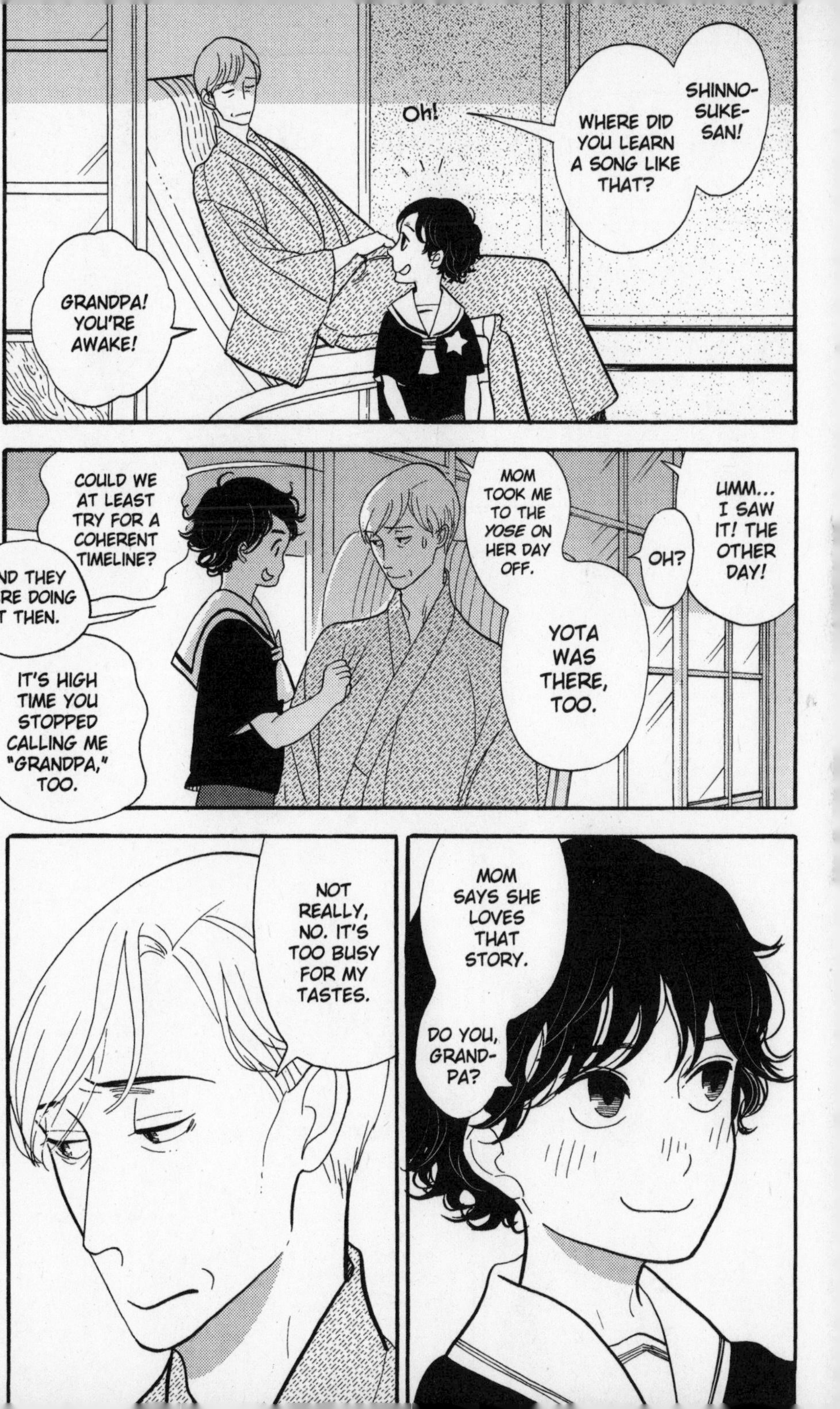
SHINNO-SUKE-SAN! WHERE DID YOU LEARN A SONG LIKE THAT?
Oh!
GRANDPA! YOU'RE AWAKE!
UMM... I SAW IT! THE OTHER DAY!
OH?
MOM TOOK ME TO THE *YOSE* ON HER DAY OFF.
YOTA WAS THERE, TOO.
COULD WE AT LEAST TRY FOR A COHERENT TIMELINE?
AND THEY WERE DOING IT THEN.
IT'S HIGH TIME YOU STOPPED CALLING ME "GRANDPA," TOO.
MOM SAYS SHE LOVES THAT STORY.
DO YOU, GRAND-PA?
NOT REALLY, NO. IT'S TOO BUSY FOR MY TASTES.

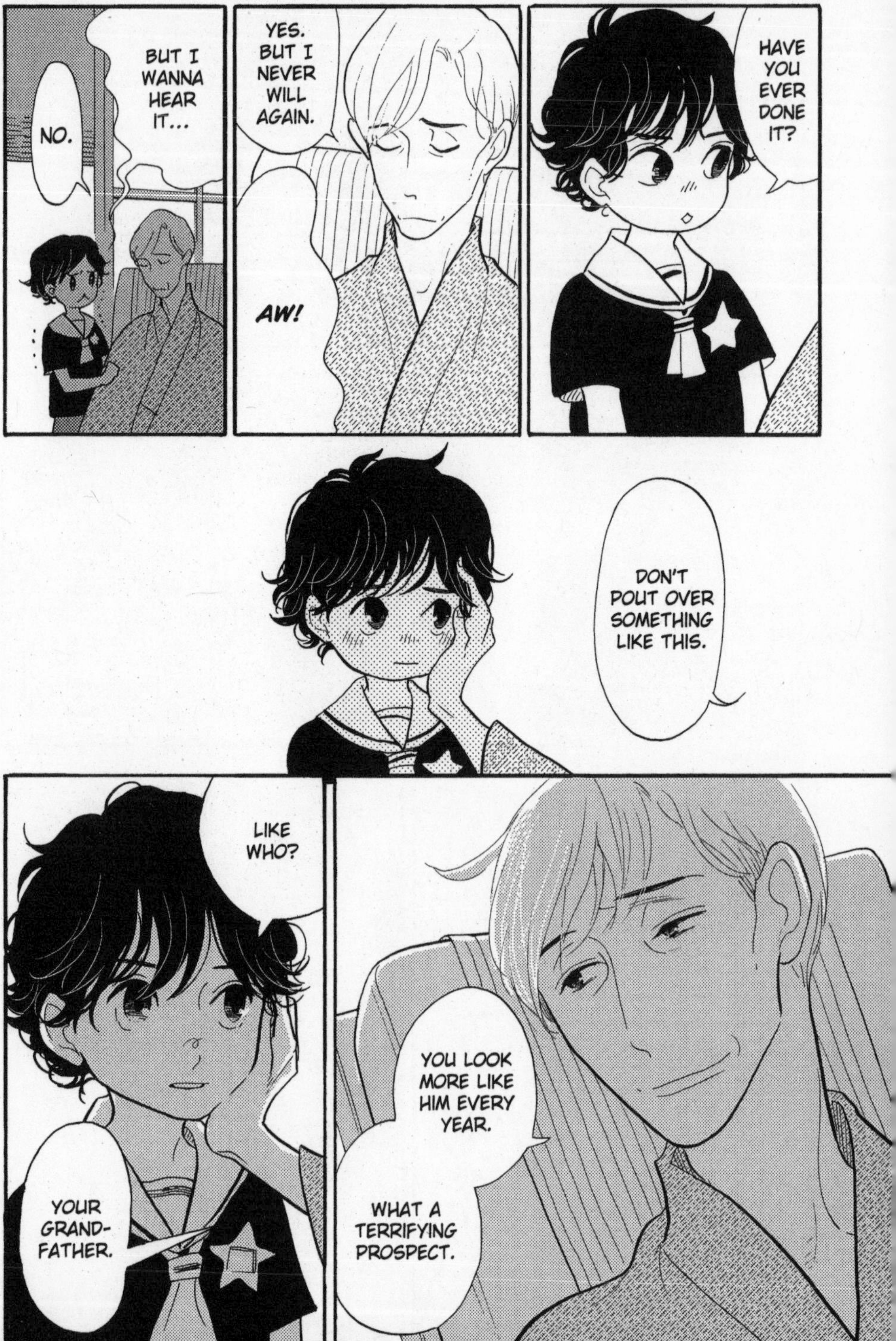
HAVE YOU EVER DONE IT?
YES. BUT I NEVER WILL AGAIN.
AW!
BUT I WANNA HEAR IT...
NO.
DON'T POUT OVER SOMETHING LIKE THIS.
YOU LOOK MORE LIKE HIM EVERY YEAR.
WHAT A TERRIFYING PROSPECT.
LIKE WHO?
YOUR GRAND-FATHER.

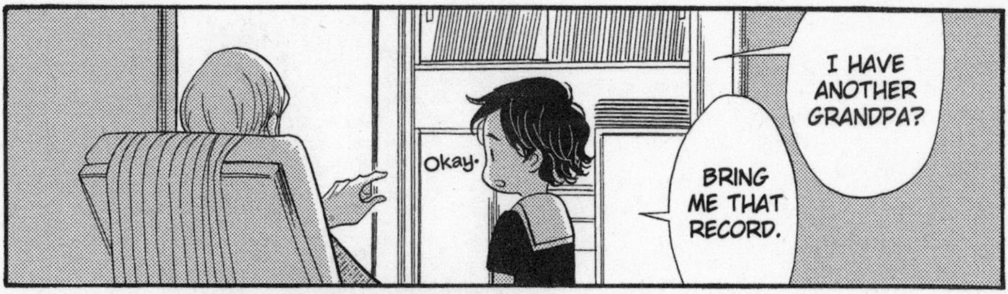
I HAVE ANOTHER GRANDPA?
BRING ME THAT RECORD.
Okay.

Album: Sukeroku: Collected Works: "The Golden Rice Cake," "The Stubborn Moxa"

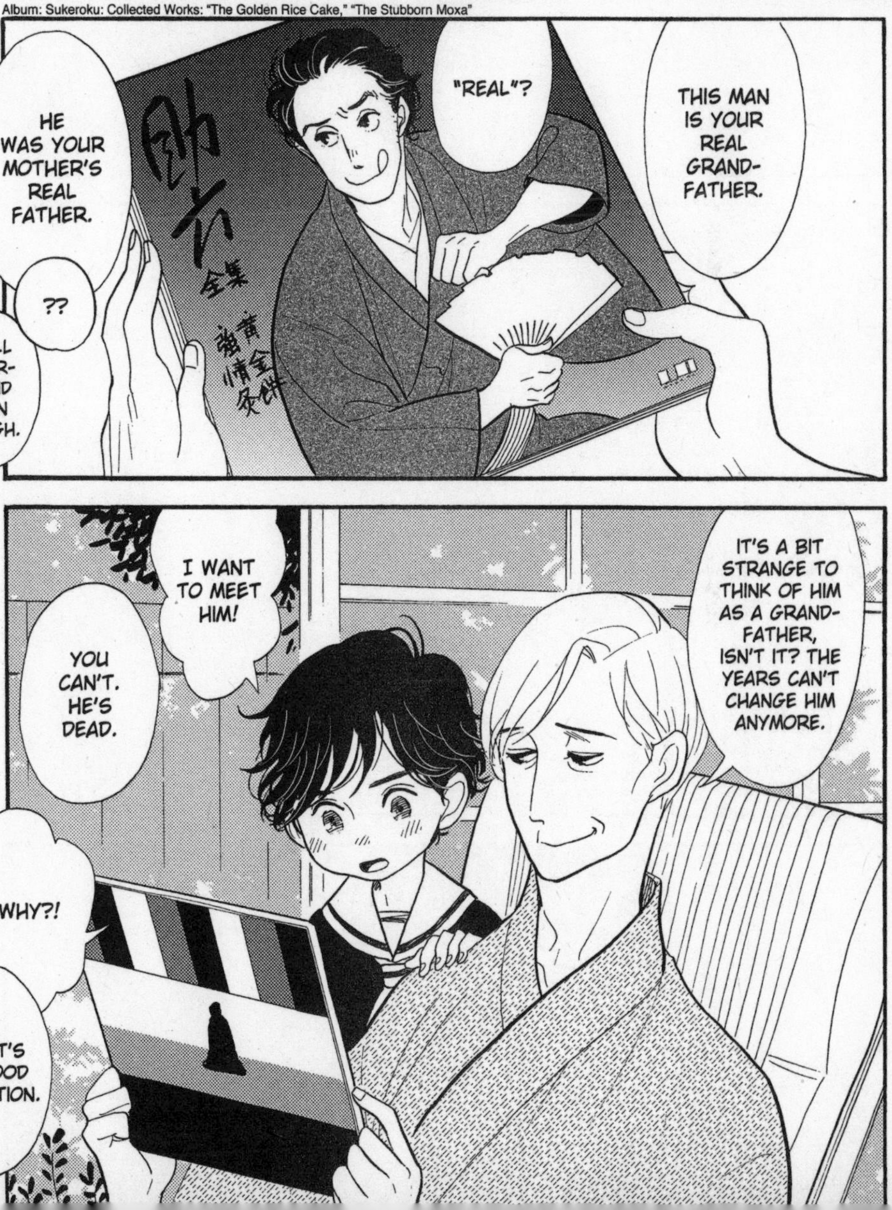
THIS MAN IS YOUR REAL GRAND-FATHER.
"REAL"?
HE WAS YOUR MOTHER'S REAL FATHER.
??
YOU'LL UNDER-STAND SOON ENOUGH.
IT'S A BIT STRANGE TO THINK OF HIM AS A GRAND-FATHER, ISN'T IT? THE YEARS CAN'T CHANGE HIM ANYMORE.
I WANT TO MEET HIM!
YOU CAN'T. HE'S DEAD.
WHY?!
THAT'S A GOOD QUESTION.

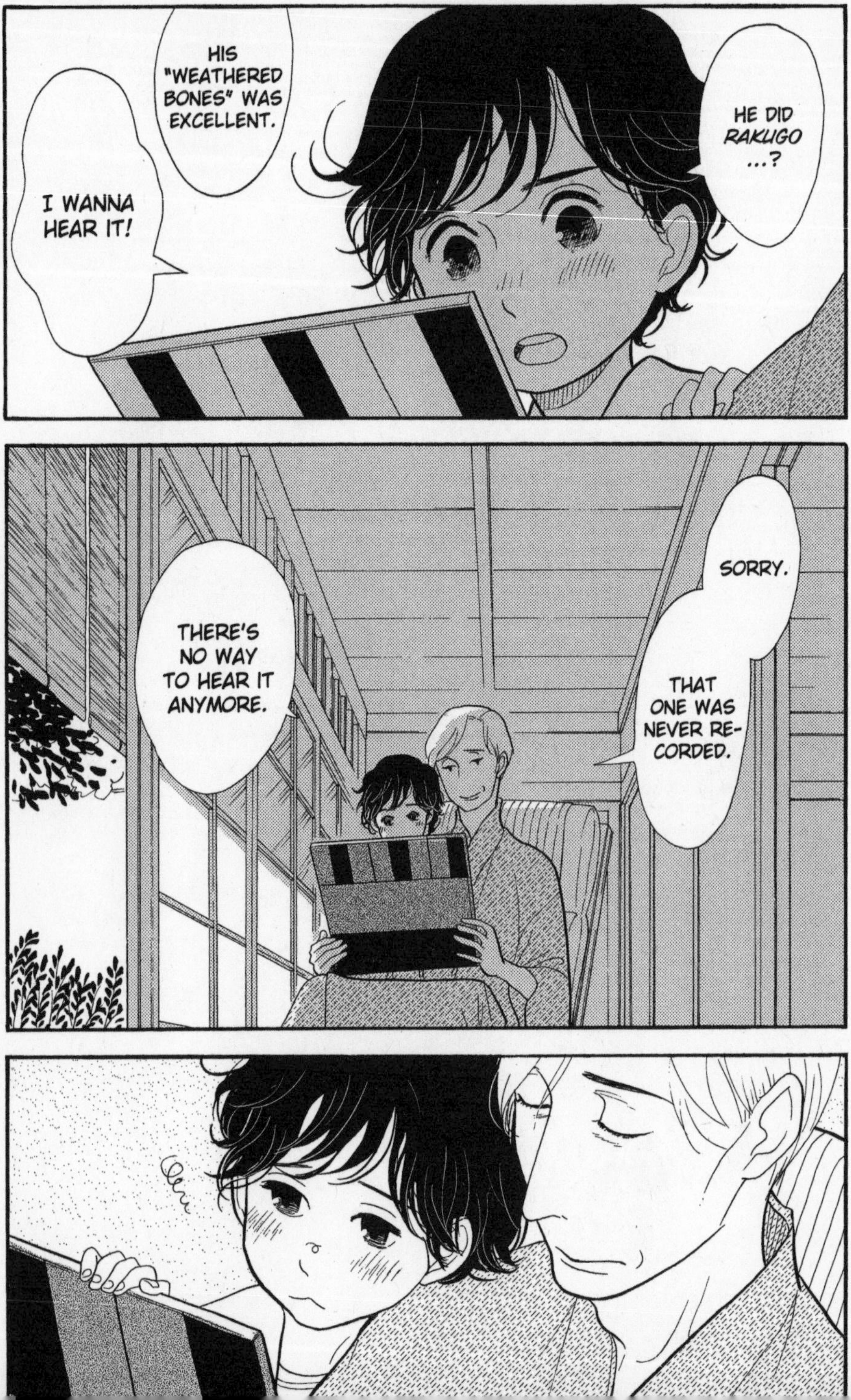
HE DID *RAKUGO* ...?
HIS "WEATHERED BONES" WAS EXCELLENT.
I WANNA HEAR IT!
SORRY.
THAT ONE WAS NEVER RE-CORDED.
THERE'S NO WAY TO HEAR IT ANYMORE.

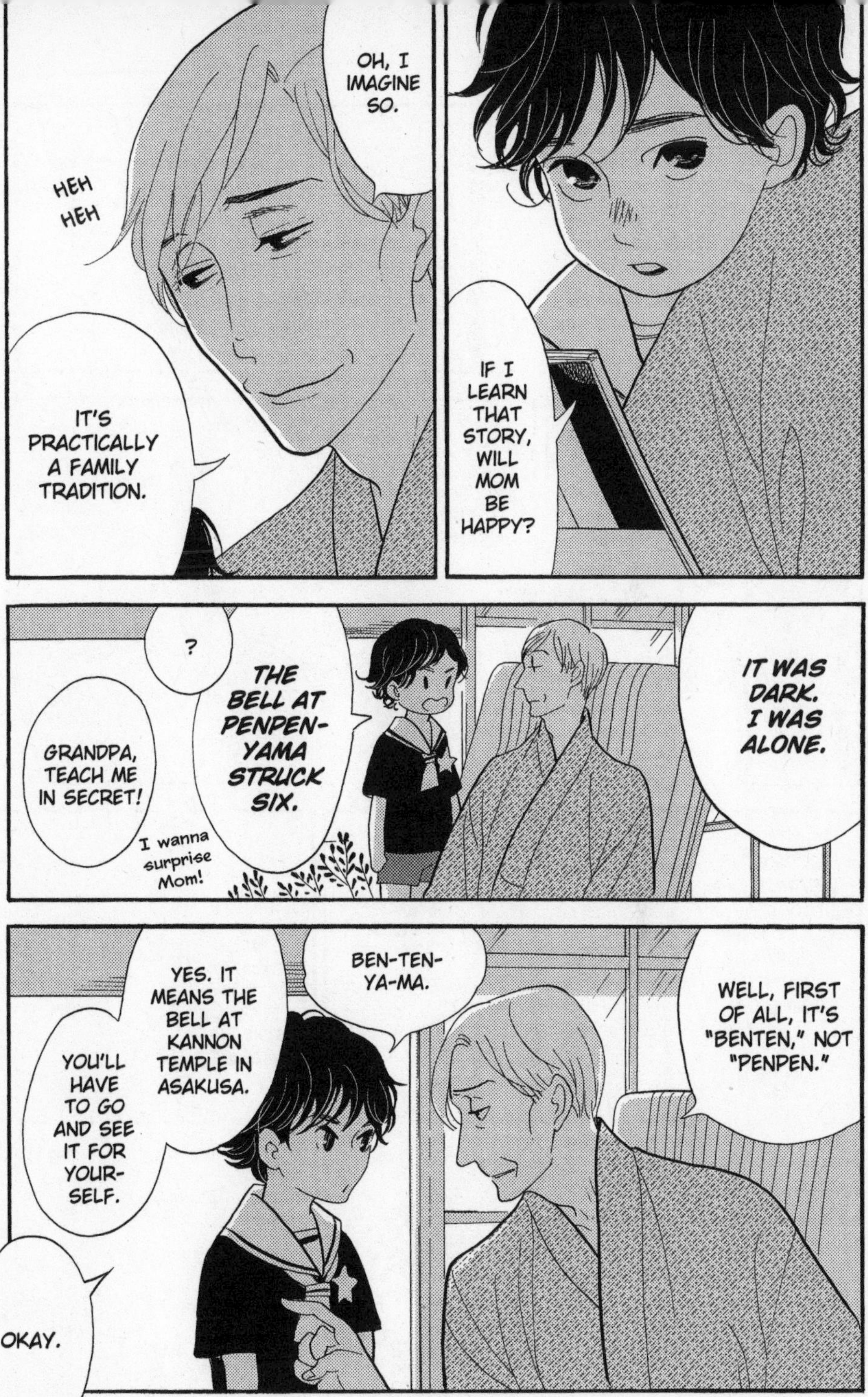
IF I LEARN THAT STORY, WILL MOM BE HAPPY?
OH, I IMAGINE SO.
HEH HEH
IT'S PRACTICALLY A FAMILY TRADITION.
IT WAS DARK. I WAS ALONE.
THE BELL AT PENPEN-YAMA STRUCK SIX.
?
GRANDPA, TEACH ME IN SECRET!
I wanna surprise Mom!
WELL, FIRST OF ALL, IT'S "BENTEN," NOT "PENPEN."
BEN-TEN-YA-MA.
YES. IT MEANS THE BELL AT KANNON TEMPLE IN ASAKUSA.
YOU'LL HAVE TO GO AND SEE IT FOR YOURSELF.
OKAY.

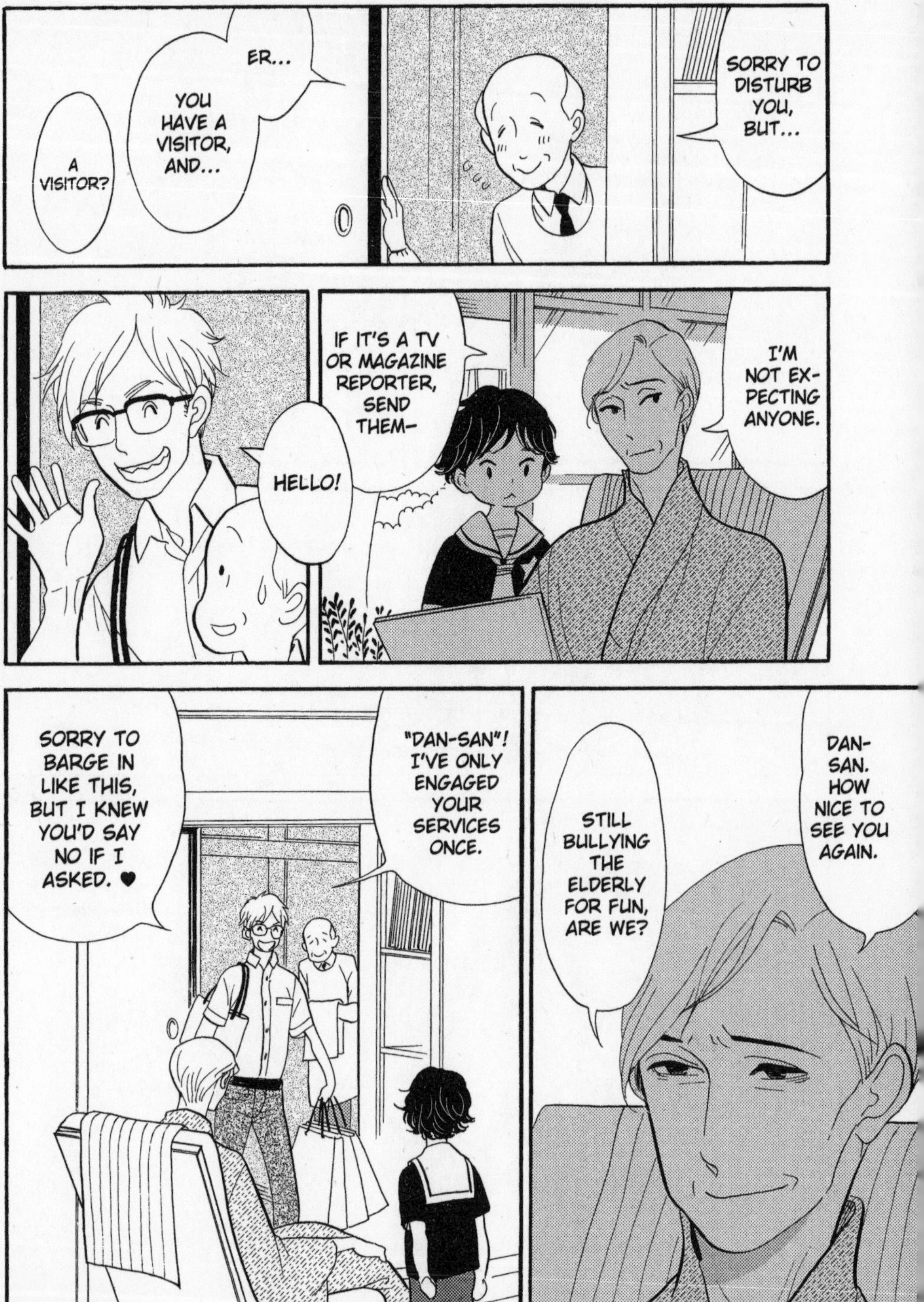
SORRY TO DISTURB YOU, BUT...
ER...
YOU HAVE A VISITOR, AND...
A VISITOR?
I'M NOT EX-PECTING ANYONE.
IF IT'S A TV OR MAGAZINE REPORTER, SEND THEM–
HELLO!
DAN-SAN. HOW NICE TO SEE YOU AGAIN.
STILL BULLYING THE ELDERLY FOR FUN, ARE WE?
"DAN-SAN"! I'VE ONLY ENGAGED YOUR SERVICES ONCE.
SORRY TO BARGE IN LIKE THIS, BUT I KNEW YOU'D SAY NO IF I ASKED. ♥

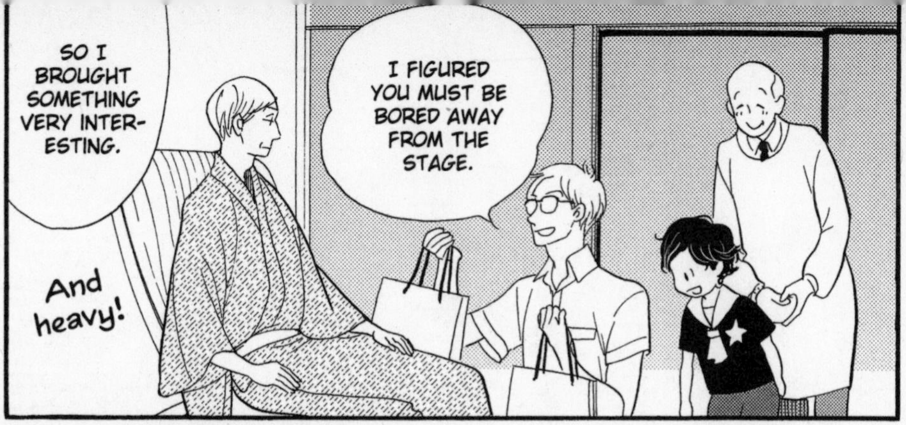
I FIGURED YOU MUST BE BORED AWAY FROM THE STAGE.
SO I BROUGHT SOMETHING VERY INTERESTING.
And heavy!

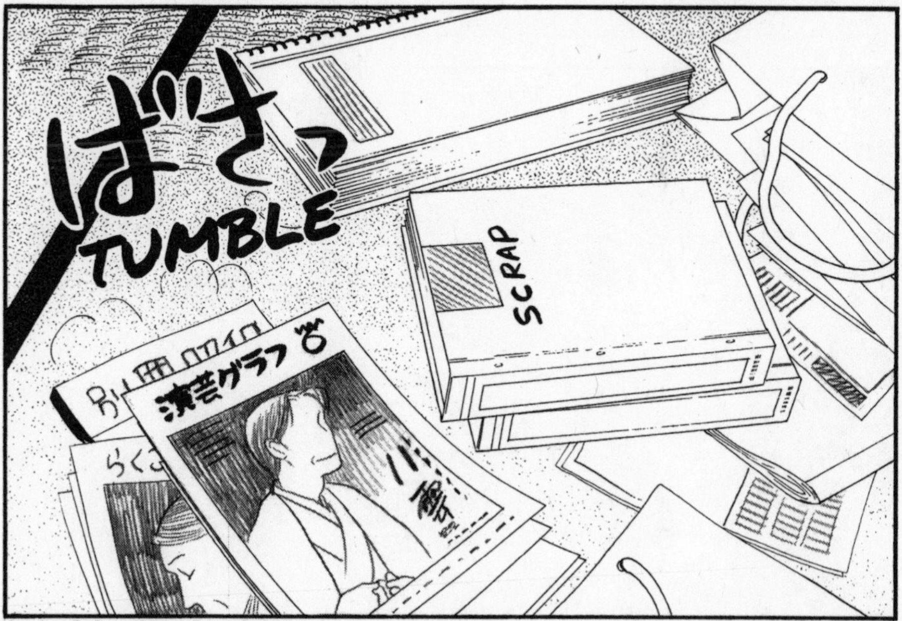
ばさっ
TUMBLE
SCRAP
演芸グラフ
Magazines: On Stage: Yakumo; *Rakugo*; Bonus Issue

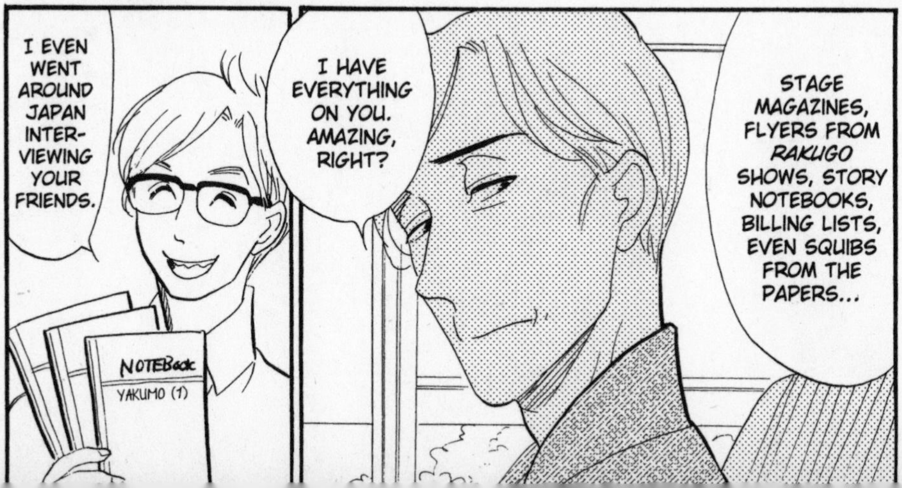
STAGE MAGAZINES, FLYERS FROM *RAKUGO* SHOWS, STORY NOTEBOOKS, BILLING LISTS, EVEN SQUIBS FROM THE PAPERS...
I HAVE EVERYTHING ON YOU. AMAZING, RIGHT?
I EVEN WENT AROUND JAPAN INTERVIEWING YOUR FRIENDS.
NOTEBook
YAKUMO (1)

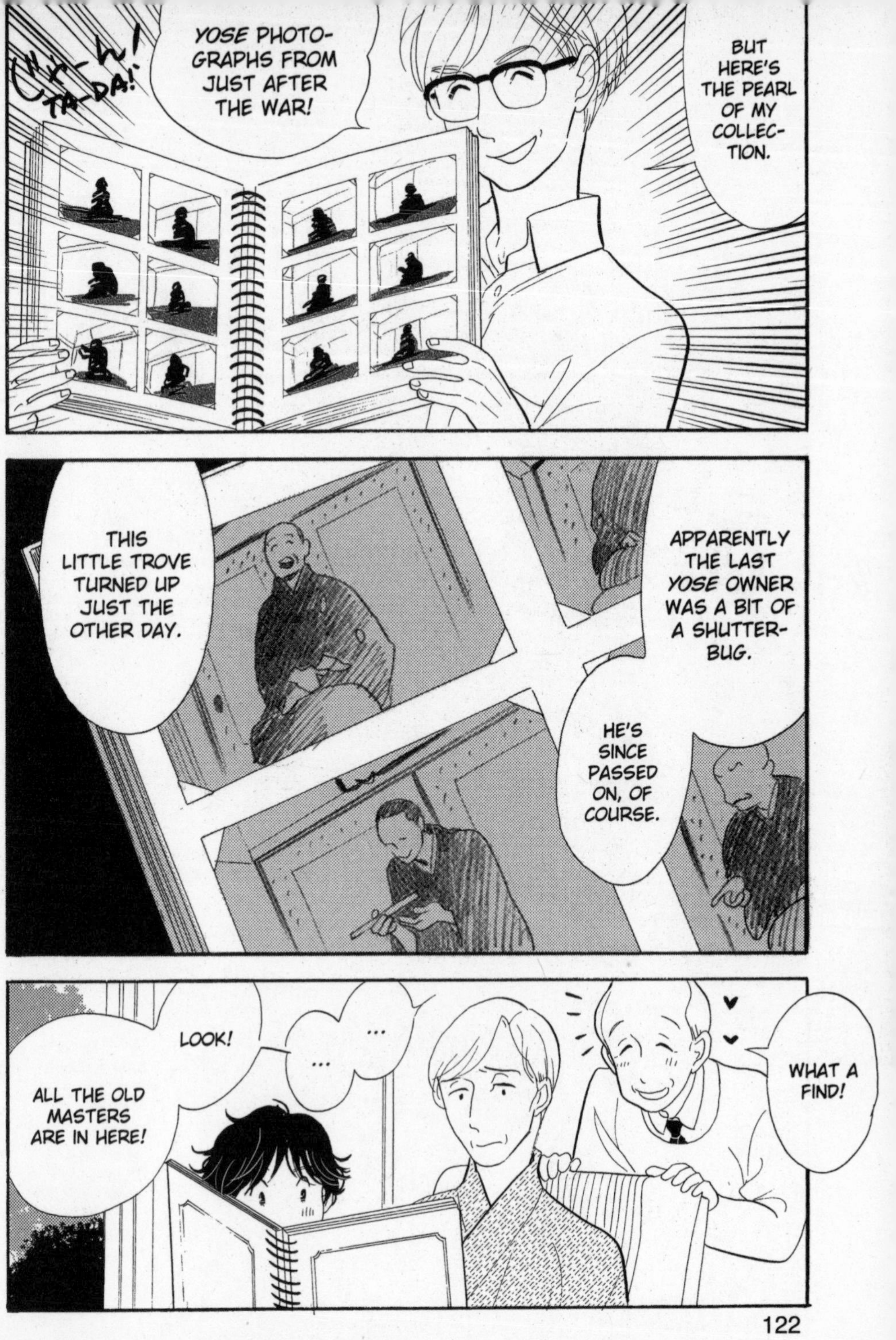
BUT HERE'S THE PEARL OF MY COLLECTION.
YOSE PHOTO-GRAPHS FROM JUST AFTER THE WAR!
TA-DA!
APPARENTLY THE LAST *YOSE* OWNER WAS A BIT OF A SHUTTER-BUG.
HE'S SINCE PASSED ON, OF COURSE.
THIS LITTLE TROVE TURNED UP JUST THE OTHER DAY.
WHAT A FIND!
...
...
LOOK!
ALL THE OLD MASTERS ARE IN HERE!

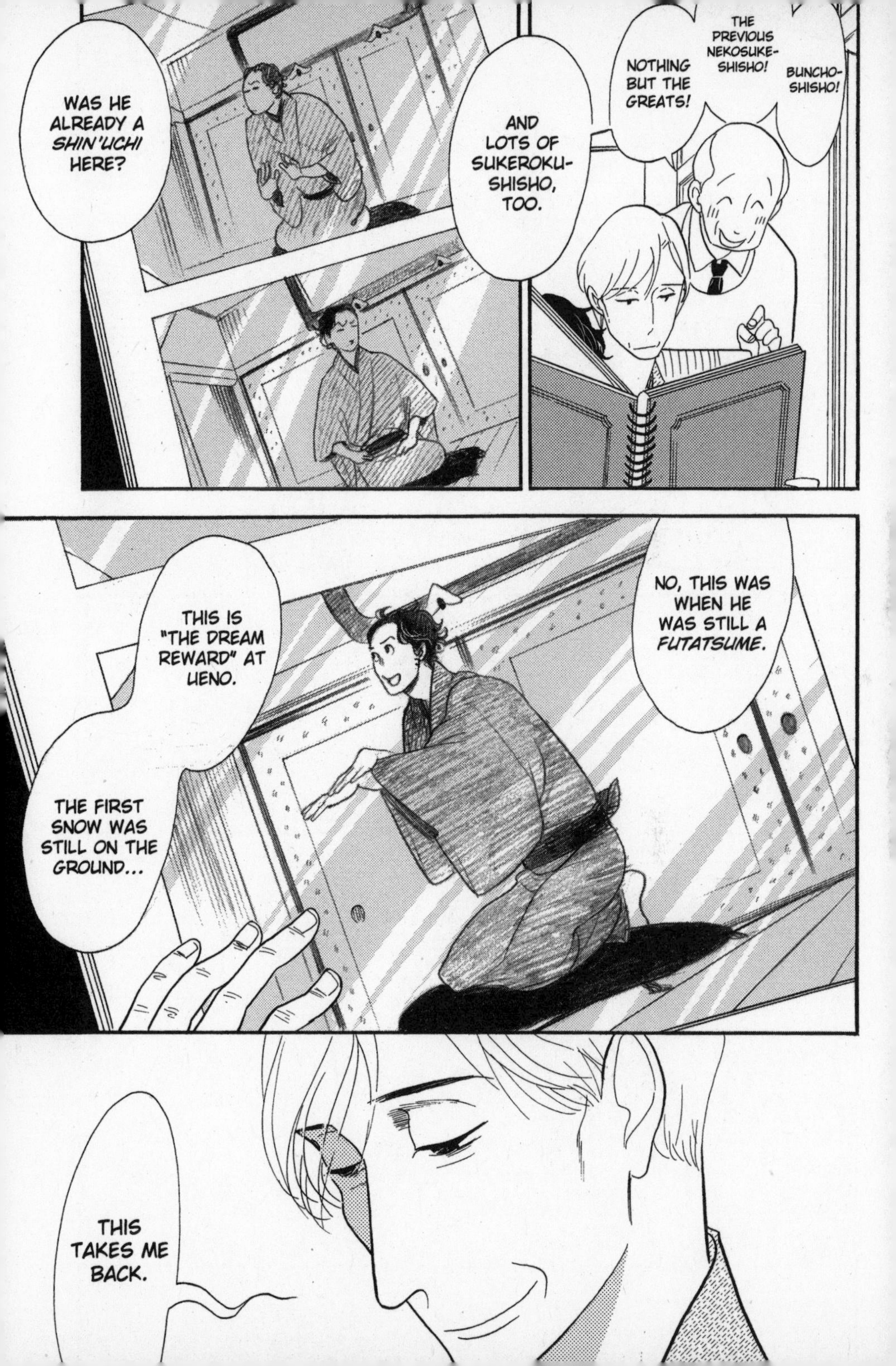

BUNCHO-SHISHO!
THE PREVIOUS NEKOSUKE-SHISHO!
NOTHING BUT THE GREATS!
AND LOTS OF SUKEROKU-SHISHO, TOO.
WAS HE ALREADY A *SHIN'UCHI* HERE?
NO, THIS WAS WHEN HE WAS STILL A *FUTATSUME*.
THIS IS "THE DREAM REWARD" AT UENO.
THE FIRST SNOW WAS STILL ON THE GROUND...
THIS TAKES ME BACK.

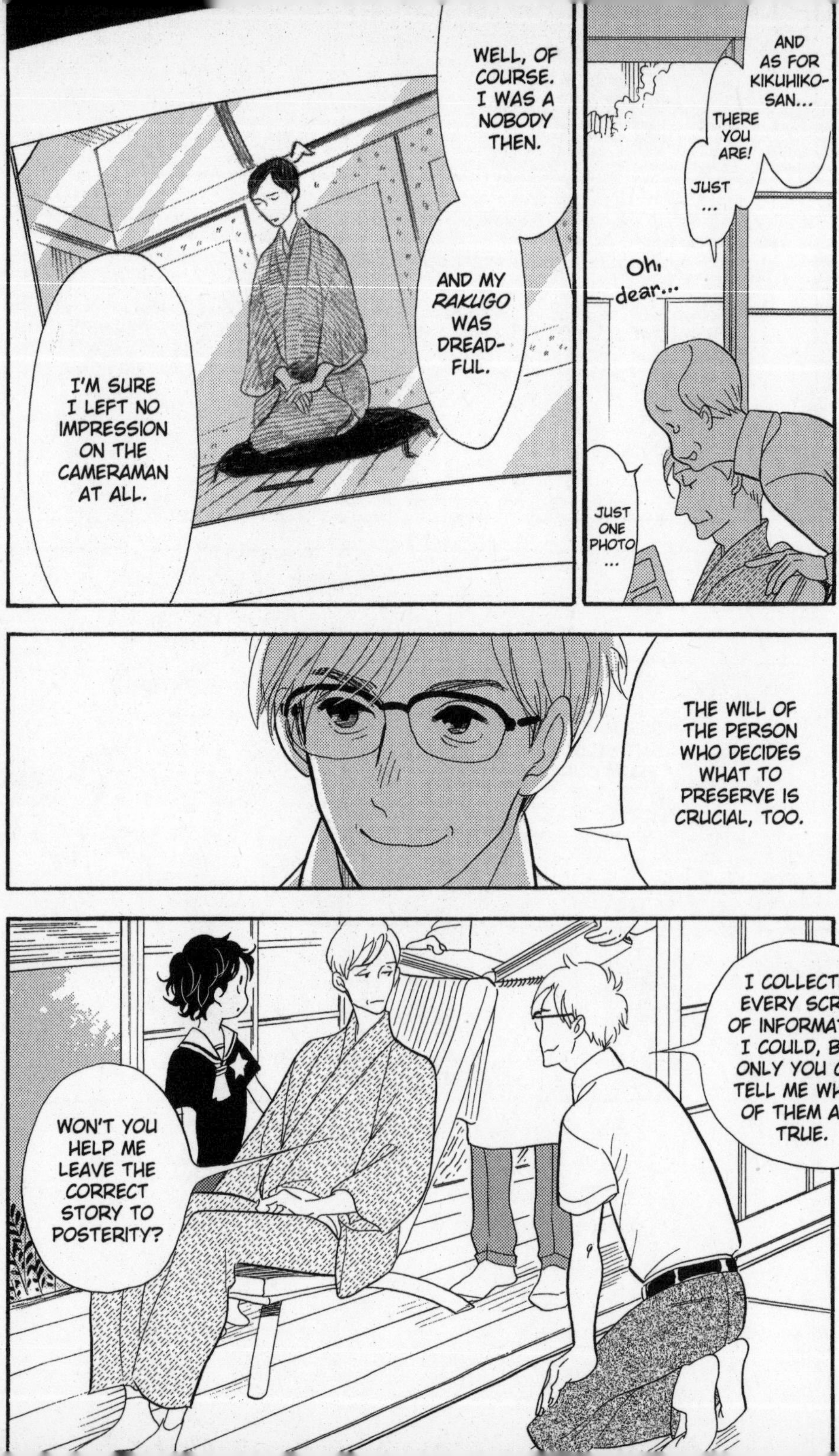
AND AS FOR KIKUHIKO-SAN...
THERE YOU ARE!
JUST ...
Oh, dear...
JUST ONE PHOTO ...
WELL, OF COURSE. I WAS A NOBODY THEN.
AND MY *RAKUGO* WAS DREAD-FUL.
I'M SURE I LEFT NO IMPRESSION ON THE CAMERAMAN AT ALL.
THE WILL OF THE PERSON WHO DECIDES WHAT TO PRESERVE IS CRUCIAL, TOO.
I COLLECTED EVERY SCRAP OF INFORMATION I COULD, BUT ONLY YOU CAN TELL ME WHICH OF THEM ARE TRUE.
WON'T YOU HELP ME LEAVE THE CORRECT STORY TO POSTERITY?

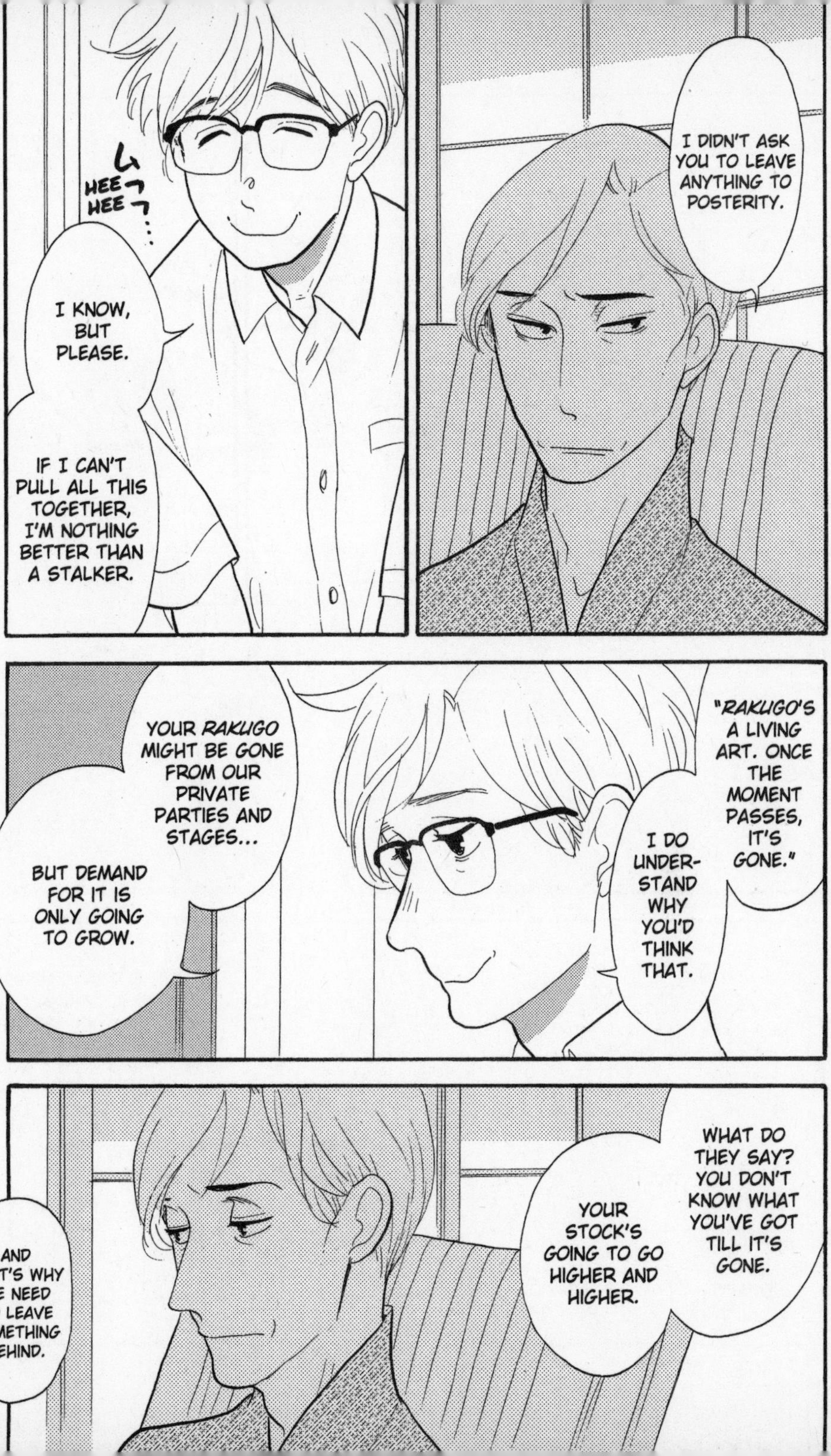
I DIDN'T ASK YOU TO LEAVE ANYTHING TO POSTERITY.
HEE HEE...
I KNOW, BUT PLEASE.
IF I CAN'T PULL ALL THIS TOGETHER, I'M NOTHING BETTER THAN A STALKER.
"*RAKUGO*'S A LIVING ART. ONCE THE MOMENT PASSES, IT'S GONE."
I DO UNDERSTAND WHY YOU'D THINK THAT.
YOUR *RAKUGO* MIGHT BE GONE FROM OUR PRIVATE PARTIES AND STAGES...
BUT DEMAND FOR IT IS ONLY GOING TO GROW.
WHAT DO THEY SAY? YOU DON'T KNOW WHAT YOU'VE GOT TILL IT'S GONE.
YOUR STOCK'S GOING TO GO HIGHER AND HIGHER.
AND THAT'S WHY WE NEED TO LEAVE SOMETHING BEHIND.

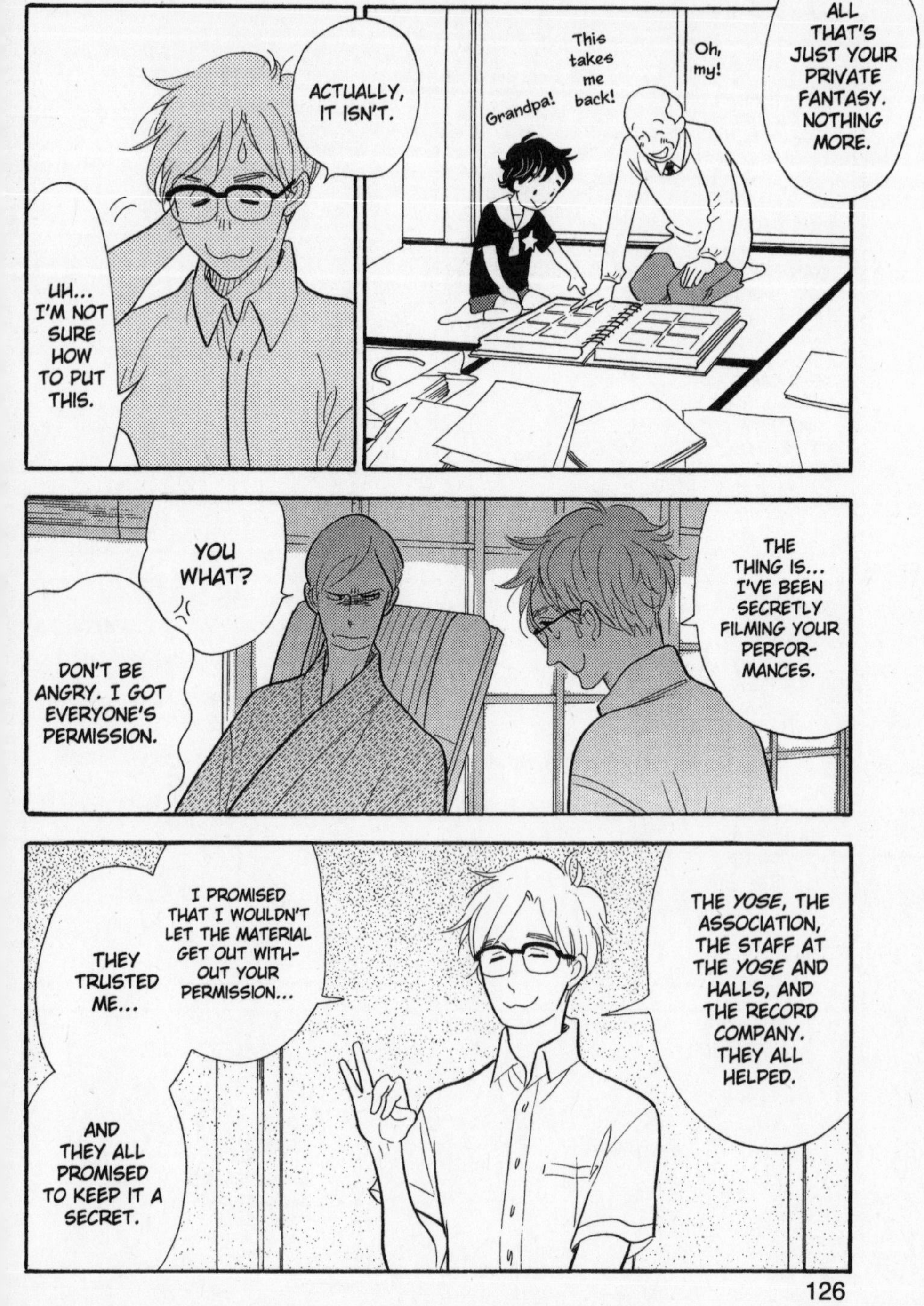
ALL THAT'S JUST YOUR PRIVATE FANTASY. NOTHING MORE.
Oh, my!
This takes me back!
Grandpa!
ACTUALLY, IT ISN'T.
UH... I'M NOT SURE HOW TO PUT THIS.
THE THING IS... I'VE BEEN SECRETLY FILMING YOUR PERFORMANCES.
YOU WHAT?
DON'T BE ANGRY. I GOT EVERYONE'S PERMISSION.
THE *YOSE*, THE ASSOCIATION, THE STAFF AT THE *YOSE* AND HALLS, AND THE RECORD COMPANY. THEY ALL HELPED.
I PROMISED THAT I WOULDN'T LET THE MATERIAL GET OUT WITHOUT YOUR PERMISSION...
THEY TRUSTED ME...
AND THEY ALL PROMISED TO KEEP IT A SECRET.

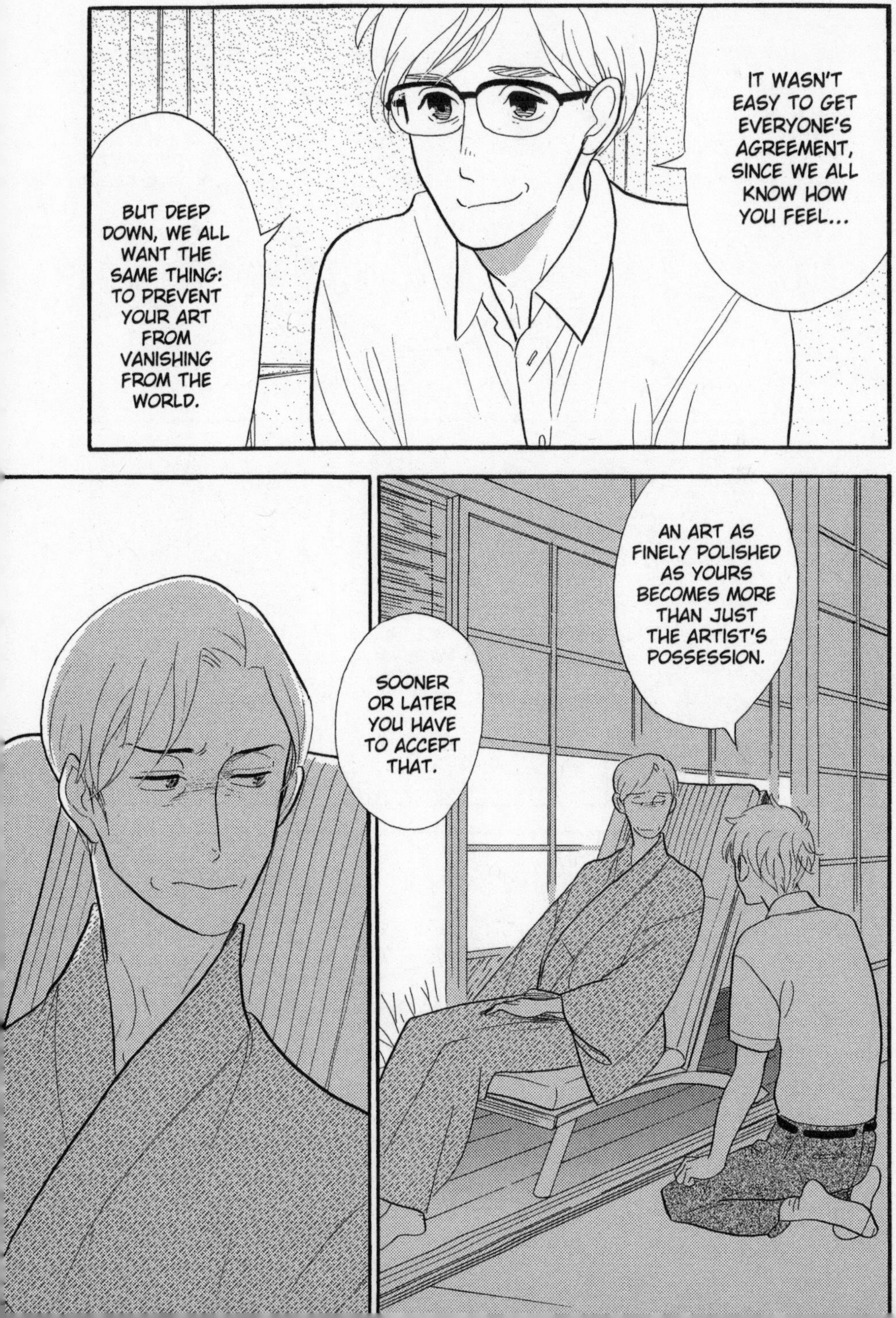
IT WASN'T EASY TO GET EVERYONE'S AGREEMENT, SINCE WE ALL KNOW HOW YOU FEEL...
BUT DEEP DOWN, WE ALL WANT THE SAME THING: TO PREVENT YOUR ART FROM VANISHING FROM THE WORLD.
AN ART AS FINELY POLISHED AS YOURS BECOMES MORE THAN JUST THE ARTIST'S POSSESSION.
SOONER OR LATER YOU HAVE TO ACCEPT THAT.

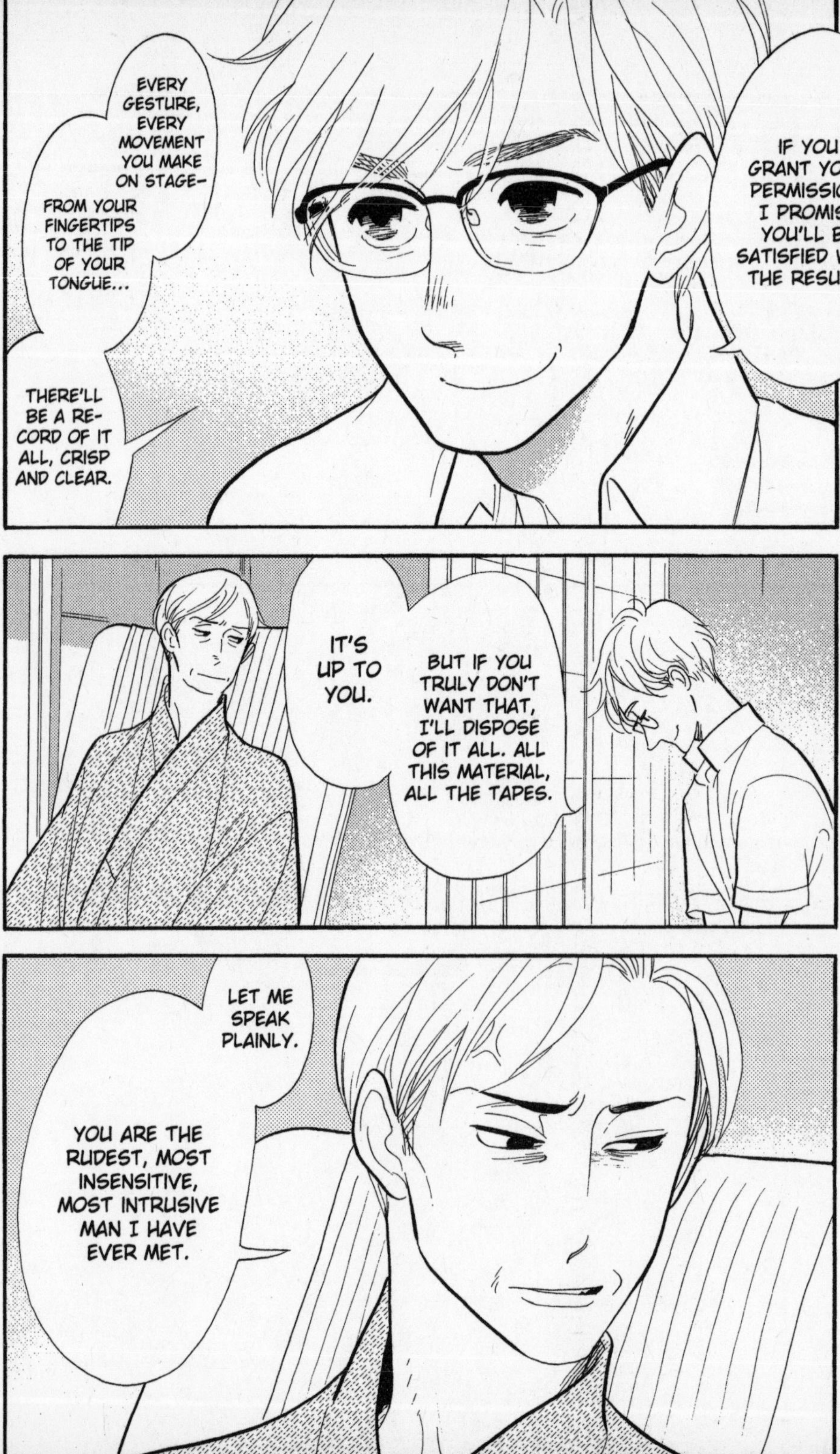
IF YOU GRANT YOUR PERMISSION, I PROMISE YOU'LL BE SATISFIED WITH THE RESULT.
EVERY GESTURE, EVERY MOVEMENT YOU MAKE ON STAGE-
FROM YOUR FINGERTIPS TO THE TIP OF YOUR TONGUE...
THERE'LL BE A RECORD OF IT ALL, CRISP AND CLEAR.
IT'S UP TO YOU.
BUT IF YOU TRULY DON'T WANT THAT, I'LL DISPOSE OF IT ALL. ALL THIS MATERIAL, ALL THE TAPES.
LET ME SPEAK PLAINLY.
YOU ARE THE RUDEST, MOST INSENSITIVE, MOST INTRUSIVE MAN I HAVE EVER MET.

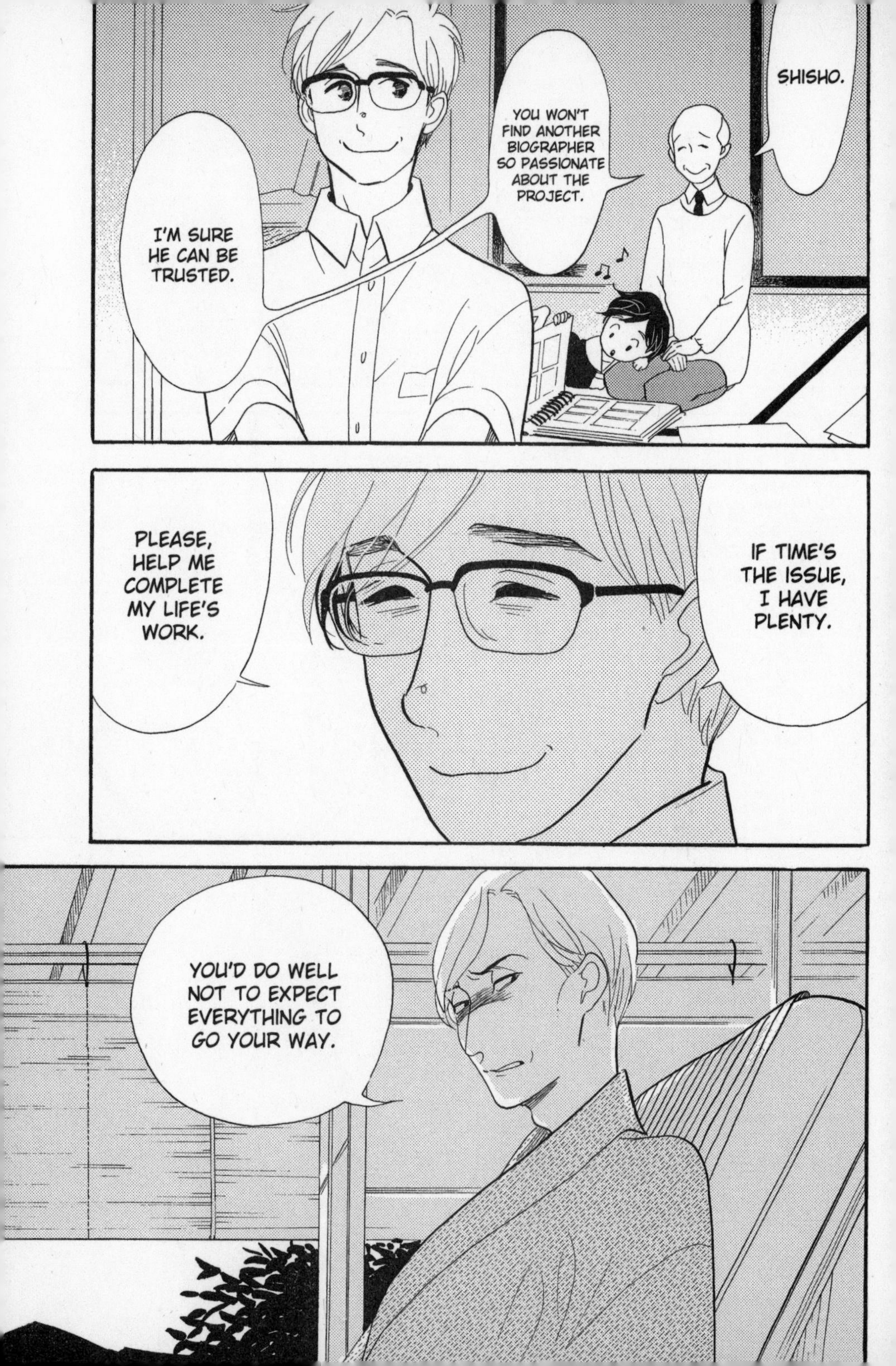
SHISHO.
YOU WON'T FIND ANOTHER BIOGRAPHER SO PASSIONATE ABOUT THE PROJECT.
I'M SURE HE CAN BE TRUSTED.
IF TIME'S THE ISSUE, I HAVE PLENTY.
PLEASE, HELP ME COMPLETE MY LIFE'S WORK.
YOU'D DO WELL NOT TO EXPECT EVERYTHING TO GO YOUR WAY.

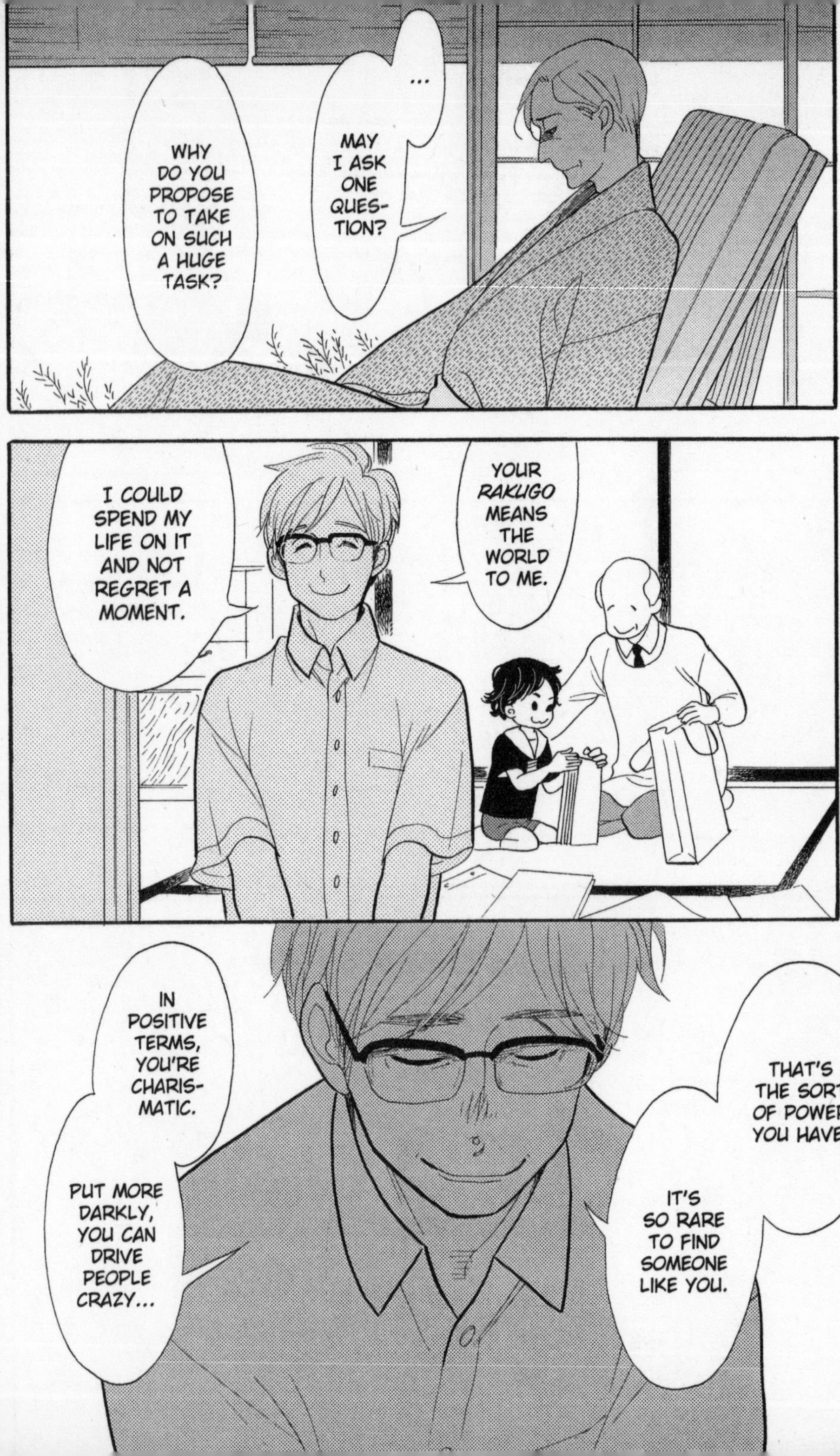
...
MAY I ASK ONE QUESTION?
WHY DO YOU PROPOSE TO TAKE ON SUCH A HUGE TASK?
YOUR *RAKUGO* MEANS THE WORLD TO ME.
I COULD SPEND MY LIFE ON IT AND NOT REGRET A MOMENT.
IN POSITIVE TERMS, YOU'RE CHARISMATIC.
PUT MORE DARKLY, YOU CAN DRIVE PEOPLE CRAZY...
THAT'S THE SORT OF POWER YOU HAVE.
IT'S SO RARE TO FIND SOMEONE LIKE YOU.

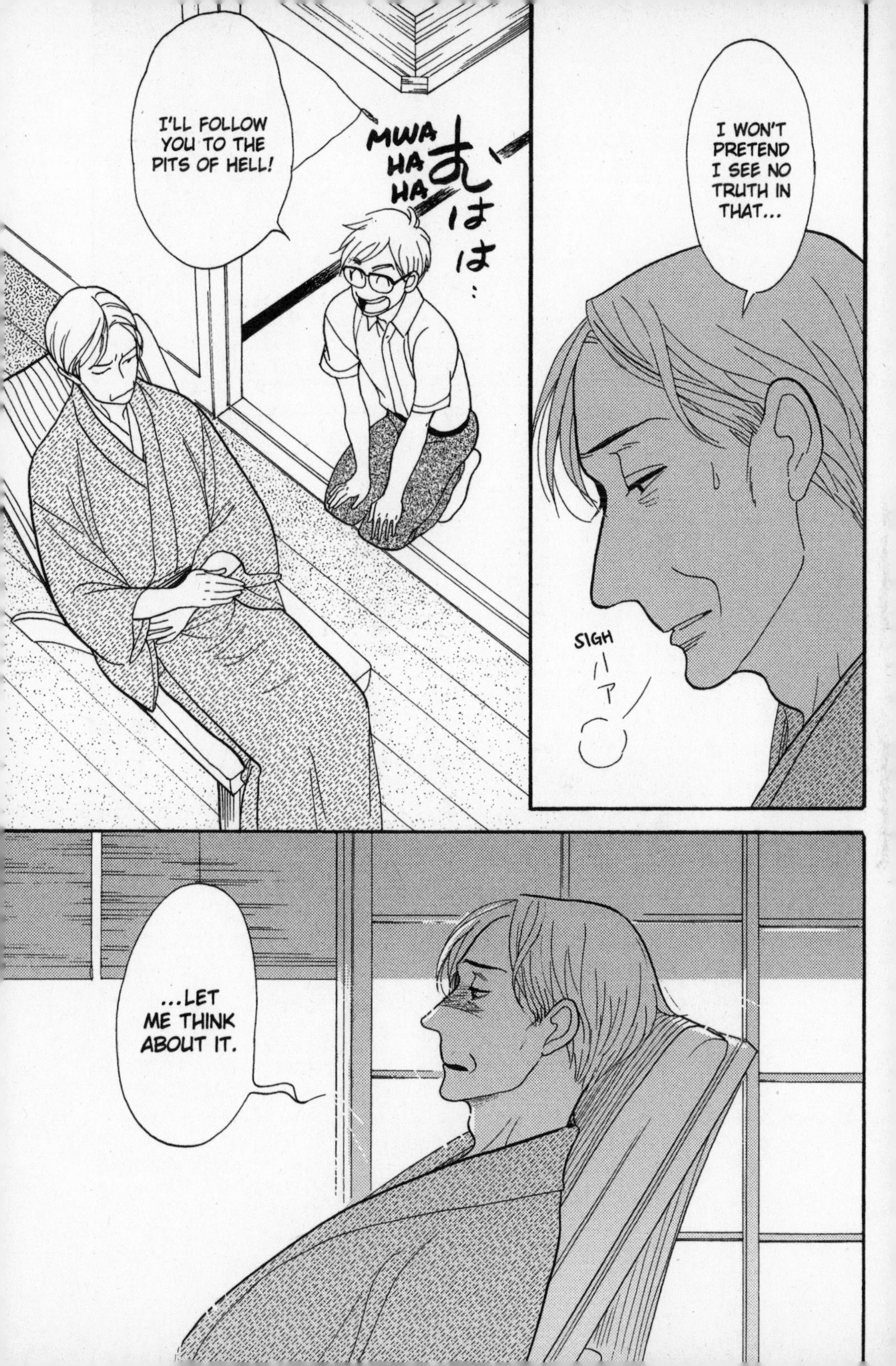
I WON'T PRETEND I SEE NO TRUTH IN THAT...
SIGH
ハァ
I'LL FOLLOW YOU TO THE PITS OF HELL!
MWA HA HA
あはは…
...LET ME THINK ABOUT IT.

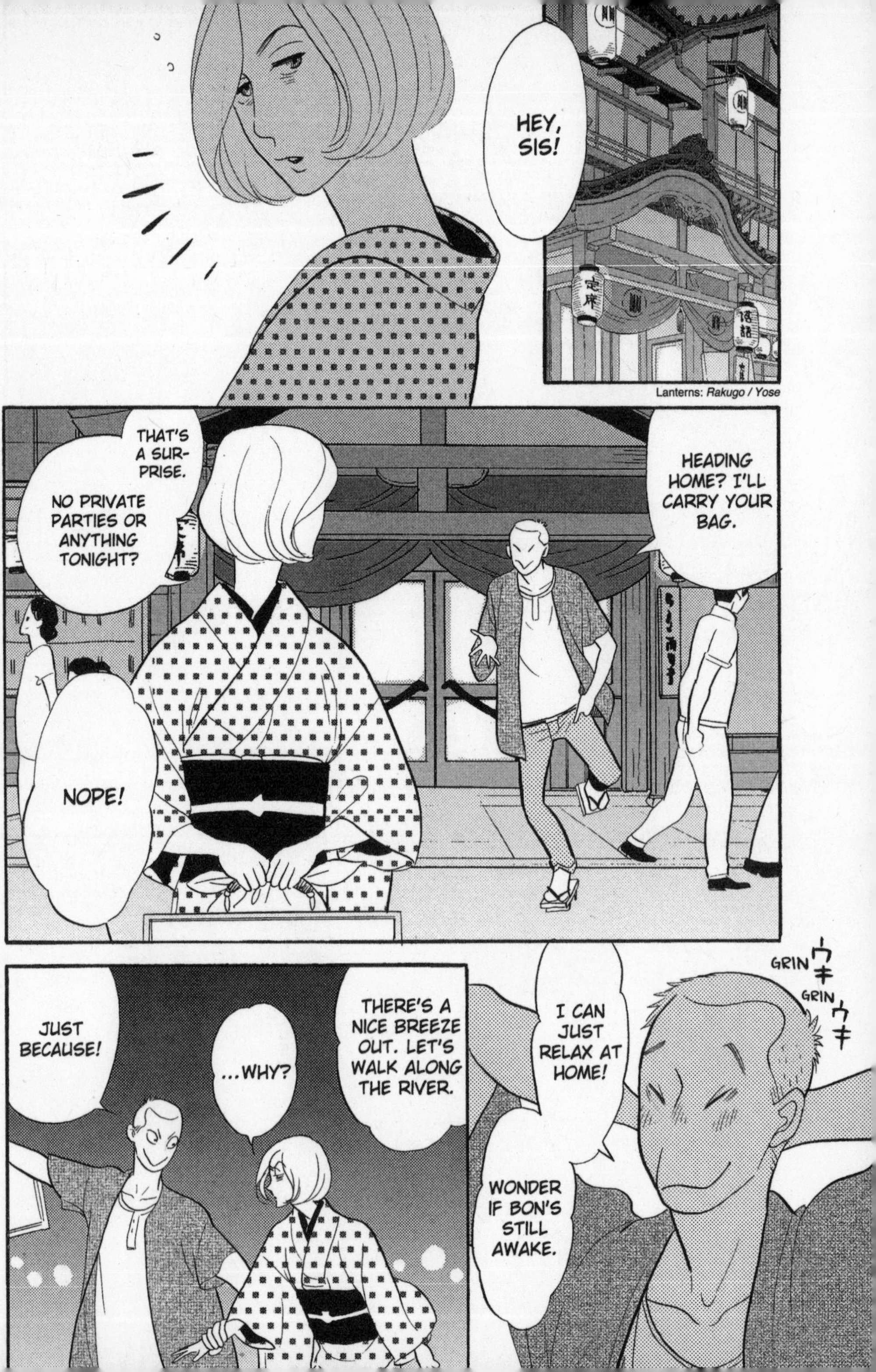
HEY, SIS!
HEADING HOME? I'LL CARRY YOUR BAG.
THAT'S A SUR-PRISE.
NO PRIVATE PARTIES OR ANYTHING TONIGHT?
NOPE!
GRIN ウキ
GRIN ウキ
I CAN JUST RELAX AT HOME!
WONDER IF BON'S STILL AWAKE.
THERE'S A NICE BREEZE OUT. LET'S WALK ALONG THE RIVER.
...WHY?
JUST BECAUSE!
Lanterns: *Rakugo* / *Yose*

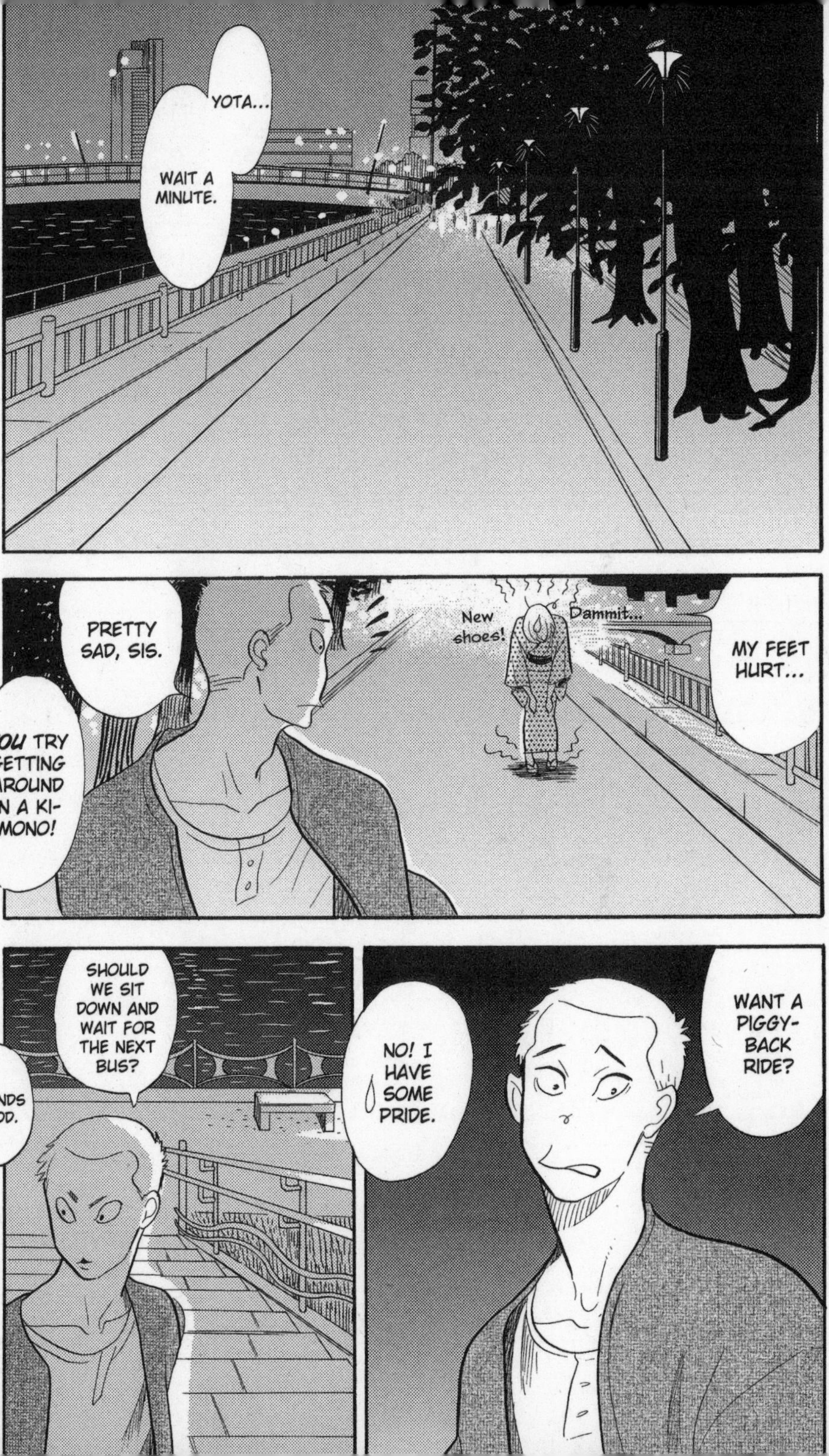
YOTA...
WAIT A MINUTE.
MY FEET HURT...
Dammit...
New shoes!
PRETTY SAD, SIS.
YOU TRY GETTING AROUND IN A KI-MONO!
WANT A PIGGY-BACK RIDE?
NO! I HAVE SOME PRIDE.
SHOULD WE SIT DOWN AND WAIT FOR THE NEXT BUS?
SOUNDS GOOD.

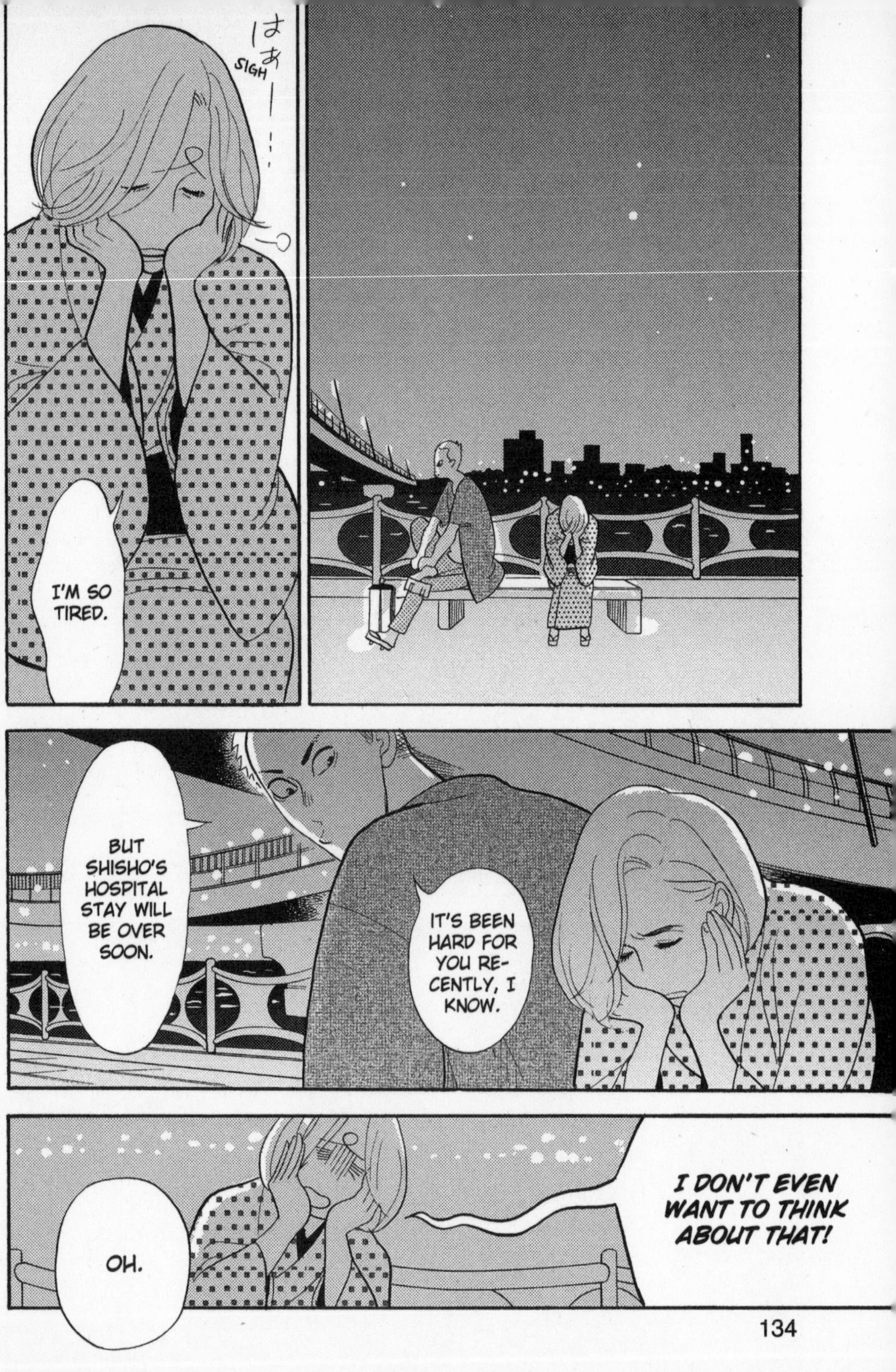
はあー!!
SIGH
I'M SO TIRED.
IT'S BEEN HARD FOR YOU RE-CENTLY, I KNOW.
BUT SHISHO'S HOSPITAL STAY WILL BE OVER SOON.
I DON'T EVEN WANT TO THINK ABOUT THAT!
OH.

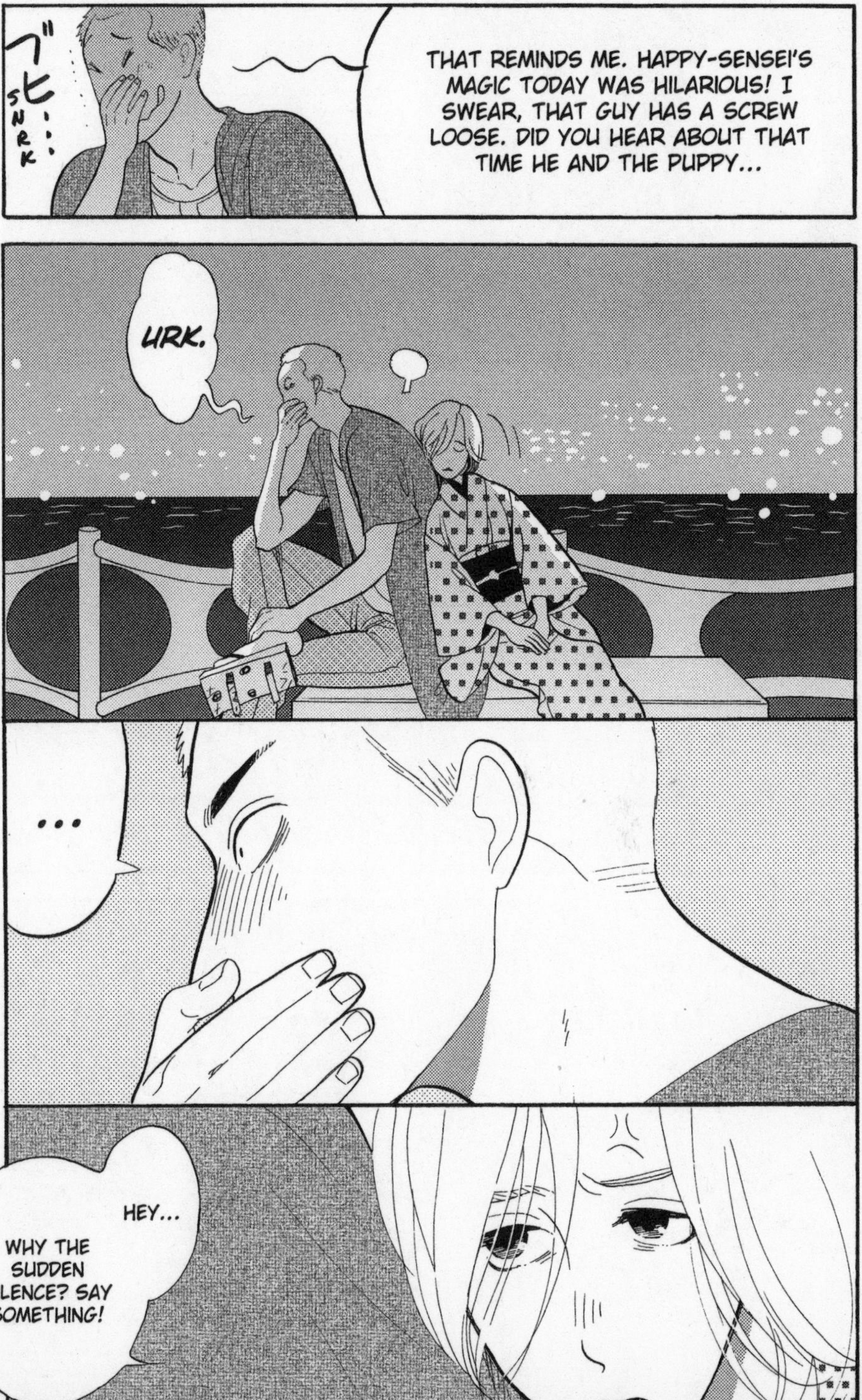
THAT REMINDS ME. HAPPY-SENSEI'S MAGIC TODAY WAS HILARIOUS! I SWEAR, THAT GUY HAS A SCREW LOOSE. DID YOU HEAR ABOUT THAT TIME HE AND THE PUPPY...
ブヒ
SNRK
URK.
...
HEY...
WHY THE SUDDEN SILENCE? SAY SOMETHING!

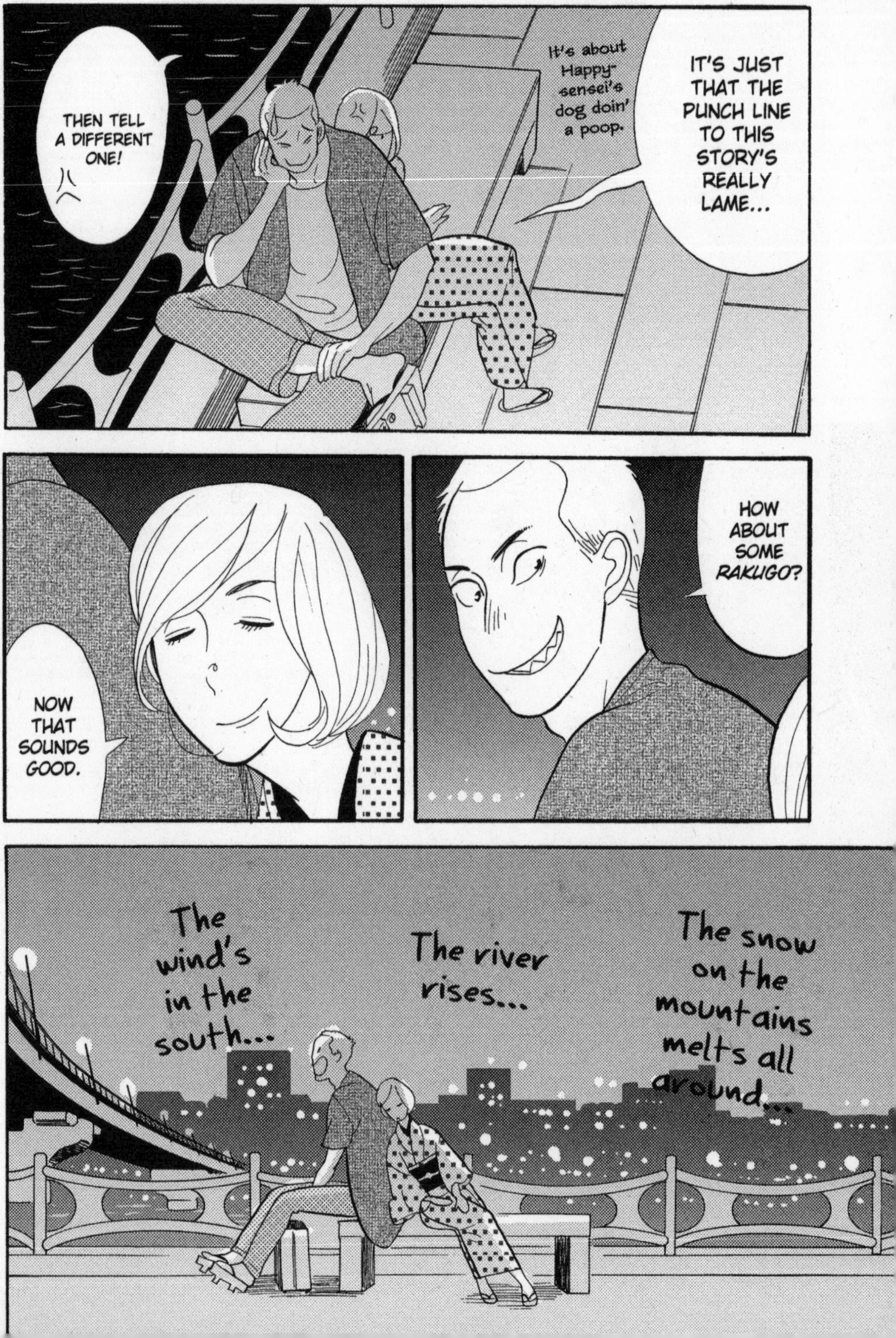
IT'S JUST THAT THE PUNCH LINE TO THIS STORY'S REALLY LAME...
It's about Happy-sensei's dog doin' a poop.
THEN TELL A DIFFERENT ONE!
HOW ABOUT SOME *RAKUGO*?
NOW THAT SOUNDS GOOD.
The snow on the mountains melts all around...
The river rises...
The wind's in the south...

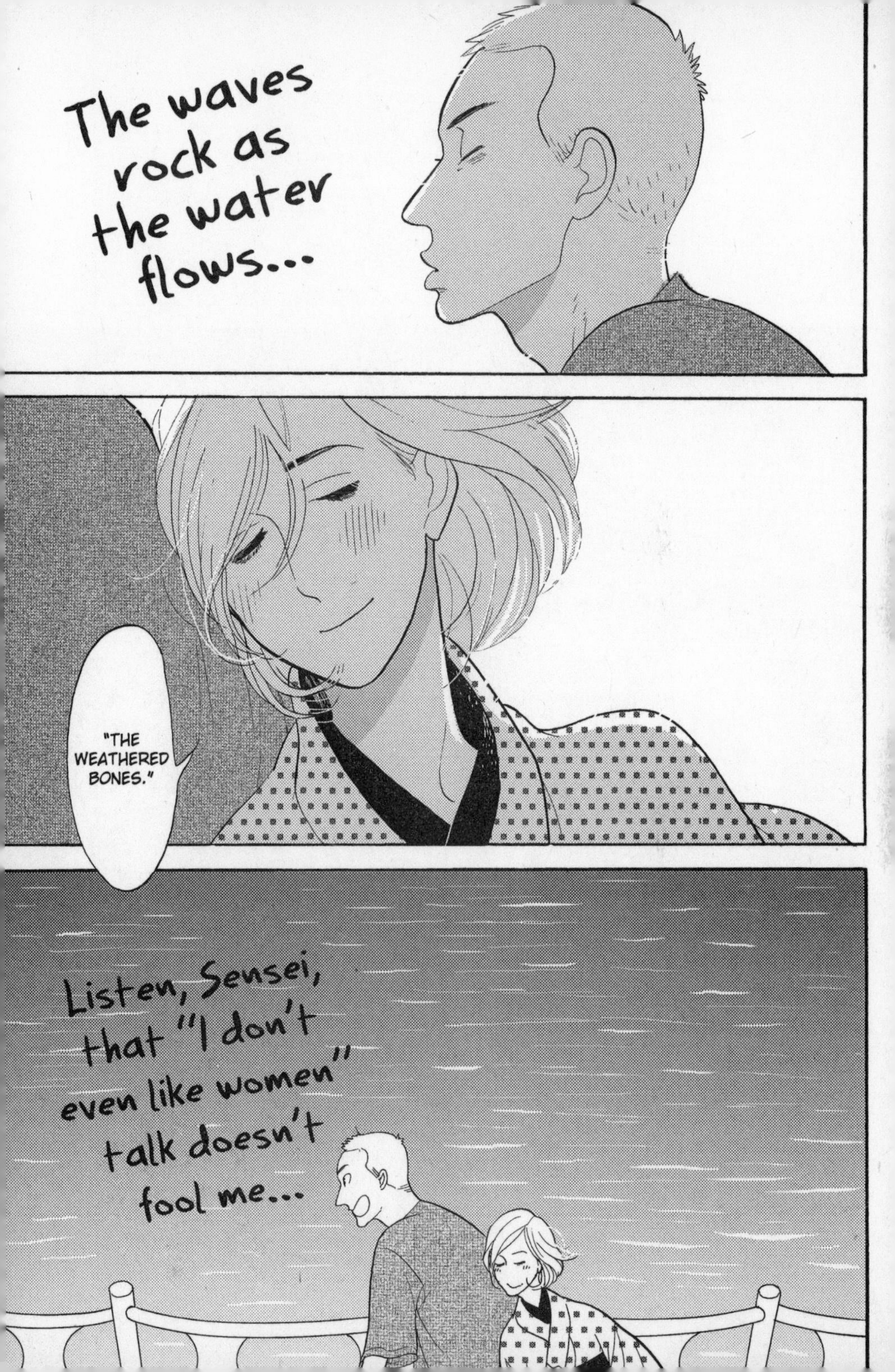
The waves rock as the water flows...
"THE WEATHERED BONES."
Listen, Sensei, that "I don't even like women" talk doesn't fool me...

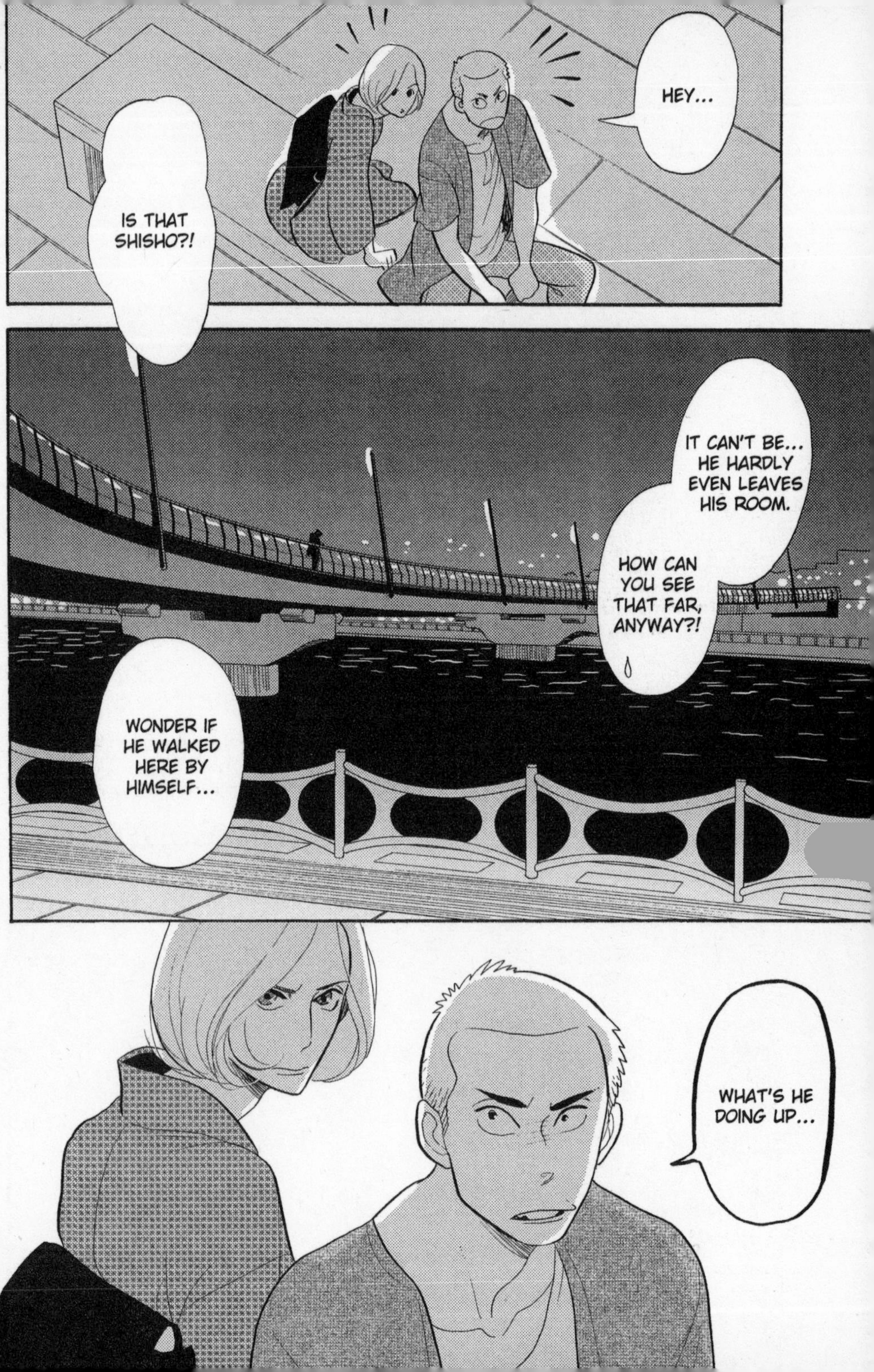
HEY...
IS THAT SHISHO?!
IT CAN'T BE... HE HARDLY EVEN LEAVES HIS ROOM.
HOW CAN YOU SEE THAT FAR, ANYWAY?!
WONDER IF HE WALKED HERE BY HIMSELF...
WHAT'S HE DOING UP...

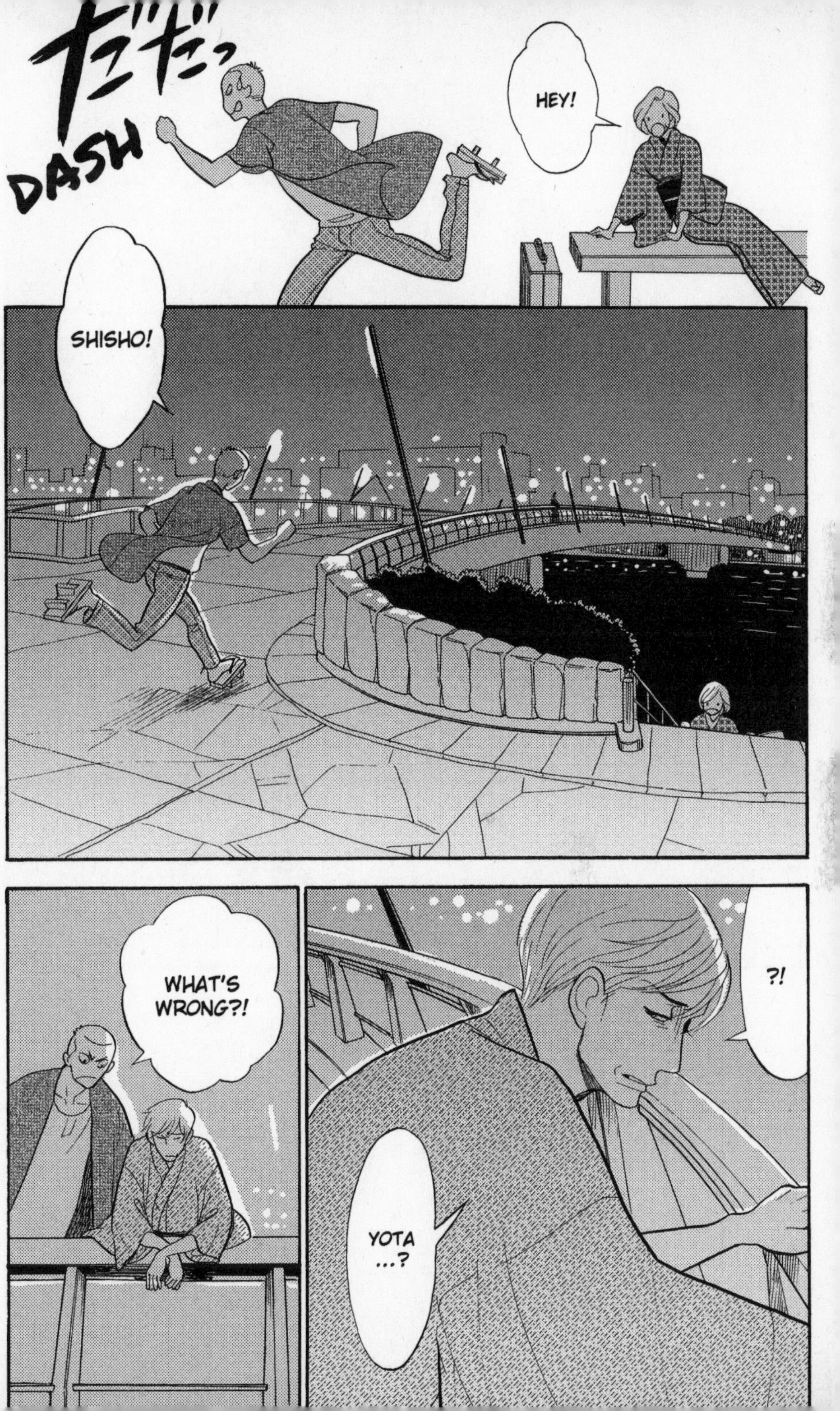
HEY!
DASH
SHISHO!
?!
YOTA ...?
WHAT'S WRONG?!

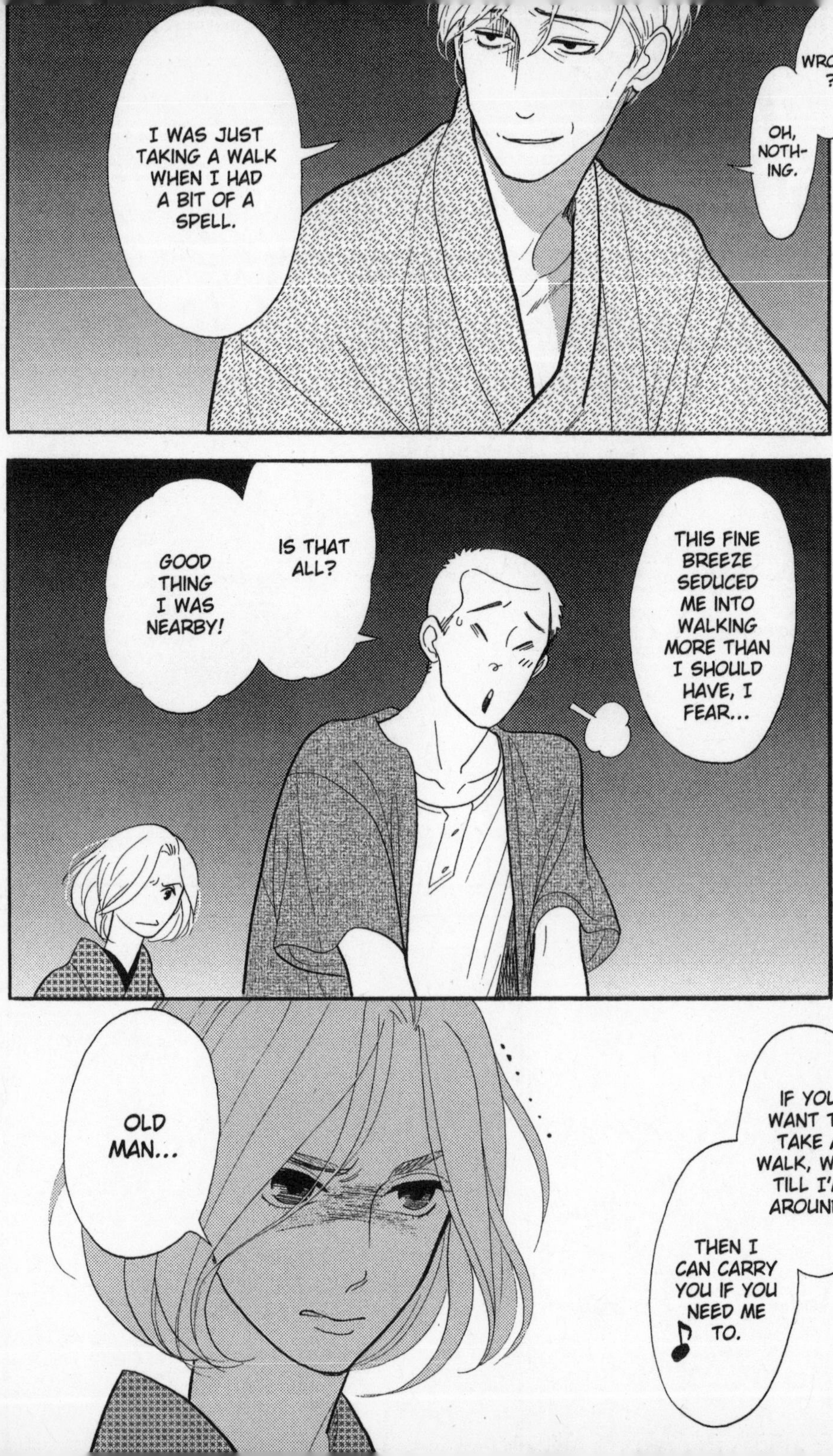
WRONG?
OH, NOTHING.
I WAS JUST TAKING A WALK WHEN I HAD A BIT OF A SPELL.
THIS FINE BREEZE SEDUCED ME INTO WALKING MORE THAN I SHOULD HAVE, I FEAR...
IS THAT ALL?
GOOD THING I WAS NEARBY!
IF YOU WANT TO TAKE A WALK, WAIT TILL I'M AROUND.
THEN I CAN CARRY YOU IF YOU NEED ME TO. ♪
OLD MAN...

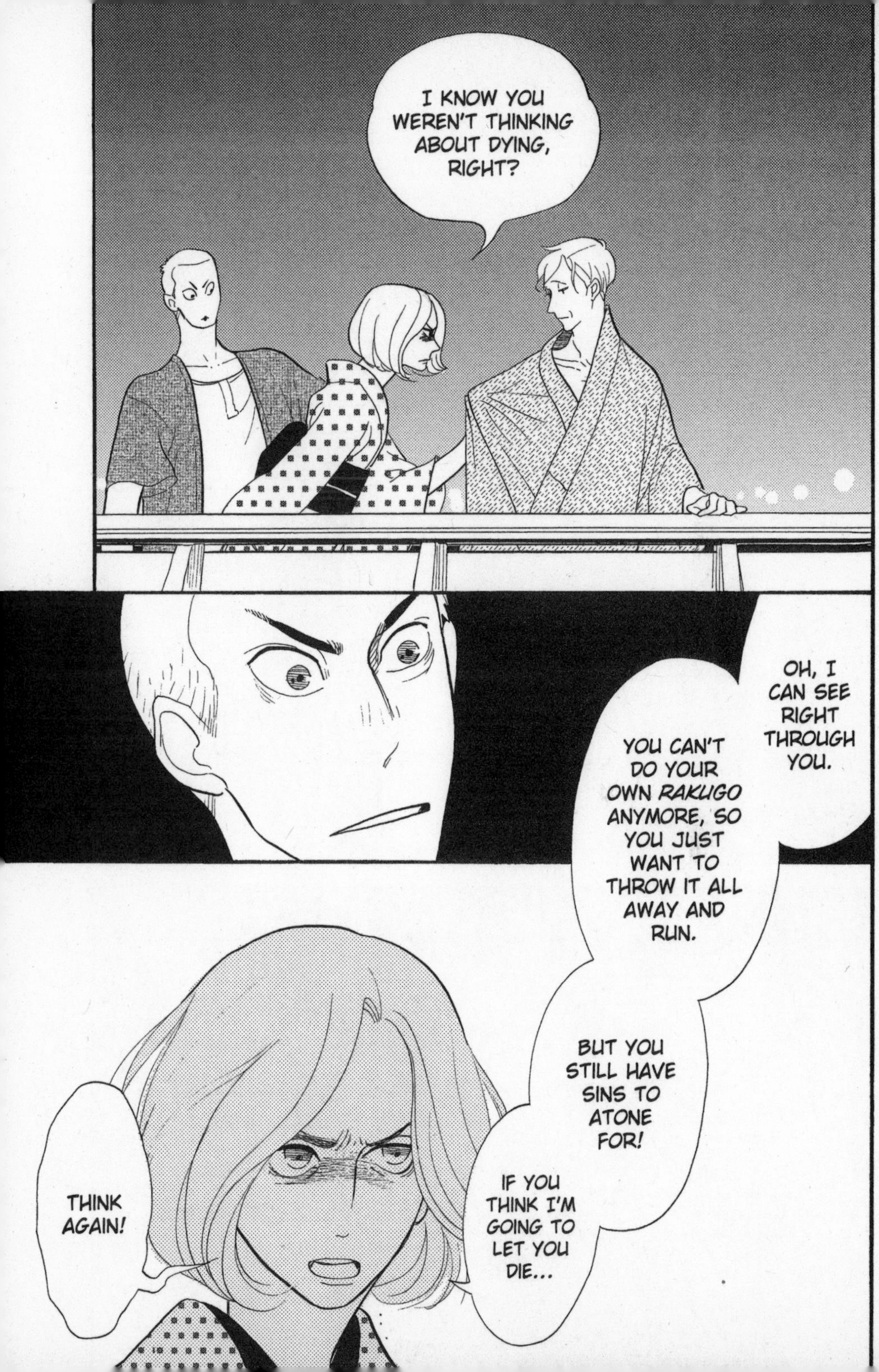
I KNOW YOU WEREN'T THINKING ABOUT DYING, RIGHT?
OH, I CAN SEE RIGHT THROUGH YOU.
YOU CAN'T DO YOUR OWN *RAKUGO* ANYMORE, SO YOU JUST WANT TO THROW IT ALL AWAY AND RUN.
BUT YOU STILL HAVE SINS TO ATONE FOR!
IF YOU THINK I'M GOING TO LET YOU DIE...
THINK AGAIN!

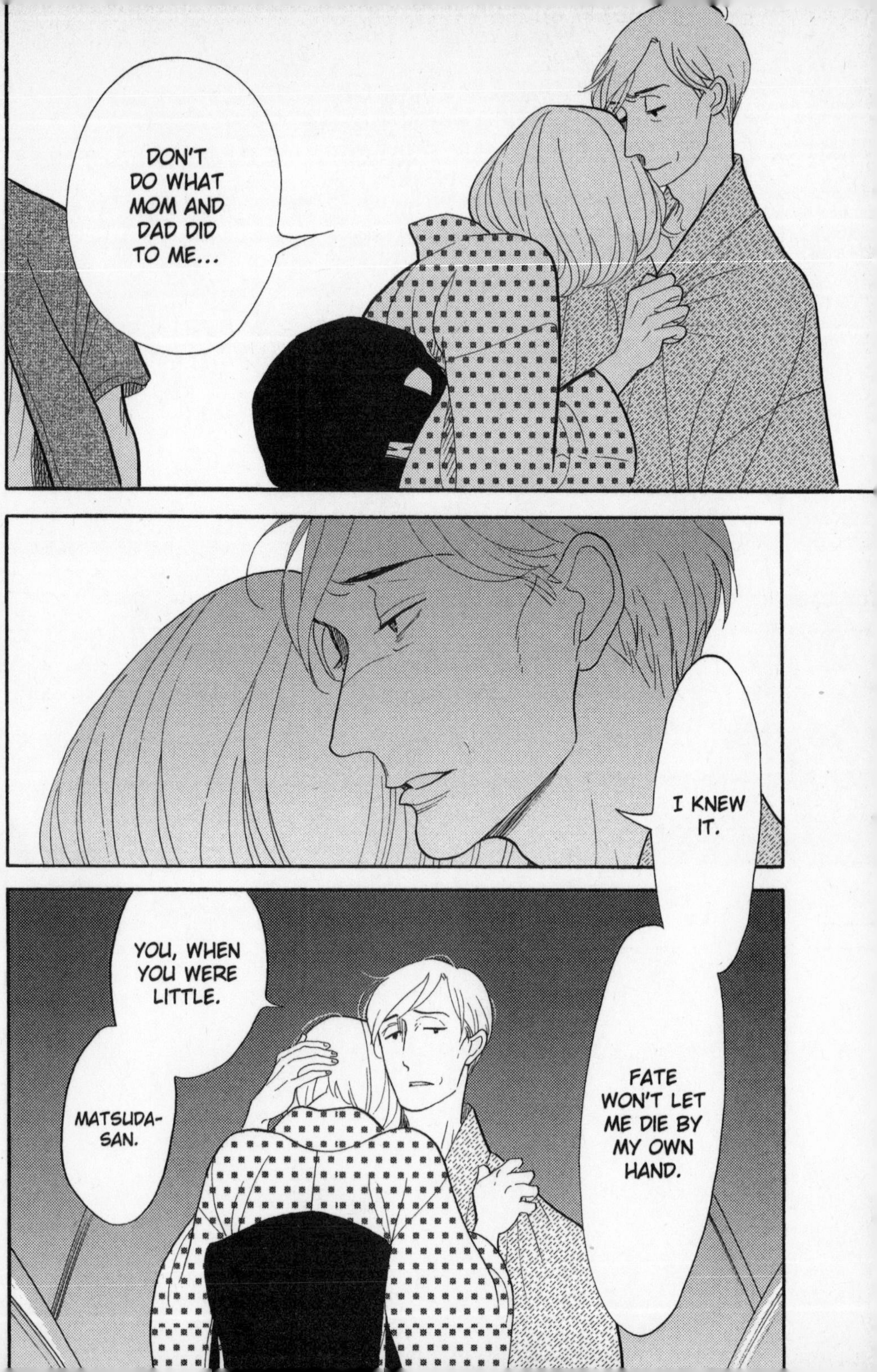
DON'T DO WHAT MOM AND DAD DID TO ME...
I KNEW IT.
FATE WON'T LET ME DIE BY MY OWN HAND.
YOU, WHEN YOU WERE LITTLE.
MATSUDA-SAN.

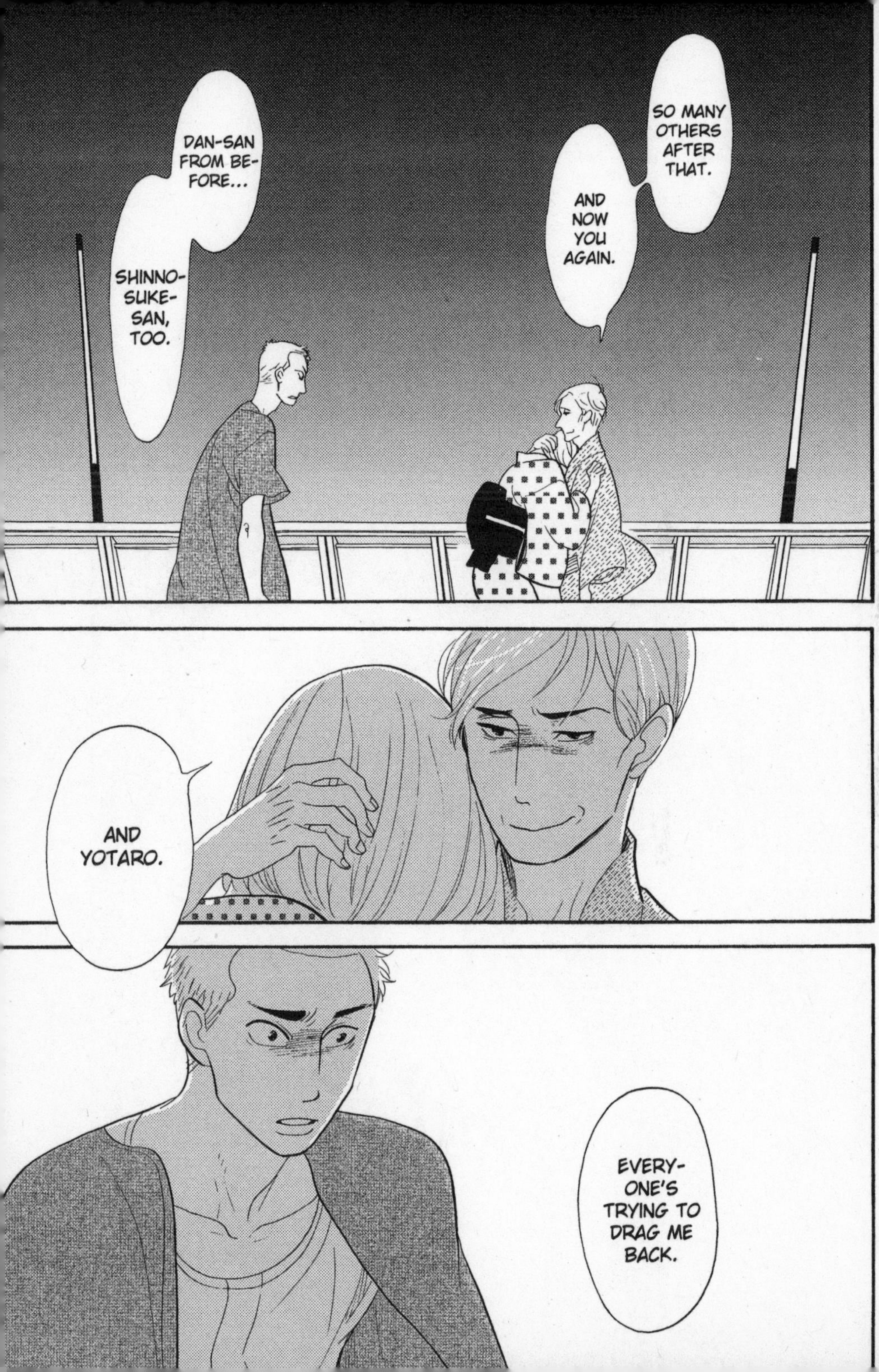
SO MANY OTHERS AFTER THAT.
AND NOW YOU AGAIN.
DAN-SAN FROM BEFORE…
SHINNO-SUKE-SAN, TOO.
AND YOTARO.
EVERY-ONE'S TRYING TO DRAG ME BACK.

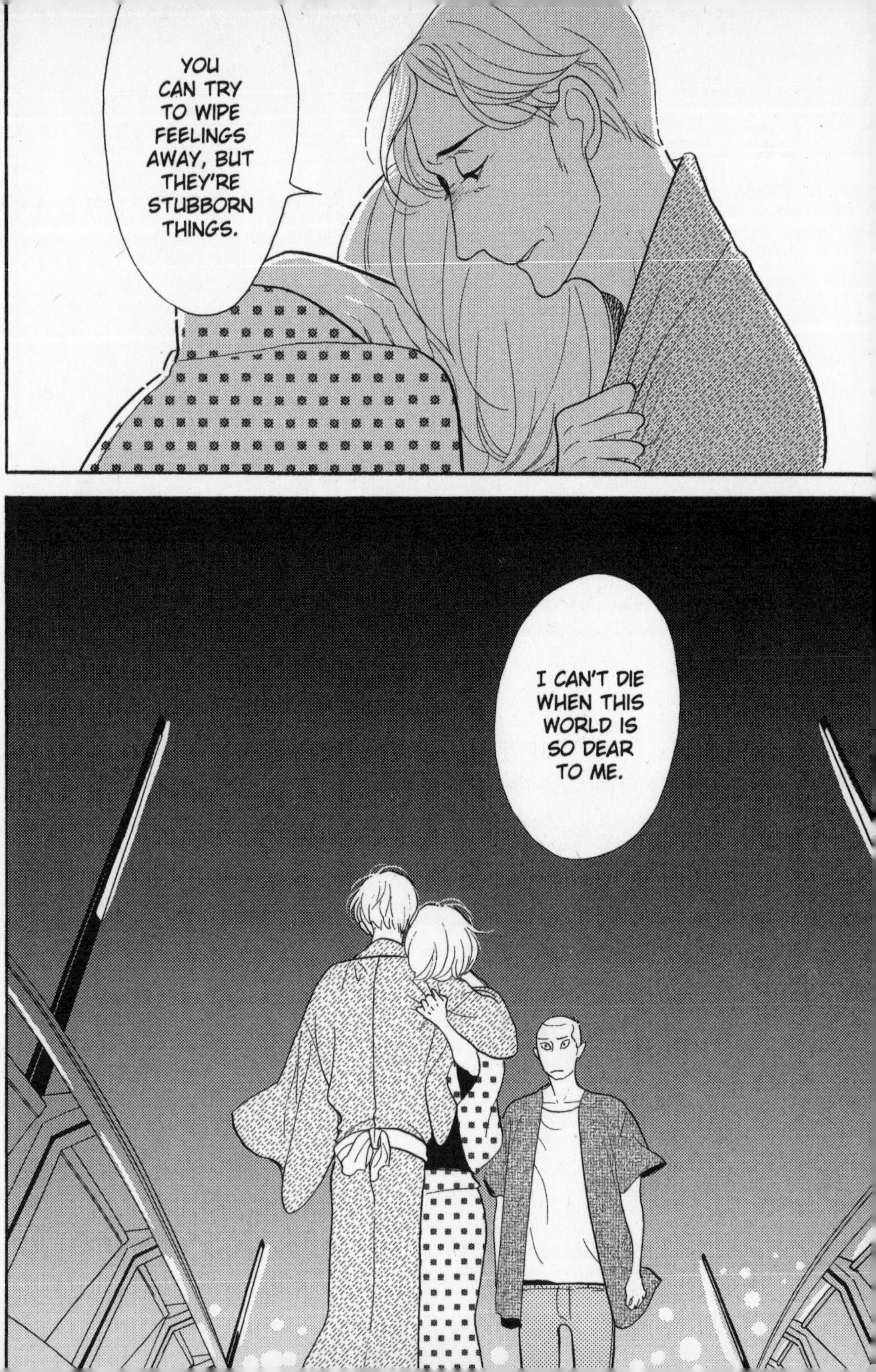
YOU CAN TRY TO WIPE FEELINGS AWAY, BUT THEY'RE STUBBORN THINGS.
I CAN'T DIE WHEN THIS WORLD IS SO DEAR TO ME.

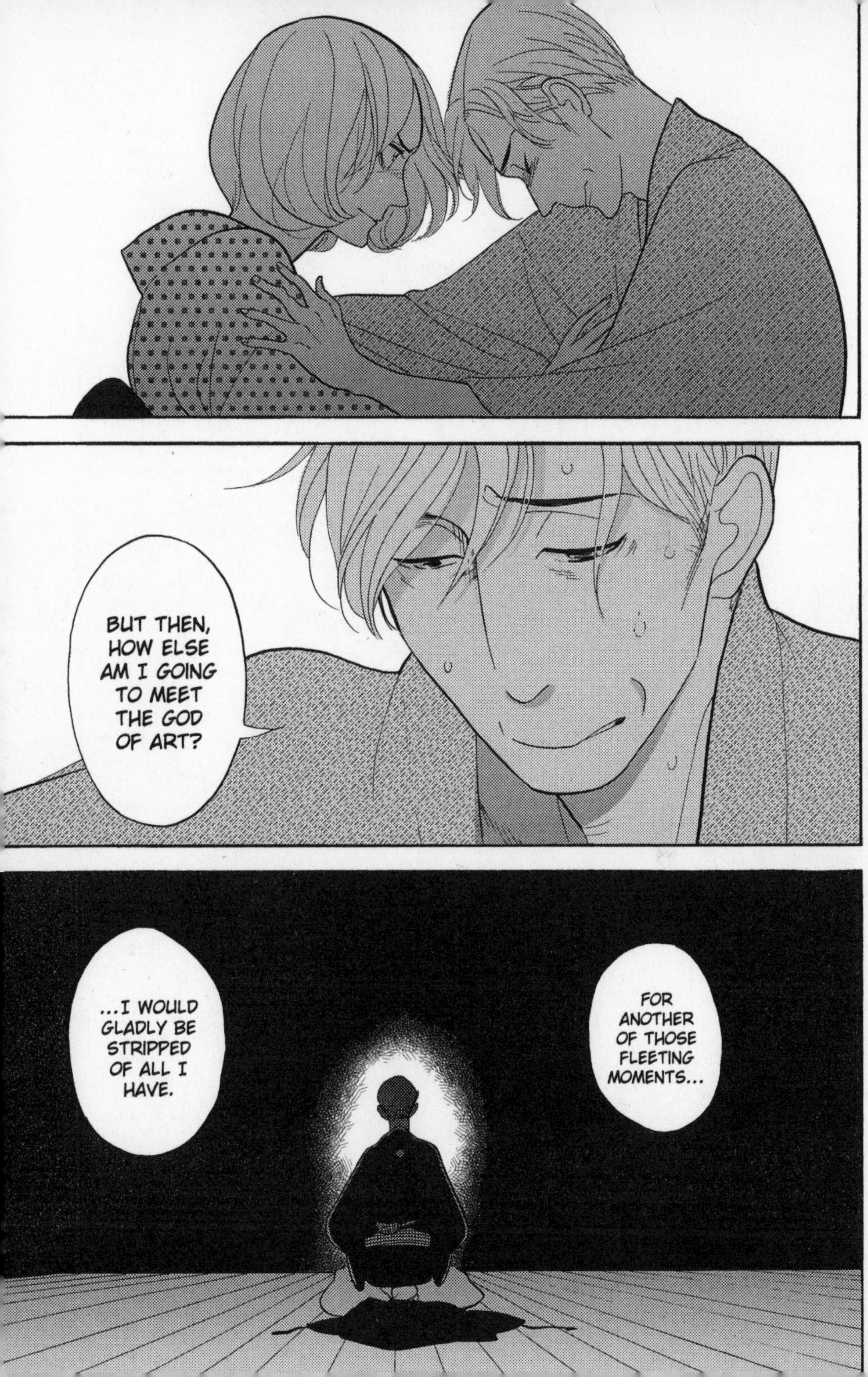
BUT THEN, HOW ELSE AM I GOING TO MEET THE GOD OF ART?
FOR ANOTHER OF THOSE FLEETING MOMENTS...
...I WOULD GLADLY BE STRIPPED OF ALL I HAVE.

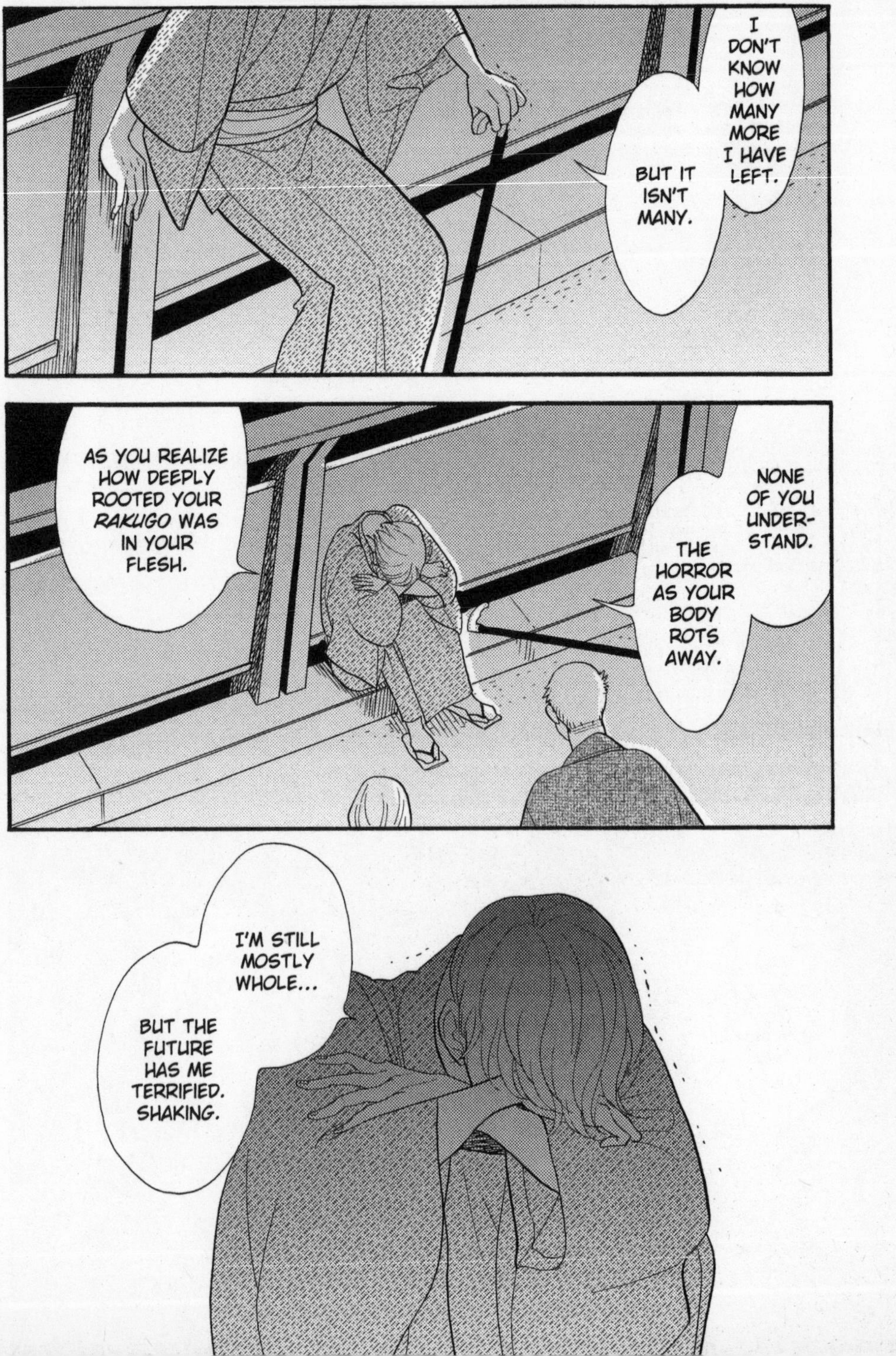
I DON'T KNOW HOW MANY MORE I HAVE LEFT.
BUT IT ISN'T MANY.
NONE OF YOU UNDER-STAND.
THE HORROR AS YOUR BODY ROTS AWAY.
AS YOU REALIZE HOW DEEPLY ROOTED YOUR *RAKUGO* WAS IN YOUR FLESH.
I'M STILL MOSTLY WHOLE...
BUT THE FUTURE HAS ME TERRIFIED. SHAKING.

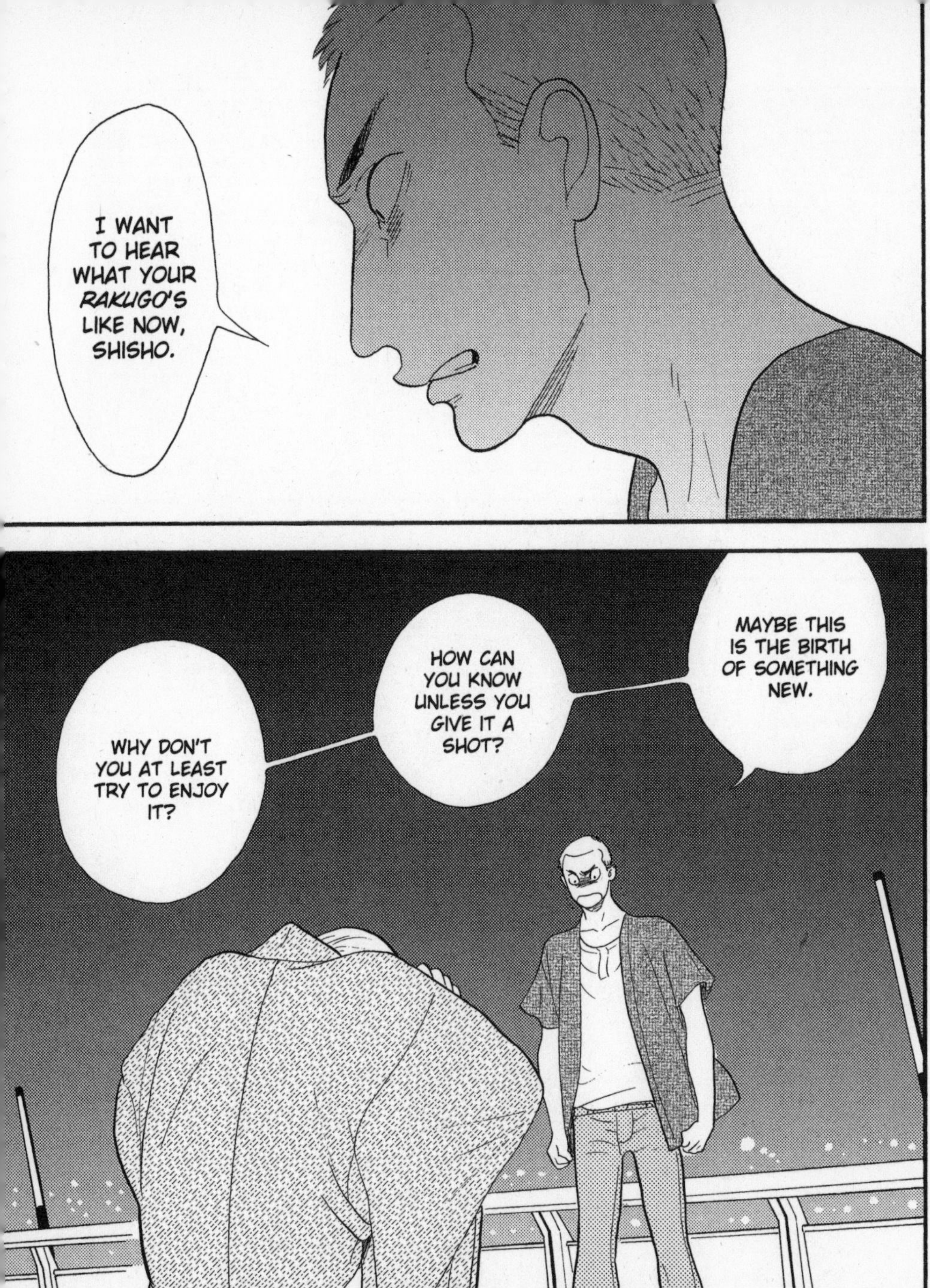
I WANT TO HEAR WHAT YOUR *RAKUGO*'S LIKE NOW, SHISHO.
MAYBE THIS IS THE BIRTH OF SOMETHING NEW.
HOW CAN YOU KNOW UNLESS YOU GIVE IT A SHOT?
WHY DON'T YOU AT LEAST TRY TO ENJOY IT?

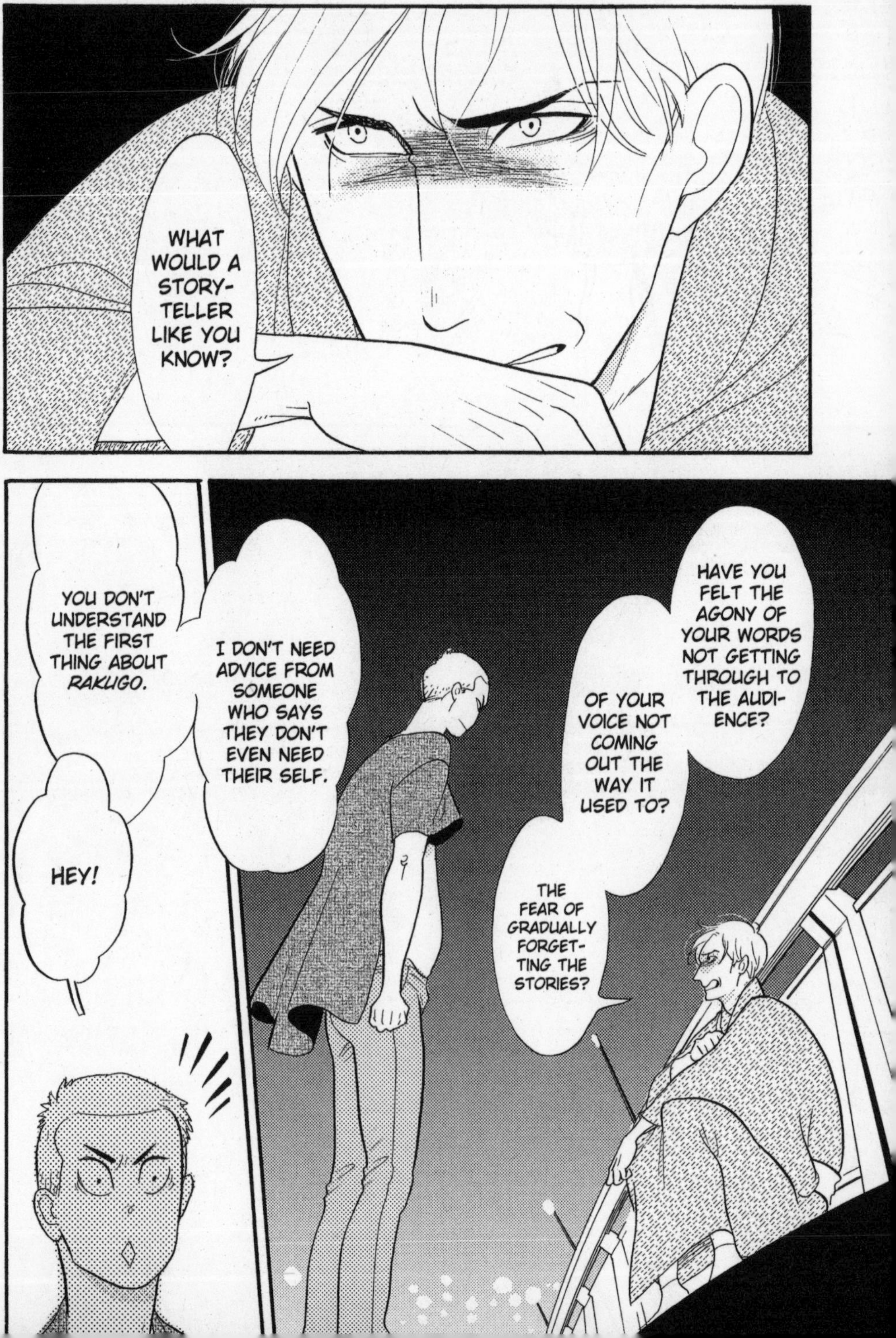
WHAT WOULD A STORY-TELLER LIKE YOU KNOW?
HAVE YOU FELT THE AGONY OF YOUR WORDS NOT GETTING THROUGH TO THE AUDI-ENCE?
OF YOUR VOICE NOT COMING OUT THE WAY IT USED TO?
THE FEAR OF GRADUALLY FORGET-TING THE STORIES?
I DON'T NEED ADVICE FROM SOMEONE WHO SAYS THEY DON'T EVEN NEED THEIR SELF.
YOU DON'T UNDERSTAND THE FIRST THING ABOUT *RAKUGO.*
HEY!

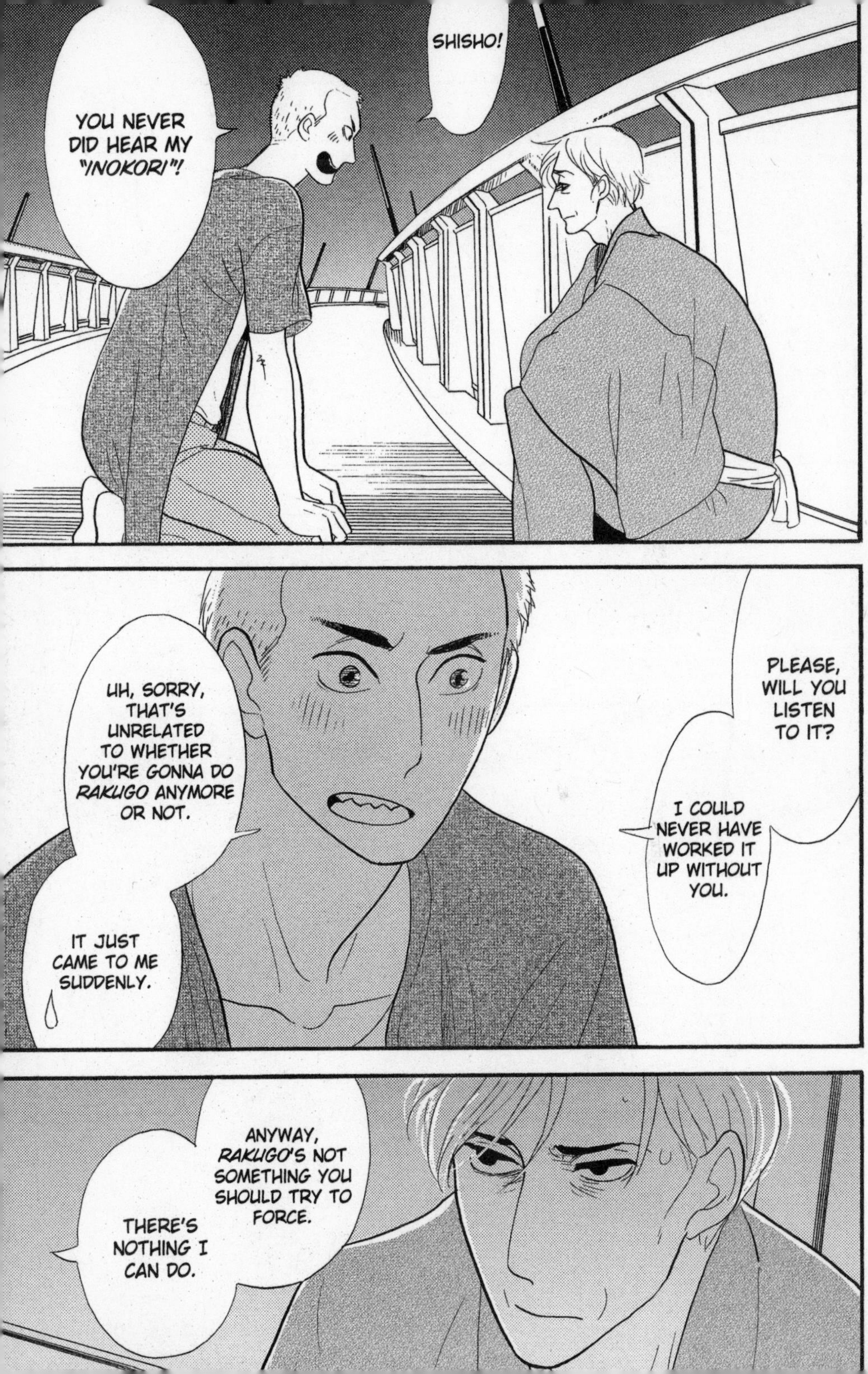

SHISHO!
YOU NEVER DID HEAR MY "*INOKORI*"!
PLEASE, WILL YOU LISTEN TO IT?
I COULD NEVER HAVE WORKED IT UP WITHOUT YOU.
UH, SORRY, THAT'S UNRELATED TO WHETHER YOU'RE GONNA DO *RAKUGO* ANYMORE OR NOT.
IT JUST CAME TO ME SUDDENLY.
ANYWAY, *RAKUGO*'S NOT SOMETHING YOU SHOULD TRY TO FORCE.
THERE'S NOTHING I CAN DO.

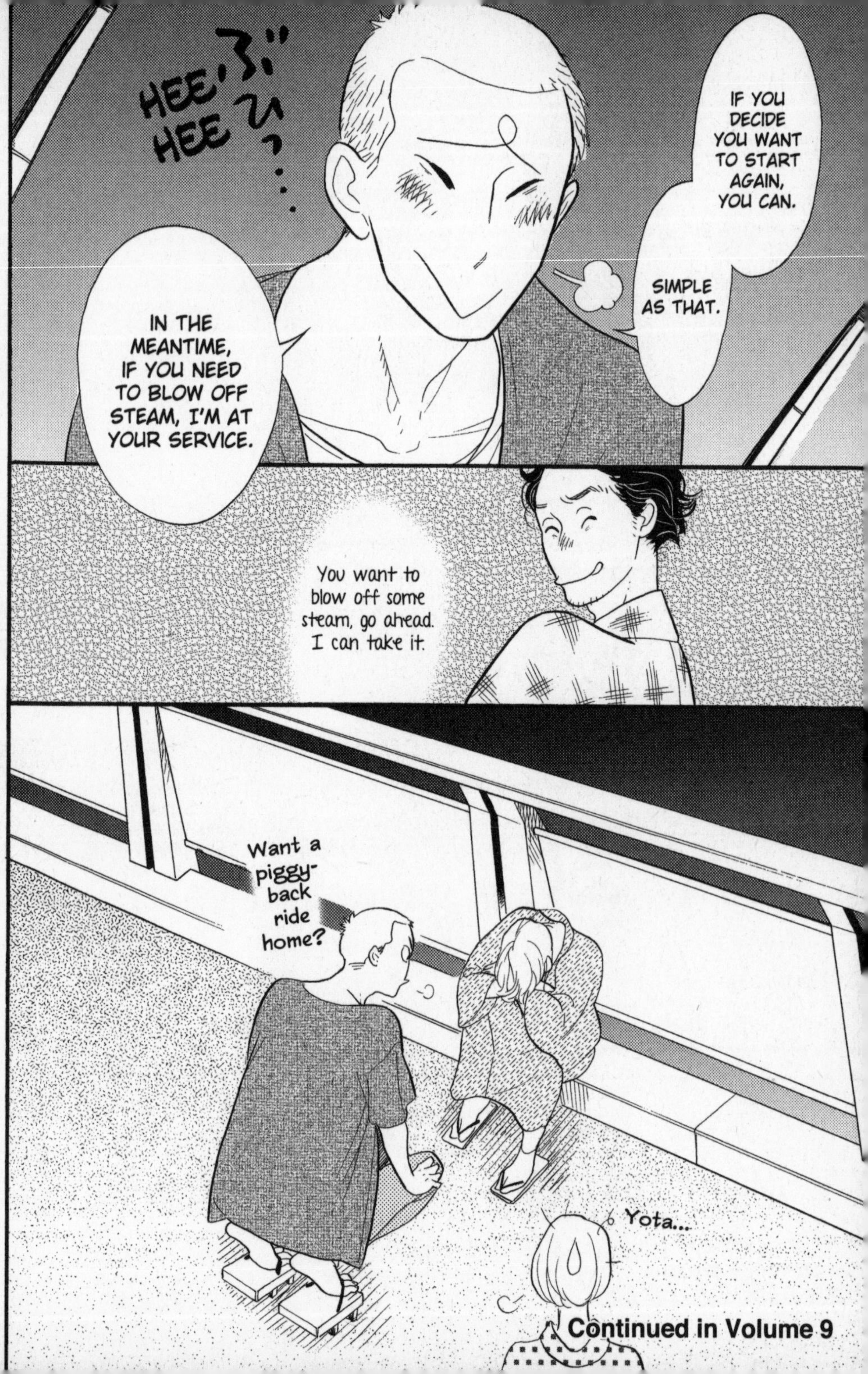
IF YOU DECIDE YOU WANT TO START AGAIN, YOU CAN.
SIMPLE AS THAT.
ぶひっ...
HEE HEE
IN THE MEANTIME, IF YOU NEED TO BLOW OFF STEAM, I'M AT YOUR SERVICE.
You want to blow off some steam, go ahead. I can take it.
Want a piggy-back ride home?
Yota...
Continued in Volume 9

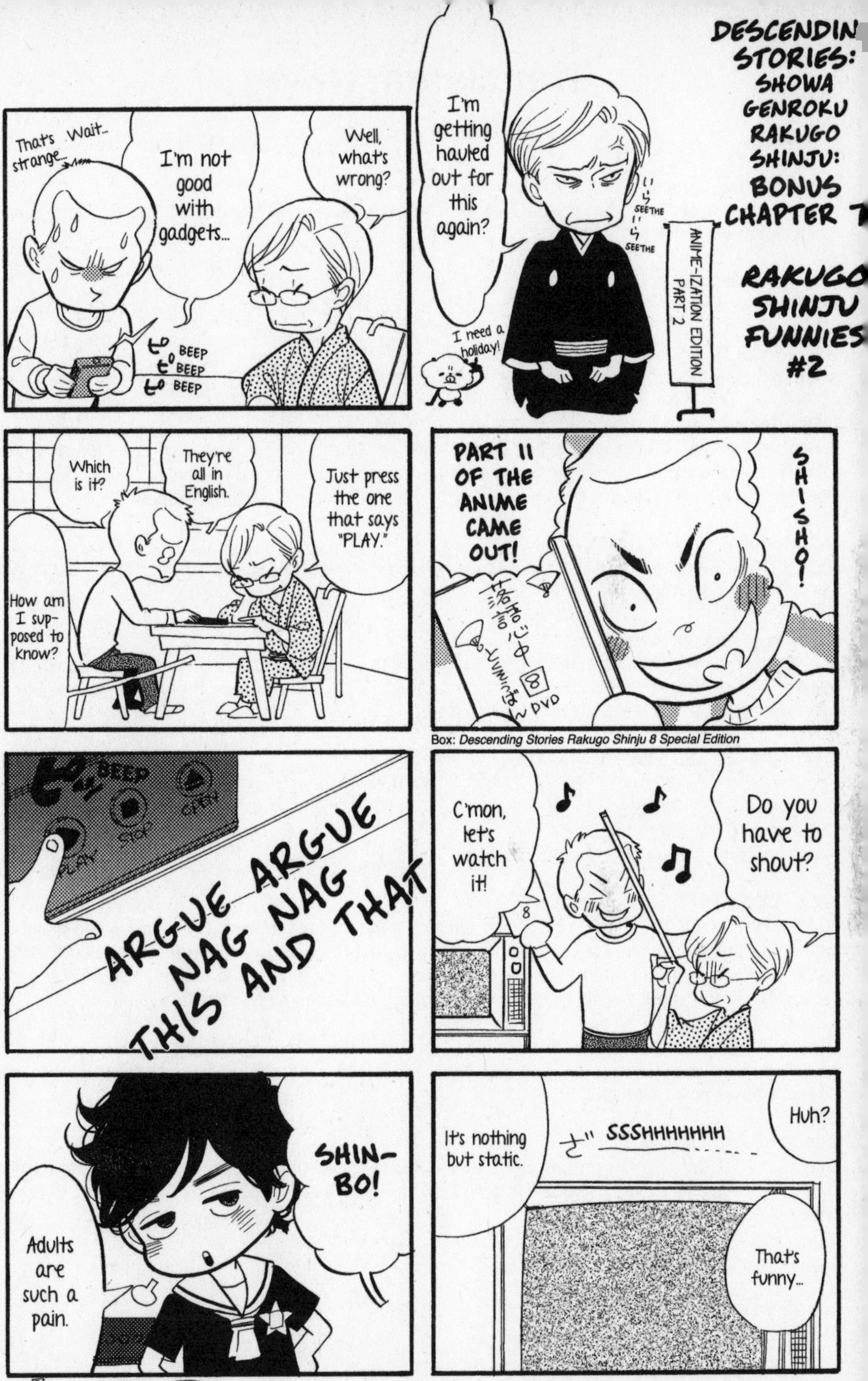
DESCENDING STORIES: SHOWA GENROKU RAKUGO SHINJU: BONUS CHAPTER
RAKUGO SHINJU FUNNIES #2
I'm getting hauled out for this again?
SEETHE SEETHE
ANIME-IZATION EDITION PART 2
I need a holiday!
Well, what's wrong?
I'm not good with gadgets...
Wait...
That's strange...
BEEP BEEP BEEP
SHISHO!
PART 11 OF THE ANIME CAME OUT!
落語心中 8
DVD
Just press the one that says "PLAY."
They're all in English.
Which is it?
How am I supposed to know?
Do you have to shout?
C'mon, let's watch it!
BEEP
OPEN
STOP
PLAY
ARGUE ARGUE NAG NAG THIS AND THAT
Huh?
SSSHHHHHHH
It's nothing but static.
That's funny...
SHIN-BO!
Adults are such a pain.

Box: *Descending Stories Rakugo Shinju 8 Special Edition*

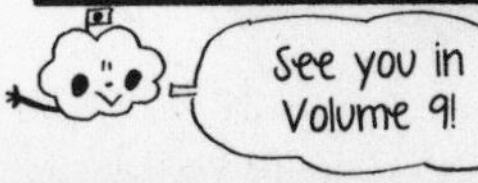
See you in Volume 9!

Thanks to: Tomizawa-sama at *Itan*, all my assistants, the anime team, Yasuko Inoue and Sawa Sakura for help with the Kyoto dialect

Translation Notes

Waka-danna, page 15
Literally "young master," this phrase can refer to a young man in general or the relatively young heir to a family business.

Kamigata, page 17
An older name for the Kyoto–Osaka region, often viewed in opposition to "Edo" (modern Tokyo).

Haori, **page 19**
A kind of jacket worn over traditional Japanese clothing.

Hatsu Tenjin **festival, page 19**
A famous festival in Osaka, the first (*hatsu*) festival of the year in honor of ancient Japanese scholar Sugawara no Michizane (whose shrines are called Tenmangu or Tenjin). "*Hatsu Tenjin*" is also the name of this *rakugo* story, which was originally from the Kamigata tradition.

O-Danna-san, page 24
Roughly equivalent to "master of the house." This is the *sekitei* or *yose* manager of the Uchikutei, where Yotaro performs.

That big quake out west, page 25
The Great Hanshin Earthquake of January 17, 1995. Over 6,000 people lost their lives and 400,000 buildings were irreparably damaged, mostly in the city of Kobe. It was the worst earthquake in Japan since the Great Kanto Earthquake of 1923.

End of Taisho…Edo period, page 26
The Taisho era lasted from 1912 to 1926. The Edo period lasted from 1603 to 1868.

Yakumo-shi, page 59
In this context, -*shi* is a shorter form of *shisho*.

Itako, page 64
"Itako-bushi," a folk song dating back to the Edo period. The name evokes the renowned pleasure quarters of Itako in Hitachi Province (modern-day Ibaraki Prefecture). Yakumo started using "Itako-bushi" as his *debayashi* (entry music) to this after the death of his own shisho, Yakumo VII—but before he went in search of Miyokichi and Sukeroku. See Volume 4 for details.

"Benkei and Komachi/Sure were dummies/Don't you think, honey?", page 65
As noted in volume 7, this slightly risqué *senryu* is based on the popular legends of Benkei and Komachi having died virgins.

O-Inari-sama, page 66
Inari is one of the most important gods in Japan, being responsible for agriculture, prosperity, fertility, rice, tea, saké, and more. Shrines to Inari are usually recognizable by their statues of Inari's messenger, the fox.

Out behind Kannon Temple, page 66
"Kannon Temple" is another name for Asakusa's large Sensoji Temple. As mentioned in a few earlier volumes, "behind Kannon Temple" was a euphemism for the old red light district.

Oiran, page 68
The highest class of courtesan.

Amanatto, page 68
Dried, candied adzuki beans. Genbei and Tasuke are having *amanatto* for breakfast.

Namu Myoho Renge Kyo, page 80
An important mantra in several forms of Japanese Buddhism, literally expressing devotion to the Lotus Sutra.

Banana vendor, page 98
Japan has a tradition of selling bananas with the same sort of noisemakers and fast talk, called *banana no tataki-uri.*

I, who have finally taken the stage…, page 100
The traditional opening of "Journey to the East," this is a complicated piece of wordplay (for example, "the monk on duty" is homophonous with what would be "the fifth act") that is more about establishing rhythm and atmosphere than conveying meaning as such.

Koban, page 106
An oval gold coin used in the Edo period with a face value of one *ryo*, which was supposed to be enough to buy a year's supply of rice.

Hokan, page 106
As noted in volume 3, a *hokan*, also known as a *taikomochi* ("drum bearer"), is essentially the male equivalent of a geisha—although they predated female geisha by hundreds of years. In earlier centuries they served as advisors and conversation partners to feudal lords, but by the Edo period, the job chiefly involved keeping party guests entertained with jokes, skits, and games.

"Dan-san"! I've only engaged your services once, page 120
"Dan-san" is short for "Danna-san," a term of respect for a master; Higuchi is jokingly objecting that he doesn't deserve the sobriquet. (The "once" he is referring to is their meeting in volume 6.)

RAKUGO STORIES IN THIS VOLUME:

Hatsu Tenjin (初天神) - The First Tenjin Festival (page 19)
Shibahama (芝浜) - On Shibahama Beach (page 46)
Akegarasu (明烏) - The Morning Crow (page 64)
Higashi no Tabi (東の旅) - Journey to the East (page 100)
Nozarashi (野ざらし) - The Weathered Bones (pages 114, 118, 137)
Kogane Mochi (黄金餅) - The Golden Rice Cake (page 117)
Gojo-kyu (強情灸) - The Stubborn Moxa (page 117)
Yumekin (夢金) - The Dream Reward (page 123)

DESCENDING STORIES

SHOWA
GENROKU
RAKUGO
SHINJU

Haruko Kumota

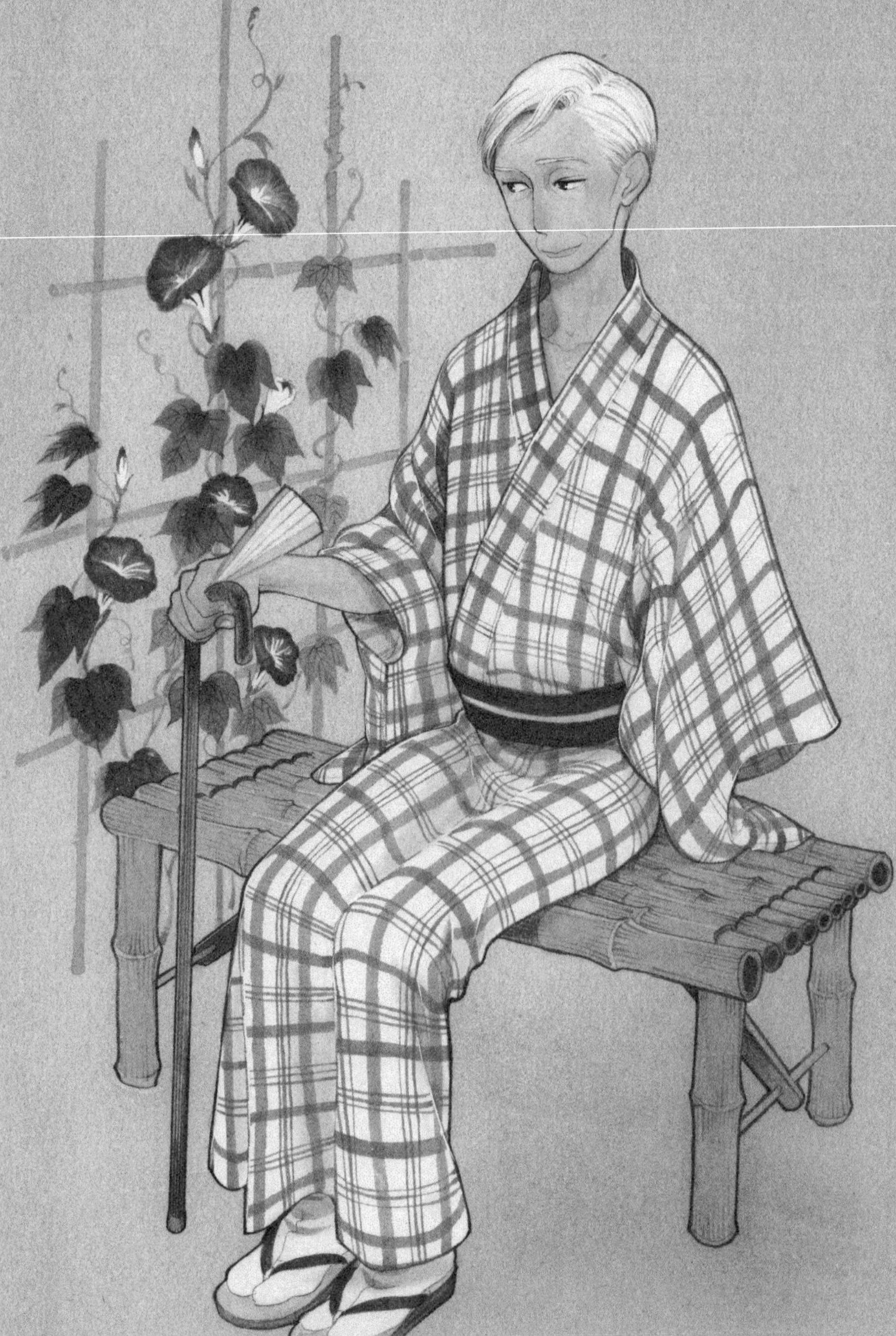

It is said that the roots of the current *Rakugo Kyokai* Association can be traced to the Tokyo *Rakugo Kyokai* formed thanks to the efforts of Ryutei Saraku V following the 1923 Great Kanto Earthquake. Yanagiya Kosan IV was later appointed its chairman and established it anew as the *Rakugo Kyokai* Association. It received permission to become an incorporated association with the Agency for Cultural Affairs acting as its competent authority in 1977, and its stated goal was to "advance the spread of popular performing arts with a focus on classical *rakugo*, contributing to the cultural development of our country in the process." It later became the general incorporated association it is today in 2012. It conducts performances in four theatres (*yose*) in Tokyo, as well as in halls, assembly spaces, schools, and more around the country.

For an overview of the *Rakugo Kyokai* Association, please visit:
http://rakugo-kyokai.jp/summary/

Descending Stories: Showa Genroku Rakugo Shinju volume 8 is a work of fiction. Names, characters, places, and incidents are the products of the author's imagination or are used fictitiously. Any resemblance to actual events, locales, or persons, living or dead, is entirely coincidental.

A Kodansha Comics Trade Paperback Original.

Published in the United States by Kodansha Comics, an imprint of Kodansha USA Publishing, LLC, New York.

Publication rights for this English edition arranged through Kodansha Ltd., Tokyo.

First published in Japan in 2015 by Kodansha Ltd., Tokyo.

ISBN 978-1-63236-546-0

Printed in the United States of America.

www.kodanshacomics.com

9 8 7 6 5 4 3 2 1

Translation: AltJapan Co., Ltd. (Matt Treyvaud, Hiroko Yoda, Matt Alt)
Lettering: Andrew Copeland
Editing: Tomoko Nagano and Megan McPherson
Rakugo term supervision: Rakugo Kyokai Association
Kodansha Comics edition cover design: Phil Balsman